THE UNKNOWN SHE
Eight Faces of
an Emerging Consciousness

THE
UNKNOWN SHE

*Eight Faces of
an Emerging Consciousness*

HILARY HART

THE GOLDEN SUFI CENTER

First published in the United States in 2003 by
The Golden Sufi Center
P.O. Box 456, Point Reyes Station, California 94956.
www.goldensufi.org

Third printing 2012.

Cover design by Anat Vaughan-Lee.

Printed and bound by Thomson-Shore, Inc.

Library of Congress Cataloging-in-Publication Data

Hart, Hilary, 1963 –
The unknown she : eight faces of an emerging consciousness / Hilary Hart.
     p. cm.
Includes bibliographical references.
ISBN 1-890350-06-0
1. Women--Religious life. 2. Mysticism. I. Title.

BL625.7 .H38 2003
291.4'22'082--dc21

                                                    2002192754

CONTENTS

INTRODUCTION

THE UNKNOWN SHE

 Is there a mystical consciousness particularly natural to women? If so, how is it affecting women's spiritual transformation, and the spiritual transformation of all humanity?

These questions led me from a Buddhist monastery in the golden-green foothills of the Himalayas to Glastonbury, England, a place of Arthurian legends; from the mayhem of Las Vegas to the warm darkness of a sweat lodge in Denver. For almost two years I worked closely with eight mystics—seven women and one man—from a wide range of traditions including Lakota Sioux, Sufism, Buddhism, and West-African Shamanism, all the time looking for clues that would help unveil the many faces of a spiritual consciousness one contributor calls the *Unknown She*.

I stayed with almost everyone I interviewed, sometimes for days, sometimes for weeks, giving myself over to their ways of living and to the energies that flow through them. I wanted to convey a spirituality not just taught, but *lived*, a spirituality shared through presence and simple ways of being. Together, as we ate, laughed, walked, and meditated, I came to see who these people are, and more importantly, how they are being used to influence the spiritual evolution of our world.

Each chapter demanded my constant attention, tested my endurance, and required a level of surrender I had not anticipated. From the bright swirling darkness of Jackie

Crovetto and the smooth flowing nourishment of Pansy Hawk Wing, to the intoxicating joy of Andrew Harvey and the wild emptiness of Lynn Barron—these energies were unrelenting, pulling me more and more deeply into myself and beyond.

Lost as I was for months and months in a kaleidoscope of the unfamiliar, in continuously forming and reforming patterns of knowing and being, I slowly began to recognize common threads and common features. And though the questions that drove this book are best answered within the following chapters, I can say by way of introduction that a mystical consciousness seems to be emerging through women and through what we tend to identify as 'female' qualities of men and women alike. A mystical consciousness that is love itself, a new energy and power of oneness, of spiritual transformation, of pure being.

While this consciousness is in essence beyond duality, beyond the distinctions of masculine and feminine, it seems to be manifesting now through ways of being and relating that are most familiar to women. As this higher energy pours into the created world from the silent emptiness of the beyond, it is unveiling itself through the mysteries of feminine understanding, emerging from the depths of the unconscious wrapped in a new luminosity one can most simply refer to as *She*.

THE NEED OF THE TIME

Most contributors in this book recognize the urgent potential for humanity to step into a new relationship with the divine and with all life. We can realize this potential in consciousness by accessing an energy of love and oneness that is present, "a huge web of light, connection, and wisdom," as Sobonfu Somé describes it. Andrew Harvey refers to this energy as "the force, the power, the majesty, and the extreme compassion of the Mother." And Jackie Crovetto says simply, "There is a new energy coming into the world." Like others in the book, Lynn Barron explains it is not really new, but has always been present, mostly hidden. "It is an ancient, ancient wisdom," she says, "that will come into our modern time."

Spiritual traditions have long understood that mystical life leads us back to the beginning again and again, returns us to where we started with deeper understanding and expanded horizons. When the Buddha held up a flower to his assembly of disciples, was he offering his students an experience of something other than returning to the simplest truths, the simplest elements of being? Isn't this what Rumi meant when he wrote, "beggars circle tables, dogs circle carrion, the lover circles his own heart..."?

So it makes sense that we are returning to something ancient for a new purpose, that in the evolution of our consciousness we are spiraling back around to something that seems familiar as well as full of potential. If we are able to free ourselves from old patterns of perception, outdated ways of living and relating, we might be able to participate in the revelation of the infinite in this moment in time.

Andrew Harvey, Pansy Hawk Wing, Lynn Barron and others insist that without a change in how we live and how we interact with each other and our world, we will continue to destroy the resources—human and otherwise— of our planet. By realizing this potential in consciousness, we can take a step into a relationship with life on earth that is infused with divine love and grounded in the knowledge of oneness. For fundamentally the new energy is relational, not autonomous. It flows and works through organic, non-hierarchical systems like life itself. It can wake us up to our fundamental nature, which is, as the Buddhist and indigenous traditions have always pointed out, not independent, but interconnected through all beings within a greater wholeness.

The energy that is now available is a consciousness of love. Like the interconnectedness of life, love reflects the reality of oneness, for in love there is no duality, no separation. As Ginny Matthews says, "In the vastness of love we can really meet each other." Love flows beyond borders, beyond definitions. It brings people together, always emphasizing how we are not separate but essentially similar. And this is why, as Jackie Crovetto explains, this energy allows for a new way to relate to differences and potential antagonism. "It is an energy that indicates we can hold polarity without conflict," she says. "We can all need different things, but nobody has to lose."

Within a consciousness of love and oneness we have the potential to experience a deep balance between our own interests and the interests of the whole. Our communities can reflect this potential as we learn to live with an understanding of how we are all connected. Ani Tenzin Palmo explains by way of describing a well-run nunnery, "We can live with others in an accommodating manner which at the same time gives each enough individual space."

This emerging consciousness is essentially egalitarian and not hierarchical, undermining all distinctions between what is seen as holy and what is seen as base. In this way it helps us bring our attention and awareness to what we have rejected for so long. Through our attention, we can help the consciousness of love flow through all levels of life, revealing and awakening the light hidden in the densest planes of existence. For Andrew Harvey, this is a process of "descending transcendence." In Angela Fischer's words, we recognize what many women intuitively feel, that "the love of God is the love for life itself." And we come to know, as Ani Tenzin Palmo shows us, that spiritual practice does not separate one from life. For in real practice, she says with shining eyes, "nothing is left out, everything partakes. All of reality is transformed!"

Mystics understand that our real responsibility is to be in service to the needs of the moment. And in this time in the history of the evolution of consciousness as well as in the political, social, and economic dimensions of life, certain needs are revealing themselves with dramatic insistence. If we don't re-orient ourselves within a new relationship with life and the divine, we will remain caught in patterns of separation and violence and destroy our world's resources. We will remain constricted by our old systems of spiritual progress and achievement, which, more and more, seem infused with materialistic patterns of domination and self-destruction. But if we can see with new eyes we might notice how the divine is suddenly present all around us, that it has been waiting patiently for us to finally forget ourselves and really live the freedom and joy that are possible. Maybe then, as Andrew Harvey says with a smile, "We might be able to join in all the divine fun!"

A NEW DOORWAY

Human beings have a great responsibility in the process of divine incarnation, for the divine enters creation through the consciousness of the human heart. It is our responsibility to receive what is being given, but we need new ways to recognize and contain what is now available. As we are warned in the Bible, Matthew 9:17, "Neither do men put new wine into old bottles, else the bottles break, and the wine runneth out..." The current manifestation of the divine needs new doorways, new pathways to enter our world. We are being asked to change our ways of thinking and being so that we can contain the new consciousness that is now available. The qualities, attitudes, and states of being that will most effectively receive, hold, and transmit this consciousness are described by most in this book as *feminine*, or *female* in nature. As Sobonfu Somé explains, "Feminine spirit is a rising energy." It is rising to answer the need of the time.

Within a traditional spiritual context, we have become used to distinguishing feminine consciousness, or the ways of the Mother, from patriarchal consciousness, or the ways of the Father. Patriarchal consciousness has generally located the divine in a transcendent state, above creation, accessible through states of detached consciousness most often achieved through ascetic or other practices that drive a person beyond physical and instinctual life. In patriarchal systems spiritual power and energy are transmitted through relationships of authority; spiritual transformation happens through knowledge, and spiritual progress through individual effort. Masculine spirituality, as Pansy Hawk Wing describes it, is "the way of the Warrior," which tends to drive energy outward through expression and achievement.

In contrast, the wisdom of the Mother is a receptive, internal energy, drawing the divine deep into all levels of life, including physical and instinctual dimensions. Therefore, feminine elements of divine consciousness recognize no distinction between that which is sacred and that which is ordinary.

Feminine energy is essentially relational, and transforms through love, not knowledge, for as Lynn Barron explains, "the female element is love itself." Many women instinctually understand this, having direct experience of how the ego is burned away in the fires of unconditional love as one gives oneself from the heart, again and again, to the unending demands of life's relationships.

Additionally, feminine traditions recognize that energy and power are transmitted through non-hierarchical systems rather than relationships of authority. And they always consider the individual as part of the divine whole, rather than as autonomous or separate.

At this point in the evolution of our consciousness we can participate—in a new way—in how the divine flows into life. We can open our minds and hearts and receive the light into every aspect of our being, and in turn recognize the divine wholeness of which we are a part. It is not surprising, then, that the qualities we have traditionally defined as feminine will be the qualities we need to develop and value in order to help this process to take place. For the ways of the feminine have traditionally honored all life as sacred, have emphasized receptive states of being rather than expressive states of doing, have reflected the inter-connectedness of life, and have not allowed the community to be forgotten in the pursuit of individual achievement. This is why it is important that we look with new appreciation to a feminine understanding of spiritual transformation that has been, for so long, generally hidden from our collective consciousness.

Because the ways of the Mother are often more familiar to women than men, more alive in their bodies, instincts, and the ways they love and live in the world, women have a particular role to play in the potential of our time. Women must really live who they are without hesitation, leave behind the patterns of insecurity, dependency, and fear that have inhibited them from expressing what they know is real. For this reason I think this book can be particularly helpful to women, for women can see reflected on these pages with great power and knowing what is so natural within them, and so deeply in need of recognition.

However, I feel it would be a grave mistake to emphasize women's roles too much. For more than anything, the contributors of the book point to the potential of a lived understanding of oneness that allows us to finally leave behind patterns that polarize men and women, and masculine and feminine ways. The challenges we are facing as a community are equally demanding for all of us, for we all have access to the qualities and perspectives that are needed. *Everyone's* participation is required. In Andrew Harvey's words, "The task of every human being is to come into their own unique version of the sacred androgyny, uniting the masculine and feminine within them." As Ani Tenzin Palmo warns, "Calling qualities 'masculine' or 'feminine' is fine, as long as one is very conscious that males also have very much the feminine, and females have very much the masculine within them." And as Lynn Barron says so beautifully, "Every human heart contains the wholeness of God."

BETWEEN THE WORLDS

Mystics know that what is real comes from the beyond, pours out of nothingness into the light of creation. Every time we take a step as individuals we turn towards the emptiness within our hearts, look to the unconditioned silence in the depths of our being for what we need and what is needed from us. So too, at this time in our collective history, we need to look to the beyond for our next step, for the ways to receive what is being given.

The feminine ways within men and women alike and within all life are the doorways into the beyond. For they are ways that listen, allow, and receive. And they know the unpredictability of the forces of creation, know that the divine suddenly enters the celebration through new music, new dance steps. And if we are to join the party, if we allow ourselves to become, as the Sufis say, "drunk with the wine of the Beloved," we have to unburden ourselves from our outdated approaches to life, the divine, and even to love.

As this book was coming to an end, I remembered that the first chapter begins with laughter and that the presence of laughter is a common thread that winds through every meeting. I laughed with Angela Fischer, bewildered, while we tried to discuss something that is really beyond communication. I watched in wonder as Pansy Hawk Wing leaned back in her chair, chuckling as though in communion with a hidden guest. I was often buckled over in tears with Lynn Barron, drunk on the energy in her house. And I sat with Andrew Harvey in the desert park, barely able to breathe through the fits of what he calls "divine hilarity." Through all the contributors in this book I saw the intense joy that arises when one lives from a place of real freedom, from fearlessly living as oneself despite the difficulties and obstacles one faces. Their common message is that a direct relationship with life itself is full of joy, the profound and deeply precious joy of being from which we have distanced ourselves in the last two thousand years of spiritual striving and achieving. Spirituality does not need to separate us from this joy. As Angela Fischer asks, "Why not go to God while embracing life? Why not surrender to Him while dancing, so that He can celebrate His beauty and His joy through us?"

Silence and freedom live together in this place of receptivity, where we wait in two worlds to live what needs to be lived, not for our sake, but for something beyond ourselves. The practices and perspectives within this book can help us become more comfortable at resting, working, and even laughing, at the juncture where we can receive the light of what is higher into ourselves and into life. We are all familiar with this space in meditation and prayer where we sit in deep silence, attentive and awake, listening within the darkness. But we can also live in this state of deep receptivity, relying on what we hear inside our hearts, not just in prayer or meditation but in all aspects of our lives. While we are at work, making love, eating dinner, and taking the children to school.

And this is what is needed of us now: to turn our mystical awareness into all corners of our lives so that everything is included. To allow the divine to flow into the world and awaken us all within the oneness and joy of That which is at once both infinite within the silence of our own hearts, and visible in the sparkling moments of light and love that are creation.

ENTERING *the* SECRET

a meeting with

Angela Fischer

ENTERING *the* SECRET

*"Is there a spiritual science grounded in the knowledge
that transformation for women can happen in accordance
with our nature as women? Yes, it exists. It is an ancient
science as old as human consciousness itself. And
for some women it is the way home."*

Angela Fischer

STEPPING INSIDE

Angela Fischer and I are sitting by the woodstove
in her living room laughing. We have been talking
about spiritual transformation in women and
our seriousness has given way to elation. I find myself on
continually shifting ground as I try to understand and
conceptualize what comes so naturally to her, and she tries
to explain a way of being that is beyond explanation and
beyond conceptualization. So we end up laughing—again
and again—at each other and ourselves as we cycle from
bewilderment to concentrated effort with a willingness to
work together until something essential within her heart
has been revealed and recognized.

Angela communicates from within a spiritual terrain
that is often unfamiliar to me, describing a process of
transformation that is in its essence a way of being. Organic
and sometimes deeply hidden, the path to God as Angela
lives it draws a person fully into life, includes a nurturing
and instinctual relationship with the physical world, and

21

reveals the divine in the most ordinary things. God seems to come to Angela, a wife and mother of four children, in the sigh of her child as often as in the depths of meditation.

This path of transformation, this way of living, is infused with joy and driven by love, has little or no outer form, and relies on a continual state of inner attention and receptivity. There are no goals and no expectations; rather one offers oneself to what is Real by relating to what is present within every moment. It is a path of surrender, in which one embraces the wholeness of one's own being rather than striving for anything beyond oneself.

As Angela tells me, awakening this wisdom within the collective consciousness of the world can bring a new balance to our lives and reveal how God is present in His creation in this particular moment. It is an ancient path as well as a path suited for the specific needs of our world today. And for some women it is the way home, a way of transformation that recognizes and values elements of being a woman that our Western culture and its spiritual systems have largely ignored.

I spend almost two weeks at the end of the summer with Angela in the small village in northern Germany where she lives with her family, talking about her life and her relationship to God. One of those weeks is set apart for a retreat with fifteen people, mostly women, from nearby cities and towns. I stay with two friends of Angela who live next door and I spend much of my time with them, with other women from the retreat, as well as with Angela and her family.

Angela and I meet for at least a few hours every day, usually in her house, to meditate and talk. Sometimes we talk over tea or dinner; sometimes we walk together, alone or with her children as they ride their bicycles along beside us. When I am not with Angela or the other people from the group, or writing about our conversations, I run or walk alone on the endless trails in the woods nearby, explore the local shops, or ride a bicycle down long village roads past the farms and fields.

Her family's brick house sits on a small street surrounded by an incongruous mix of farms and newly built suburban homes. Less than a mile from her home, beyond a field of Shetland ponies and the railroad tracks, the village ends at the edge of the vast wood where she and I often walk together.

Angela is a strong woman in her mid-forties with graying hair and translucent blue eyes. She has a physical power and presence that manifest in the way she moves through the many tasks of her day, and she seems consistently attentive whether she is roller-skating with her daughters or leading a meditation meeting. Despite the demands of this book and the retreat, she stays closely involved with the routines of family life. Her husband and children remain a constant presence in our time together, and her children especially swirl around us in a continual reflection of love and life.

For twenty years Angela has been a guide, helping people, mostly women, find and follow the thread within themselves that leads them deeper into their hearts and allows them to live their love for God more fully in the world. Since meeting Irina Tweedie, a Naqshbandi Sufi, in 1985, she has combined her own experiences and understanding of feminine wisdom with the wisdom of the Naqshbandi Sufi path.

Throughout our meetings Angela is increasingly open with me, and yet there are times we both feel the inaccessibility of what she knows and lives so naturally. Some of the frustration and confusion we experience together are a natural part of the emergence of feminine power and wisdom, which often lives in secret, and expresses itself in mysterious and unexpected ways, sometimes revealing itself openly and sometimes seeming to work from a place of darkness.

Entering Angela's physical house echoes my own confusing passage towards that which she holds most dear. The front door of the house opens into a very small space, and one must immediately pass through another door to enter the dining area. To step into the living room, one must open two doors back to back. Some of the doorhandles turn one way; at least one handle turns the opposite way. I often feel turned around and halted, sometimes laughing, sometimes frustrated when I come to meet and meditate with her.

I visit Angela in her home, and later we speak in my home when she comes with her family on vacation to California. Our discussions and our time together lead us around and around, spiraling us to a deeper meeting ground, through growing openness. Throughout the process, some particular dynamics of women's spirituality reveal themselves, and yet we are both struck by the feeling that something essential is beyond view. But that which comes so naturally to Angela is elusive in part because of its naturalness. As with everything simple and natural, the thread of the miraculous is woven throughout, not as something separate, but as something essential to its simplicity.

TRANSFORMATION AND THE PHYSICAL BODY

One evening Angela and I sit in her living room, she occasionally feeding the woodstove that fills the room with a strong heat—a relief from the late-summer chill outside. It is dark now, and we can hear her husband cleaning in the kitchen after our dinner together, and her children playing upstairs. We sit for a while, listening as the noises of the house recede, and enjoy the way the room slowly warms from the stove.

"These are interesting times, aren't they?" Angela asks me. "It seems there is a need now for something ancient to come into consciousness. But talking about feminine wisdom, feminine ways of being, is not for the purpose of returning to how things have been. There were times when women's spiritual traditions thrived, and had great influence in the community. But those times are lost, and they are lost for a reason. Humanity is elsewhere, at a different point of evolution. But an essence remains—an essence of feminine power and understanding that can be re-awoken now, for a new purpose. And if women come into contact with this essence within themselves, they can be of service in a new way. For these reasons I think it can be helpful to remind us of this ancient wisdom within ourselves, wisdom that is the root of spiritual transformation in women.

"Every soul has her own way to God," she tells me. "Everyone is treated differently on the path and every path is unique. This is why it can be difficult to generalize about spirituality. Yet for some women there is a need to recognize that who we are *as women* plays an important role in our journey home. And there are hints and traces pointing to how ancient feminine traditions have recognized this, have always understood that spiritual transformation can happen in accordance with our nature as women, which is different from men's nature. What is natural for women, what we know so deeply, can be the basis of how we grow. And sometimes these things are easily overlooked because we take them for granted, because from one point of view they are so simple, so ordinary. But from another point of view they are truly precious.

"Of course from an absolute perspective it does not matter if you are a man or a woman," she continues, as though addressing a concern I had not yet voiced. "Our essential nature is the same. On the level of the soul, it is the same. But we are born into this world as human beings. We begin with either a male physical body or a female physical body, and we know there are some important differences between the two. We go back to the source from *here*, from this physical world. The spiritual path includes the physical world, and spiritual realization includes the physical dimension. Otherwise we would not be here. So the path can be different for men and women because we begin from a different point, a different starting ground.

"The body is the earth within spiritual life. The earth that gives ground, receives the heavenly light, and nurtures the spiritual process. The physical body is of tremendous importance for the spiritual transformation in women, yet it is the element that is most often overlooked.

"Of course, when I talk about the physical body I also mean something much more expansive than we are used to associating with the word 'physical.' The physical world reflects other levels of truth in its own particular way. The physical differences between men and women are not just biological, but much more complex and multidimensional. But the physical dimension has been ignored for so long within our spiritual systems that I feel it is helpful to bring it back into consciousness, so that transformation can be recognized as inclusive, a process that works within wholeness.

"For women, everything is included," she tells me. "We just need to live who we are. Of course we need to come to know who we are, and this is the journey. Coming to know who we are means we come to know how God has made us. We come to know the secrets of creation, the mysteries of how God reveals Himself in this world, for these secrets are put into the female body. God has entrusted these secrets to women as a physical consciousness. Women's spiritual transformation means to make the mysteries real, to make them conscious. It is a process of going back, or returning to the source, but at the same time it is a process of realizing creation. And without the physical body there is no realization."

The room is warm now; Angela closes the stove to bring the fire to coals and we both push aside the small blankets we have been sitting beneath. "Women have a particular knowledge about creation and the miracle of creation," she says. "We know the ways God reveals Himself in the world. This knowledge is in all women because we give birth. And I don't mean one has to become pregnant to live this wisdom; it is inherent in who we are. This knowledge exists at the deepest level of our consciousness, and the spiritual process can help us become more and more aware at this level, awakening this consciousness which is, in essence, the Creator in His creation, the divine in physical form. It is like a secret gift, a specific way that God is part of His world through women.

"This consciousness gives women a unique role to play within creation. It allows us natural access to the creative darkness from which all life emerges. We can access this darkness, and work within its silence to guide life from the emptiness. We live in two worlds, helping light enter existence, wherever it is needed, and we are attentive—with great care—to all that is born."

WHOLENESS

Women's particular responsibilities in the process of creation reflect an inherent wholeness and a natural access to all levels of life. Angela explains that spiritual transformation for women naturally reflects this wholeness as well.

"Most everything in a woman's life is included in her spiritual path. So she does not need to go from here to there," she says, gesturing across the room. "She has the ability to go just where she is, to go without going. It is important for all of us to break this conditioning that we have to become someone or something *else*. A woman can walk her path within where she is. Of course through discrimination and attentiveness she comes to know and live her real self, which is free. But her transformation includes who she is in a unique way.

"You see, it is often not like this for men. Men's journeys are of course towards themselves, but at the same time they seem to journey away from themselves, leaving their bodies behind. They master their instinctual nature—which is an expression of the body in the world—and transform these energies. Most of the practices given in all kinds of traditions are designed to assist this process. They are easy to recognize, emphasizing ascetic trials like fasting, physical endurance, and controlling sexuality. And we consider these as general spiritual practices, not recognizing that they might be inappropriate for women. Women often don't need these practices, because they stay where they are; their connections within life, within the created world, provide the ground for their transformation. Our bodies can be included because they do not need to be purified as men's do; they are already pure.

"Working with men, you can push them, just push them with a lot of energy, yah? Just—umph!" Angela says, thrusting her open palm into the space between us. "You cannot do it with women like that. Women lose connection to life and their physical body. They need the container of being connected to life. And in this container the whole transformation process takes place. The flow of the process is, in part, guided and fed by the sacred substance within our bodies. If a woman disconnects from her body she cuts herself off from this essential source of spiritual energy, the divine potential that allows her direct understanding of her own divine nature and the sacredness of all life.

"The alchemical process of transformation for women happens within a container, a vessel. The container is like a basket woven by the threads of life and earth, woven by women's connection with their feminine instincts. Or you can see it as a cocoon within which the transformation of a caterpillar into a butterfly takes place, secretly. Like a cocoon this container of life spins around the inner process. The cocoon is the protecting cover within which the deep process of purification, melting, and creation takes place. It is the container that carries, embraces, and feeds, but also hides and somehow veils for a while what really happens. At the same time the cocoon maintains the connection to earth, to the body. In this way whatever happens on the inner planes—on other levels of reality—has an effect on the body, on the world of matter."

Angela tells me that spiritual exercises which stress renunciation or disdain for the body or the world can sometimes be harmful for women. "If a woman does practices that encourage a detachment from her body or her everyday life, she can cut her instinctual connection to life. If this happens, she denies the energy of life itself, and the love that is in life and in really living who one is. For a woman it is often the stream of life that connects her to the Absolute. Women know that this stream flows from the circle of the uncreated eternal into this world and with this world back again to God.

"Women know we are in relation to life around us. For example, meditation is very important. But what's the point of sitting on your meditation cushion, your attention somewhere else, when your child is hungry, or when your plants need watering? Women instinctively know that life itself can be a meditation. It is part of feminine wisdom that the spiritual world and the material world come together in the wholeness of life where neither is sacrificed for the other.

"I have found that many women are helped when, at the beginning of their path, they feel that everything is embraced, when they understand that they don't have to cut their lives, or themselves, in parts, and leave some behind. Spiritual conditioning can tell us that we have to turn away from our ordinary lives. And in the beginning for some women it might appear as a kind of relief to turn away from the demands of life that confront us again and again with our restrictions and attachments. But women often know, instinctively, that this is not right for them, and they are so relieved to see this wisdom reflected back.

"So then how does a woman's process look?" she asks. "It takes on as many forms as there are women. But one thing is the same, and that is love. The great Sufi master Bhai Sahib said that women need only a few spiritual practices. They are taken by the way of love."

LONGING

One of the first steps on a woman's journey is to understand that she already embodies the most essential dynamic of her spiritual evolution—the natural capacity of longing that manifests throughout every level of her experience.

"The feminine aspect of love is longing," Angela says one morning, as we walk with her dog along a dirt road that cuts across a cornfield near her house. "Longing is part of the nature of women. Sometimes women are so close to this quality of love and being that they can't even see that it is longing, yet they are somehow longing all the time."

The aching emptiness, need to be loved, sense of loss or incompletion that women so often experience as second nature can be the longing to go Home, the longing of what is real calling for them to return. This longing will lead a woman where she needs to go; it will bring her to the experiences she needs in order to fulfill her life here on earth.

"The Sufi Irina Tweedie used to explain that the masculine side of love says, 'I love you, I am coming to you, wait for me,'" Angela tells me. "And the feminine side of love says, 'I am looking for you, I am waiting for you, come to me.'" In Sufism, longing is considered to be not just a quality within women, but the state of every soul before God, the pull of the soul to come Home and be united with her Beloved. Longing draws into itself the love of God, like a magnet. The soul cries for God as an echo of God's longing for us, and God answers. Angela tells me that for women, this longing is a natural state of being and manifests on many levels in a way men's longing does not.

"Longing is the way women *live*," Angela explains now as we sit in the quiet of her kitchen, drinking tea. "Longing carries the feminine qualities of openness and the power of attraction as it is lived through the passion and sometimes also the suffering of love. At the most obvious level this longing manifests in a woman's sexuality, in her sexual receptivity. She gives her body and her love through receiving. A woman loving a man, procreating a child, lives as one who receives. The nature of her love and creative power is to open herself, to become a vessel and to be at one with what is maturing within her. This is the way of the feminine on all levels. On the level of physical nature it seems simple and clear; so how could it be otherwise on the inner planes?"

Angela and I discuss how the feminine side of love is a dynamic emptiness that waits to be filled, an emptiness that plays a specific part in the process of creation through its capacity to receive. In a woman's body this emptiness is the womb, the creative space which draws life to it and from which life emerges. Instinctually and psychologically this emptiness can manifest in a woman's sexuality, and in her relationality—her receptivity, her natural capacity to listen, to be attentive, and to attract.

Women's tendency to feel that something is missing, the tendency to yearn for greater and greater fulfillment, is the thread of the heart leading to the only real source of completion—the wholeness of the Self, or the closed circle of love that is the core of the Sufi relationship of lover and Beloved. In part, a woman's journey is to follow this thread and to trust where it leads her.

"The longing is just there," Angela tells me. "Women don't need to do things to gain the longing or achieve the longing or to work for it. It's just there. And it is the direct way to God, to go with the longing, to flow with the longing, to live the longing. It is the fire that is already burning.

"Women are so close to life," Angela says, softly. "We know so much about life. We know about the earth, about creation; we are the echo of His longing for us, and we are called to live in a way that reflects something of our lives back to Him. And so the longing in a woman, I found, often appears first as a longing for life, for living *our* lives fully. And there are so many ways to live a life! And women think we're not allowed to have this longing, or we're ashamed of it. We have this image that to live in God does not go together with longing for life. But it's just nature; we belong to life in a way. At the same time we feel our longing for God. It's the same.

"I remember when I was younger, some of my children were born and were still babies. My life was fulfilled, but from time to time I realized that I looked at my friends who didn't have families with some jealousy. They were very busy with their spiritual lives, meditating for hours, visiting seminars and retreats and spending time with their teacher. A certain anxiety had sneaked into my mind, unnoticed by me, that this great fulfillment of having children and a family could become an obstacle for my spiritual path.

"But the day came when I was able to see Mrs. Tweedie again, to ask her for spiritual practices. I was so eager!" she says, shaking her head and smiling. "I was starving for spiritual nourishment, for practices beyond this everyday chaos. I had so little time then to meditate, or travel to groups or seminars, and I thought I would be given something I could take home with me, a special practice so I wouldn't fall behind, so that I could come closer to the Beloved.

"And Mrs. Tweedie said to me with such love, 'You don't need practices. Love your children and your husband, this is your practice and your yoga path. If you wash your children, remember you're washing the Beloved. If you love your husband, remember that you love Him.' And so that's what I tried to do, and still try to do. That has been my main practice for years. It has been the most powerful exercise I could be given, and life itself has given it to me.

"Every woman has her own way to connect with life through her longing," Angela continues. "Mrs. Tweedie said, 'Everybody has to bring back to Him his or her own fragrance from life, the essence of the experiences of the soul, which comes back as a certain fragrance or scent.' And I like this picture; it reflects that what we bring back has something to do with our lives, our lives *here;* otherwise it can't have a fragrance, because a fragrance belongs to the created. Each fragrance will be different, and we are here to make conscious that every aspect of life is a reflection of God.

"For women, longing is also in our bodies, holding the tension between the uncreated and the created. Every cell calls out for Him, waits and longs for Him. Through our longing we awaken this divine love within us. Our bodies are included; our bodies are filled with His love for us, our love for Him. And this fulfillment takes place in the most ordinary parts of our lives, in the simple ways we live. He comes to us with many faces, many forms. We just need to recognize Him and embrace Him."

LOVE AND VULNERABILITY

One day I have brunch with three other women who have come to be with Angela during her workshop. We sit at the garden table outside the house next door to Angela's, where I am staying. The table is filled with an array of pastries, cereals, juices, and we each have a cup of strong dark German coffee that I bought from an expensive café in a nearby town the day before. It is late morning, the washing is hanging on the line behind us, drying in the warm sun. Angela's sons are riding their bicycles around the block, circling us, laughing with us each time they pass by.

I can feel a deep devotion in these women as we sit in the sun, enjoying the food and talking about the workshop. Their joy at being together with each other and Angela is as full and palpable as the warmth of the morning. Many of the women from the retreat live in this town, or near-by, drawn to be physically close, to be able to run into each other at the shops and on the street. It is as though the love flows through the group especially when they are physically near, and creates a distinct container of strength, attentiveness, joy, and care.

In the afternoon I go to Angela's house and we talk about women's natural openness and vulnerability, and the need to allow this openness as much as possible, for it is the way love enters into the heart.

"We are loved, all of us," she says. "Love is the divine energy within us; love is the fuel for the journey, the beginning of the journey, the end of the journey. Love is the energy of the path, the fabric of the universe, the way God lets Himself be known in the world. Our longing to go Home, our longing for God, our longing to be ourselves completely will guide love to us, will increase the love within us, and will allow love to transform us. But we know the tendency to turn away from love; there is always the danger that we don't trust it.

"It is so important that women allow themselves to be loved. That is the way we give ourselves in complete trust. For many of us it is much easier to identify with someone who loves, who is actively giving. But how is it to be loved, without control, without limiting what flows to us in abundance? And to not care about being vulnerable to love, to accept the bewilderment of love, and even to accept the violation that comes with love?

"We like the side of love that is tender, soft, and embracing, the love that gives us what we want," Angela says, smiling. "But love has this other side as well that we sometimes forget. It is the violent quality of love, uncompromising and allowing nothing but the truth. Love is a quality of light, and when light enters the darkness it can hurt. A ray of light can be very painful for eyes that are used to the dark. Light can come in and split us open. In this way, the violent side of love destroys our sense of wholeness. But even our sense of wholeness evolves, and there is a transformation into a consciousness of oneness in which even more can be included.

"Once we have tasted the sweetness of love, we want it always and forever. But it is not in our hands, not a matter of choice or will. Love is unpredictable, and it is given and taken away as God wills. Our part is to give ourselves unconditionally, give ourselves to union and to separation equally, for together they hold the tension of creation. And the more we love, the more we feel that we are loved, the more we will suffer from separation. We become more and more conscious of love, of its intensity, and this goes together with the dynamic of feminine longing, with passion and power coming from deep within the feminine nature.

"When we face separation, when we face that we might not get what we want, this is the place of incredible opportunity. Here, we choose to give ourselves unconditionally, or we go back to patterns of power dynamics to protect ourselves and control our environments. Women know how to be creative; they can often create what they want. This is the feminine shadow, how we use our understanding of creation to create for ourselves.

"Just as individual women face these moments of choice, so have ancient feminine traditions faced these moments in the past, when the power of feminine spirituality was used for self-protection because it was threatened by changing times. These patterns within the collective feminine must be let go of, for we all stand at a point when something new can come into consciousness. There is an essence within the feminine ways that will always remain, but the essence has to be freed from the power structures that come along with those traditions.

"You see, violation on an individual as well as collective level will deepen the longing and lead us to new states of consciousness. The longing is always there, but longing needs to be increased by love, and this process is not always easy, or safe, and can go against deep conditioning in women, conditioning that serves to protect her wholeness, her security. So there is a fearlessness involved, a willingness to be loved and to love without conditions, to accept unconditionally what God gives you, even when it is painful."

I ask Angela to speak a bit about the dangers for women to become abused, to give themselves to love in an unhealthy way. "It is very important to not confuse the vulnerability before God and the acceptance of violation through love with taking abuse from people," she tells me. "Psychologically, women have been conditioned by a great deal of abuse. This is why the topic of vulnerability in a spiritual context is very delicate. But what I mean by the unconditional acceptance of love's violation is something beyond psychological dynamics. Women need to cross a certain threshold in order to enter into this land of freedom—an aspect of their own nature in which they are naked, pure, powerful, and vulnerable all at the same time.

"I think a certain degree of psychological integration is required in order to live this potential of freedom which leads to a surrendered state—in which one unconditionally accepts what is given before God. On the level of the soul, there is a place within all women that is uninjured and inviolable. It is from here that psychological wounds of violation and abuse can be healed. Yet some wounds might never be healed, and this does not matter because we belong to God, and in His hands we do not suffer self-pity. A woman must be very mature to live from this place of vulnerability that is far removed from being a victim. It has nothing to do with being in an abusive relationship that continually keeps one from growing or living who one truly is. It is a place of surrender and freedom, in which the power of the soul flows in.

"It can be helpful if women are conscious of this difference, and women themselves will know the difference between the vulnerability of the soul before God and the psychological patterns of being a victim. Just ask your heart and you will know. Are you living who you really are? Also, this is why it is important to have an experienced spiritual guide whom you can trust. She or he will take you to this threshold. This is so important in the current spiritual atmosphere, where there is so much abuse."

Later, Angela and I speak about this state of vulnerability as a natural state, a state of freedom and power. "Women *are* vulnerable," she says. "Vulnerability is a state of being that we discover in time, as we let go of our defenses, as we allow the path to reveal our basic nature which is simple and vulnerable. This state of vulnerability, our capacity to bear what love brings us, can not be attained through spiritual practices. In fact, it often reveals itself as we let go of our dependence on practices, as we let go of our identification with discipline, and let go of our compulsion to *do*. Then we become aware of who we really *are*.

"We do so much to protect ourselves. Women are used to carrying so many forms of self-protection. And we know there are good reasons to protect ourselves. It is very difficult for women in the present time to open up to this aspect of their nature because there are so many experiences of violation of the feminine on a collective and individual level. They are stamped so deeply into the psyche of women. So we build habits to protect ourselves from even ourselves, from our very own nature. But if we live our vulnerability before God, consciously, in the light of His love, it is a state of real spiritual strength and power. As the Tao Te Ching says, 'The softest thing in the universe overcomes the hardest thing in the universe.'

"Women have direct access to this intimate relationship with God, a relationship of love," Angela tells me. "A woman knows what it means to attract love from a place of longing, a state of vulnerability, with the courage to be empty. On a good spiritual path, with a real teacher, we can follow love where it leads us, and we trust this love in all its forms."

SERVICE

Angela assures me that women can trust their longing and follow it where it takes them. And yet there is a special danger for women that their connections to life and to the activities of the world through which their love and longing often manifest will trap them in attachments that limit their capacity to really live their spiritual potential— their potential for unconditional love and a life in service to something beyond themselves.

"It has been said that attachments are a woman's greatest obstacle," she says, the afternoon light spreading across us and the couch where we sit. "Men's consciousness tends to detach from the world more easily, and their spiritual transformation requires this detachment, this capacity to disconnect from and transform the instincts of the body. But women are closer to matter than men, connected within the material world more directly. So the danger of being caught in attachments is greater. There is not just the danger of being attached; women *are* attached.

"It can be helpful to understand that this attachment goes both ways. It is not just that women are attached to matter, but also that matter is attached to us. Matter needs women, life needs women, because we know about creation, and we participate in creation. The feminine ways of transformation are not necessarily about becoming detached; rather, they help bring a person to a state of freedom. We can learn to deal with attachments, and live attachments responsibly, joyfully, as expressions of our love for something else.

"When my children were young, I was nearly overwhelmed by how much they needed me. The need was so great, and it was for *me*. I had to be there for them completely. And I was afraid of being limited somehow, trapped, by this incredible need, by the way I was connected to them through my body, through my own natural ways of caring for them. Limitations exist within these instinctual relationships. And the point is to go beyond these limitations, not by rejecting them or pushing them to the side, but by surrendering to them, consciously, responsibly. In this way we become free within these relationships through a process of giving up control, and letting go.

"When my first child was a baby she had a hard time falling asleep at night. And I was drawn to be with her, to stay with her, to give whatever I thought she needed. So I would sing to her, and hold her, and lie beside her. And nothing worked. So I asked, I prayed, and the answer from within was that I was holding on to her, not letting her go. I was thinking I had to be with her so she could go to sleep. But in fact I had to let her go on her own, be free to sleep. I had to trust that she was being taken care of by God; I had to put her in God's hands. I had to trust something beyond my own instincts so we could both be free. So I left her alone. And of course this was difficult for me! I had to grow up then as well, to let go, to open the situation up to something higher than myself. But from then on she could sleep."

The Sufi master Bhai Sahib said that the greatest limitations allow for the greatest freedom. Ordinary life with its constant demands is the arena for spiritual training. The relationships within life can teach acceptance, patience, attentiveness, help a woman develop her capacity to listen and respond immediately to the need of the moment, provide a ground for mystical states, and most importantly deepen her experience of unconditional love.

"The spiritual potential of a woman in part lies in the transformation of attachments to relationships of love and service," Angela tells me. "She doesn't need to transmute

her energy, or do practices designed to pull her away from
the limitations of living her life, in the way men sometimes
do. She needs to accept, and really live from, the unconditional love and longing that manifest in her life, in her
work, and her relationships with her children, her partner,
her teacher, and her connection to nature. This way she
allows her spiritual essence, her love and longing for God,
her desire for union with the source, to transform her
attachments within those relationships.

"Yes, so often we want to get away from the demands
of life; we think we can be free if we leave them behind.
And so many spiritual traditions—monastic traditions, for
example—encourage this. But for many women cutting off
from life cuts off the energy of transformation, the love that
lives inside us. To accept our limitations, our attachments,
our simple human needs, provides the ground for offering
our lives back to God, and He helps us become free if it is
His will."

The limitations of life, the simple elements of being a
human being with all our vulnerabilities and inadequacies,
are opportunities for us to live from a deeper vulnerability,
the place where we need the help of something else, the
help of the divine. If we see the illusory nature of the
objects of our desires and let our attachments awaken us to
the truer need, the need for guidance and love directly
from the source, then the ordinary moments of life are
continual opportunities for grace and love to come into
the world. Our need draws this higher love into our lives.
This is how we can be in service; this is how our limitations
allow for the limitless to manifest in the world.

Angela tells me that while we draw God's love to
us, it is also within us already. "Real love, God's free and
limitless love, is in all of us," she says. "It is in our bodies
and connects us in service to something far beyond our

egos. As attachments mature into unconditional love and servanthood, this divine consciousness in our bodies awakens. This is the natural source of our understanding of real love, of the love for God and God's love for us. We don't need to look for it because it is already inside us."

DARKNESS

It is evening. Angela and I sit in her living room, while her children are upstairs. We have had a day off from the retreat, and people are out for dinner, spending time alone, or home with their own families for the night. Angela and I ate dinner with her children while her husband was working. Now he is home, putting the children to bed, and we begin talking about women's unique work within the process of creation that includes a familiarity with darkness—the darkness of the Absolute as well as the darkness of the physical plane.

"Darkness is real," Angela says, with sudden tenderness. "Darkness is the ultimate reality. Everything comes out of darkness. Light and love come from the darkness. In the darkness there is so much light, so much love, because nothing gets in the way of the light, nothing reflects or refracts it. It is pure blackness, like the sun coming through outer space. The light is there, but you can't see it, because there is nothing for it to reflect off of. In the dark nothingness we can experience real love because even we are not there to limit it." This is the mystery of being and non-being at the same time—a mystery, Angela tells me, that women embody.

"Everything comes from the darkness," she says again. "This is why you can call this darkness 'She,' because everything is born from Her. The ways that form comes from this formless darkness are the hidden ways of creation.

And women know of these ways just as we know how to give birth. This is knowledge within all women, knowledge of how something is born from darkness, born from emptiness. The image of a child emerging from the womb is one of the easiest ways to illustrate what I am talking about. Although we don't see what happens during pregnancy, we are completely involved, and our bodies know what to do, how to be. And our involvement does not end when the child emerges, but it takes on a new form of care and love in a place of closeness, relationship, and separation.

"And women's involvement does not begin with the pregnancy. It begins before. At times when there are no physical signs at all, much before the physical conception even takes place. It really finds its source in the darkness far beyond the physical plane. Sometimes it is reflected in women's dreams in which they know they soon will be pregnant. There is a conception taking place some months before the physical conception, when the soul enters a certain plane of being that is not yet physical. This process of creation, that begins so far away in the unseen, and is yet so connected to life here on earth, is part of the mystery of women's being."

Angela tells me that women's spirituality can lead to an awakening of conscious participation in the process of creation. It is as though women no longer have to be cut off from knowing what takes place deep within as they give birth, as though they can become awake in the place of birth. "We can wake up in that darkness," she says, "and we have a specific order to guide life with love from there, from the unknown to the known, from the invisible to the visible."

I ask Angela how one can wake up in this darkness, this state of emptiness. "All kinds of spiritual traditions use meditation, prayer, and other practices to merge into this emptiness, the deep blackness that gives birth to light. You see it in all traditions, throughout the world. And meditation is another reflection of the vulnerability we were talking about earlier, the vulnerability of love, the receptivity and openness that is who we are before God. Because when we meditate we are completely alone before Him, we are attentive only to His needs, and in this state we can be used.

"It might take years of meditation to wake up in this darkness, yet it is a living potential in us all right now. And women have a natural affinity to it, as it is so much a part of our being. Whether you are a man or a woman, the process of merging depends upon feminine qualities of receptivity, stillness, vulnerability, and longing. Through our own vulnerability and longing we connect ourselves with the darkness within us, with the roots of all being."

Angela explains to me that merging is just one element in a spiritual process that includes full and complete participation in creation. Conscious merging into the darkness of the Absolute is one element; guiding the love and light from the Absolute into the world is another. "It is as though we spin inside the center of darkness, which is the merging," she tells me, "and at the same time we spin outside, guiding love into the world.

"How do we guide life with love from the formless into form?" she asks. "We can understand more if we look upon the ways we enter this state of emptiness. Through meditation, prayer, and grace we come consciously into the presence of this absolute darkness. That's so for all of us, for men and women. These practices open us more easily to our deeper nature, a nature that becomes more and more vulnerable. We open ourselves, reveal ourselves, become more receptive, and in doing so merge into the nothingness, the darkness where we are not.

"Here in the darkness we find the utmost vulnerability within ourselves, our deepest longing which is the state of our soul before God," she continues. "At the same time, we find the receptivity that allows us to receive the light. Our receptivity allows us to be used in the process of light taking on form, allows us to be used to guide light and form into the world. We die into the darkness and within the darkness die into the light so a new birth can happen."

An experience or understanding of this merging with the Absolute in which one receives divine light can include or encourage a turning away from the relative world. This has been the tendency for spiritual systems in the last two thousand years. "The transcendent and formless have become the goals," Angela says. "The world has been left behind. And yet for women this goes against our nature, which is to be involved, through love, in the entire process of creation. We can help guide the forms from the formless, and then, even further, care for what is now alive. We don't give birth to a child and then leave it alone! We instinctually care for creation. We nourish the world around us out of knowing the darkness and knowing the light, being at home in the formless emptiness where the source of everything is 'She.' From here we can guide the waters of life into the world. We live our responsibility as God has entrusted us for His sake. We become the eyes and ears of God, and bring back through our own consciousness the knowledge of the Truth.

"The danger is to dismiss this material world as incidental. But it is creation! The density of the physical plane allows the light of God, the pure light that comes from the Absolute, to be reflected so we can all see it, and so He can see it through our eyes. It is so simple—the pure light of the darkness can not be experienced unless there is something to reflect it. In the absolute darkness there is no duality, nothing to reflect His light. So it must be brought into the world of forms if His light is to be known. Experiencing God's presence includes, then, the density of form that reflects His light. How else would we know Him? How else would He know Himself?"

By this process, human beings come to know the Absolute through the relative. Without the relative world there is no divine knowledge, and no way to serve as God's witness to creation. We can only fulfill this role if we are willing to be here, in this world, with conscious care. This includes turning our consciousness towards the darkness of matter and the world of form. Towards all that we experience as solid and dense, so seemingly unlike the space and complete freedom of the Absolute.

THE LIGHT IN MATTER

I spend the afternoon on one of Angela's neighbor's bicycles. It is a beautiful clear day, bright and cool. I ride miles beyond Angela's house, down small cobblestone pathways leading past the endless fields of wheat. Hawks fly overhead and threshers move slowly along the horizon. I return late in the day, and meet Angela for tea. Her youngest daughter sits with us for a while in the back garden, curious about the American woman who has come to visit her mother. She and I try to speak with each other despite our language differences and her sweet shyness. Soon Angela's husband calls out from a window above, encouraging his daughter to leave us alone so Angela and I can talk again in private.

As the temperature cools and the afternoon turns slowly into evening, we begin to talk about the earth, and the ways our spiritual systems have largely lost contact with its real resources.

"We have for so long turned our consciousness from creation," Angela says slowly. "But creation needs the light and love of consciousness. The world needs so much light and love. We are all made of light, made of love. Becoming conscious of that and living our human feminine qualities of love, attentiveness, care, and compassion for all creation brings into light what we have rejected for so long. Shines light on the so-called 'dark places,' and makes visible the feminine ways that honor all creation as sacred. I don't mean that we need to try to improve the world, or save the world. But just to turn our consciousness towards the world with an understanding of its divinity. This way we allow love to flow through us into the world according to His will."

Every level of reality reflects every other level. As we consciously participate in this complete process of creation, in which we accept our role as the eyes and ears of God, we begin to transform our own consciousness from a consciousness of duality to a consciousness of oneness in which we see how all things reflect each other. This transformation allows us to see that the darkness of the Absolute is reflected in the darkness of the earth, that the light of the Absolute is the unrecognized light of the earth. Being present in absolute emptiness is in its core the same as being present in the emptiness of life. Density is not really dense; the endless space and freedom of the Absolute exist everywhere. The wholeness of women allows us natural awareness of the wholeness of all life, the way oneness exists within all levels of reality.

"Through our surrender to being here and to all aspects of life, we become one with what is created," Angela tells me, "if we don't reject life, regardless of what it brings us, if we invite and welcome life like a beloved friend who arrives at our door, if we don't judge, don't divide life into pleasant and unpleasant experiences, then we give ourselves to being here in this world. Then we can enter the core of creation. We descend into the inner places of the earth, and here we find the heart of the earth. We know the non-being, and we know the being, and we know the place in between where love comes into the world. We experience real love, and also we see how real love is reflected into the physical world through compassion, attentiveness, care, change, and transformation.

"It is a new way to surrender, a new way to be of service," Angela says, as she pours us both more tea. "And yet women have always known the potentials of darkness within life, within matter, because we are so close to creation. This closeness gives us knowledge about the secrets of creation, how nothing is as it appears, and how the hidden nature of this world reveals itself when we turn with love into the darkness that is here.

"You see, light and matter are not really different. This is why it's so hard to explain. We're used to seeing it differently—there is the light and there is matter. We are used to looking to the light and getting away from matter. But there is light *in* the matter. It is as though there are treasures of gold in the earth. Or like diamonds: only when you put them into light they are radiating and shining; they are pure light. But they are growing in the earth, and already in the earth they are diamonds. We just have to put the light of consciousness on them in order to make them shine."

Angela tells me that she recently took her children to an experiential museum in which visitors can explore and interact with aspects of the planet and the cosmos. "Did you know," she asks, "that if you go under water at least two hundred meters there is a darkness so complete that no sunlight can enter? But here there are strange fish that contain this light, this luminosity. It is a light that is not a reflection of the sun. And the deeper you go the more light there is in these fish. Well, that is how it is in the depths of darkness. There is a light there from a seemingly different source than the light above, originating in the darkness. Women know light like this, because it lives inside us in a conscious form.

"In spiritual transformation," she continues, "and in the transformation of matter, what is physical has to receive the light. It is like a union. But it is not really a physical thing—in fact it is light uniting with light, consciousness uniting with consciousness. This is essential in women's spiritual transformation because women receive the light within their physical bodies. The pure essence that comes in is light, and the light enclosed in matter is activated by this light. And the deeper you go into the earth the more there is the light. The deeper you go the less the light is frozen. When the light comes together with light, when the light in the matter is activated, something happens in what we call the material, the physical matter, because then you can see that matter is not just matter but it is energy flowing in a certain way. Then we become conscious of what matter really is, and how the energy structure of matter functions. And matter itself becomes conscious. This is consciousness of oneness, for in oneness where is the distinction between matter and spirit? Between light and dark?

"It seems to us as though matter becomes finer and finer, more and more transparent. In fact it is the consciousness that puts the light on it, to reveal that it's all flowing. So it's the consciousness that reveals that it is all sacred, that what you call matter is sacred, the earth is sacred, our bodies are sacred."

Angela tells me she experiences women's unique relationship to matter and the light within matter through the involvement of her own body in her work with others. "I know when I am with women that my body is involved in a different way than when I am with men. Women need the physical presence of the person who guides the process until a certain stage," she says. "There is a process of transmission between people. It is as though the light within one awakens the light within the other. It is a process within the body, including the body.

"The transmission happens through the whole body. It is not physical, and yet it is carried by the physical body. For example, when we talk to each other we are connected through sound, which comes from the voice. The voice is carried through the breath, which is in its core the transmitting substance of light. Breath belongs to both worlds and connects them, the created and the uncreated. Breath has a physical dimension and a spiritual dimension as well."

In this process, light enters a woman through her throat *chakra* and activates the light in her body. "Receiving this light is an initiation for women," Angela tells me, speaking softly. "Inwardly she is prepared; the light within her is in expectation, a state of dynamic receptivity. She receives in her heart, through her throat chakra, what is given from a heart in love. Light meets light and awakens light. Light that is kept hidden in matter begins circulating. Matter is not matter anymore. This is the transformation of women. This is how she begins living the mysteries of creation, the mysteries of what is hidden in her body, in the earth, in life."

THE SACRED SUBSTANCE WITHIN WOMEN

"There is a secret in women's bodies," Angela tells me, in the quiet of one early morning, before the children are awake. "It is a beautiful secret, a gift from God, a gift found nowhere else in creation. It is a substance that helps incarnate the divine, bring spirit into matter. It is a secret because even women themselves don't know it lives inside them. But women can come to know this gift; it is their way Home, and it is the way for women and the created world itself to become aware of its sacredness."

This substance within women's bodies is love, divine consciousness, and life itself. It is in women's bodies because women give birth, because women know the mysteries of creation. "This substance belongs to the body, to the heart, to life," Angela explains. "If a woman loves she loves with this substance. She receives love, receives light with this substance. How can you describe this substance that is not really a substance? It is not matter, but it permeates matter and is flowing between the cells of the body.

"This is my way of seeing it. For me it is more emptiness than 'something.' It just is. One can see it through its expressions, how the sacredness expresses itself in the world. Like the scent of a rose, but not the rose itself. Like the Creator in creation. Something unearthly reflected here on earth.

"In women it can be reflected through beauty. The beauty of being a woman. It is God reflected through her. Why is beauty so appealing to us, to all people all over the world, throughout all ages of time? Why is beauty so seductive, why does it fill our hearts with amazement and awe? We marvel before beauty in nature, in the arts, and in women, even if most women don't know that they are beautiful. Why? Because beauty touches our hearts with remembrance of its Creator. It is His love reflected so directly that no heart can really remain closed to it. If we are open to beauty, we sense the sacredness within. It is the sacred substance given to women that makes them beautiful. Our spiritual traditions that became focused more and more on transcendence tend to deny and neglect beauty in women as it is an expression of the immanence of the divine. But if a woman denies her beauty, she also denies the sacred substance within her which is nourishing her spiritual potential."

A woman's spiritual evolution allows greater and greater awareness of this substance, and it is her participation in life that allows the substance to transform and reveal itself into consciousness more completely.

"The only thing we can do with this substance," Angela says, "and of course we can't really do anything directly with it because it is a form of divine consciousness, is to become aware of it and then it can flow, consciously, through our natural instincts."

Consciousness has tremendous power, and when a woman brings together her instinctual nature with an awareness of the divine within herself, the creative potential of God becomes expressed through her individual relationship with life. This process intertwines the most ordinary with the most sacred so that what is real can flow through all life and all experiences.

"Spirituality for women can be so simple. Women need to be themselves. That's all. This is how we become more conscious of our divinity, of this divine substance within us. By being herself, a woman brings together her instinctual nature with this divine substance. Women are naturally connected to matter, to creation. When we live this connection we live our divine nature through our ordinary nature; they become one."

A woman's instinctual nature has the potential to reveal her sacred nature, which is itself the creative potential of God. A woman allows this by consciously honoring her body, honoring her own individual ways of knowing and being, and expressing her instinctual nature through love. She lives her instinctual nature within the relationships with family and others in daily life and with the natural world. She lives it through her sexuality, her intelligence, her passion in life, the cycles of her body, and through giving birth. Through the simple tasks of the day, the way she cooks, nourishes, and cares for herself and her environment, and through her natural creativity. Not through the desire to satisfy her own needs, but with a sense of offering herself and her experience in relationships of unconditional love. Ultimately, in service to the divine within herself and all things.

At its essence, the creative power within women is the secret of the word "Be."

"The mystery of creation is a feminine mystery," Angela says. "It is the mystery of *being*. A woman carries the secret of how multiplicity comes from oneness within her heart and body. And so she has a role to play in creation, a special responsibility for birthing the sacred here on earth."

RESPONSIBILITY TO THE EARTH

One of my last mornings in Germany, I ride the bike towards the open fields that have become my favorite place to go when I want time away from the retreat and my work with Angela. I wear a coat, and a scarf wrapped around my neck; it is cool, and the early morning mist has yet to burn away in the sun. All the landscape is soft and wet, like the air. The shapes of the trees, the edges of the pathway in the distance, all flow into each other, gentle and indistinct. Even the birds seem to come gently into view, and then melt back into the soft gray sky, disappearing for a time, maybe reappearing moments later down the path.

All the tall wheat from the day before is now gone, the farmers having suddenly finished haying for the season. Rolls and rolls of grain—each seemingly over ten feet high— lie far apart from each other across the acres of flat ground, still golden despite the muted light. I have never seen hay in these large round shapes before, being used to the rectangular bales I see in America that lie closer to the ground, and closer to each other. Wet and warm from riding, I find the smooth bit of the cobblestone path and ride slowly past these giant circular signs of harvest, returning later to Angela's house for breakfast.

We talk this morning about women's unique connection to the created world. As Angela explains, a woman has a responsibility to live her divine nature not for her own sake but for the sake of creation. Creation needs women, and women need to honor and respect this relationship.

"The key to life is within women," she tells me, after we have moved from the dining room into the living room, quiet now behind closed doors, the morning sun pouring in from behind the apple tree through the open window. "There is a certain magnetism between the earth and the physical female body, between her body and the vibrations of the earth, that is not present in men's bodies. It is as though women's energy is polarized differently than men's, the way her etheric body and physical body meet is charged differently. This puts women in a specific relationship to earth. Women take up and digest the energy from the earth differently.

"The task for women is to consciously live their unique connection with the earth. The earth needs to stay connected with consciousness. Matter is so dense, and consciousness vibrates at a much finer frequency, and matter needs consciousness. You can look at it as women providing a way for the earth to be conscious.

"It's like when there is moisture in the earth and it comes up as fog," she continues, gesturing upward, "and goes up as clouds, and the finer and more diffuse it becomes the more it separates from the earth; it goes higher and higher. And somehow it is the task of women to let the clouds rain again so that the moisture can take form again, so that it comes back to earth because the earth needs it. In the same way, the earth is suffering in women when they are disconnected. Because matter needs women in order to stay connected.

"I asked my husband one day when we were doing our shopping why it is that women are so attached to things in the world. And his answer was, 'Because someone has to be.' And I understood that it is women's role to be attached to creation, in part because men do not have this capacity, and the earth needs humanity to be attached. Of course it is a woman's responsibility to transform her attachments into connections of love that nourish.

"As a mother you learn this; your child is somehow fulfilled when you're fulfilled. It is as simple as that. If the earth, the whole of creation, needs to be taken care of, women need to take care of creation within themselves. And they do this by caring for their own bodies and their own relationships to matter through their own bodies. So we can say the world is happy when women are happy. The earth radiates with light when women radiate light.

"This connection between the earth and the transformation of women is very tangible. You can see it in the relationship between the cycles within women's bodies and the cycles of the moon. There are cycles in nature as well as in the lives of women. We have the seasons, and the cycles of ebb and high tide, which again are connected to cycles of the moon in relationship to the earth. Everything is connected.

"You see, I am living here near the northern sea coast where there are very strong tides. The midwives in this area know very well when the expected babies will be born. The delivery rooms in the hospitals are crowded at the high tide.

With my own babies, it was like this. I could be sure, each time, they would not come before the waters flooded back to the shore.

"Also, menstruation gives a rhythm in the life of a woman which flows with those cycles. Everything in creation is pulsating in the rhythm between expansion and contraction, and these rhythms determine our earthly life. Women are immersed so deeply into these rhythms of creation, into the cycles of the earth, because they experience it through their bodies for decades of their lives. For many women, the years of fertility, the years when women menstruate, are a very important time in their spiritual journey. We know how to see menstruation as something that makes women impure, and which doesn't allow them to participate in specific spiritual practices or gatherings. In fact, menstruation itself is a very efficient way of purification for women. So during this time of women's lives the work of purification and transformation flows more easily than before or after. This says something about how our bodies are important, how they are included in our own transformation as well as in the transformation of the whole."

Often women's spiritual awakening includes a new way of relating to the earth. Angela tells me that when she was in her twenties she spent two years living very close to nature, in a community that had no heating, no electricity. "The ancient feminine wisdom was reawakened through sitting at night by the fire," she says, "sitting under the starry sky, watching the ways of the stars, the changing moon at night. And in the daylight, painting, writing poems and songs, sharing dreams with other women and singing, working in the field, and caring for the animals. It was not romantic, and was not easy. We were not protected from the cold icy Scandinavian winters, from the storms coming from the ocean, from the heat of the sun in summer. But we were part of earth and nature, very deeply, and of the spirit that permeates it."

For Angela, this time in nature added to her understanding of herself and her relationship with the planet. "I had to go as close as possible to the heart of nature, to listen to her song," she says softly, smiling. "The song of creation praising the Creator. The ancient melody of the feminine mystery of creation. How things come into being and how they return. And all the while we nourished the qualities and potency of the heart—intuition, devotion, longing. The ancient knowledge of the soul.

"Some of the few practices I encourage women to do help them become conscious of their relationship to the earth, because it is such an essential and nourishing relationship. I might suggest a woman walk barefoot in grass. Or walk, slowly, consciously linking her breathing to her footsteps. These exercises can help a woman connect to the earth through her body. This is done for her own expanded consciousness, but also to serve the earth, to honor its sacredness.

"The feminine is the key to becoming alive," she continues. "But women do not really use this key, and they do not use it consciously. The world is crying out for liveliness. Spiritual consciousness wants to be lived. The world is thirsty for life itself!"

RETURNING

"The mystery of the feminine is the way of creation," Angela tells me in our last days together, "the way of becoming, of coming into this world; what women experience within ourselves, in our bodies—the ability to become pregnant and give birth, to participate in the whole process of creation. Women know this way; we know creation as it comes into the life.

"But we also know the way back," she says quietly. "And that's so difficult to put into words. It's the part that makes life complete, but it is the part that has been cut off for such a long time. And it's easy to overlook. The process of creation and giving birth—it's only half of the process. What is happening to the soul in the spiritual journey, in the process of transformation, is the way to be born again. And this process of being born again is the way the soul brings back to the source its experiences here. This is the real cycle of creation.

"What comes home on the spiritual journey is the fragrance. Or the flavor of honey which is unique to the journey of each soul. This mystery of light upon light, light awakening light, is like the bee flying back from the flower to the beehive. Something is returning. The bee is humming the secret of becoming and being, the knowing that without creation there is no real transformation, and without the essence there is no real fragrance, no sweetness.

"One of my favorite sayings within Sufism is, 'I was a hidden treasure and I longed to be known, so I created the world.' This speaks to us about why God created the world; it tells us something of His secret, and also speaks to us about why we are here. And somehow expresses exactly the secret that is planted into women, a woman's divine knowing."

All my talks with Angela turn around the central theme that women know, intuitively, the mysteries of creation, of how form is birthed from formlessness and flows back into the eternal. Women have the potential to live this wisdom consciously, for their own sake and the sake of the whole. In doing so, they can help awaken a sacredness here, reveal the presence of the divine here in this world.

I sit with Angela in California, where she has brought her family on a vacation, and where she meditates with a Sufi group. Eucalyptus trees send their sharp, clean scent on the breeze, and fog begins to lift off of the ridge behind the house where she stays.

"It is time to come down from the mountains," she tells me. "To bring the beautiful clarity, the vastness of the sky, deep into the valleys where life is waiting. The clear and icy wind of the mountaintops is still with us. But if it descends, the earth will warm this wind, and the wind will refresh the land.

"We are on the threshold of a time in which humanity and spirituality can come together in a new way. Signs are appearing everywhere, signs that our time contains a great opportunity for humanity. Life on our planet is threatened—menaced in an alarming way through greed and growing materialism. Yet there appear possibilities that are barely visible, possibilities for a new consciousness that will help us rediscover a pure flow of life and perceive the holiness of life in a new way. This new consciousness includes a more spiritual relationship to matter and a more physical relationship to spirituality because it is a consciousness of oneness.

"Just as the dark balances the light, the moon the sun, we need the feminine as well as the masculine in order to make this new consciousness alive in the world. All humanity is waiting for this, waiting for what is whole and complete to manifest here. Men and women equally need the feminine to be lived in a new way so we can recognize and live within the wholeness of love and life. Because the feminine contains a special knowledge of this balance within all of us. The feminine knows that darkness and light, matter and spirit, originate from the same source and are contained within each other, and that their coming together leads to new possibilities.

"The ways of the feminine within us all can receive and live the new consciousness that is being offered to the world, to give it the character of life and humanness, to give it warmth. This is what women know, deep in their being. They know how to receive what is being given, how to bring balance to creation, how to know God here, how to unite what we have all kept split apart for too long."

Angela and I sit quietly for a while. It is almost silent here on the porch of the house, except for the cries of birds soaring in front of us, and the wind that can pick up in the afternoon the way it does now. Her children and husband are at the beach, giving us a last bit of time alone. In the stillness I feel Angela's excitement, the anticipation of something new.

"Maybe now it is time for all of us, and especially for women, to let go of the belief and the fear that we can never enter the light of Truth as long as we embrace and are embraced by life. It is possible that we can dance in celebration of life—full and empty at once—and at the same time see through the veils that have concealed what is real.

"Why not have both?" she asks. "Why not go to God while embracing life? Why not surrender to Him while dancing, so that He can celebrate His beauty and His joy through us? So that the dance is not forgotten, so the singing is not forgotten as we come nearer to Him. When stillness and emptiness again sing in the midst of the chaos of life, then the future will dance towards us in celebration and joy."

Angela and I sit and smile at each other. The day is beginning to end, and her family will be back from the beach soon. After a time, I leave, and Angela goes inside to get dinner ready.

The mystery of feminine transformation
is the mystery of creation,
it is the secret of musk and fragrance.
The mystery of bee and honey.
The dance of matter and spirit, of unity
of light and darkness, of the luminous dark.

Divine essence is the One.
One and Alone.
The Beloved is the musk and the fragrance,
the nectar, the bee, and the honey.
The Nothing that comes into being through love,
the being that comes into the world through creative power,
the world that appears with light and shadow.

His creation is the reflection of His non-existence into existence.
This is our world, our earth, our body, our being.
These are the seasons, the songs of the birds,
the whispering of wind.
This is the laughter of children and the pain of giving birth,
the sigh of longing and the tears of separation.
The endless joy in reuniting.

Divine essence is the One. One and Alone.
The Beloved is the musk and the fragrance,
The honey, the bee, and the nectar.
This One is the essence and the fragrance as well.
It flows into the shape formed by the play of light and shadow.
It is transformation through creative power,
return of form into formlessness.
The formless being that through which love merges
into nothingness
unites, dissolves, loses itself.
Creation and complete transformation forming
the circle of wholeness and nothingness.
The mystery is a circle of love.

ANGELA FISCHER

IN RELATION

a meeting with

Pansy Hawk Wing

In Relation

PIPE CARRIER

 Pansy Hawk Wing tells the story of how the teachings of the *Canupa*, the Sacred Pipe, came to her people:

The people lived knowing that there would be a message coming. They didn't know in what form, or how it would come. One day two men—two scouts—were out looking for hunting grounds for the camp. While they were out, one of them looked to the West and there was a white cloud and as it came close they realized it was a woman dressed in white buckskin, pure white buffalo calfskin. She was so beautiful, and the one man said, "This must be something sacred, she brings us that message we are waiting for." The other one had sexual thoughts about the woman. And as the woman approached, she looked at the one who had the carnal thoughts and the smoke happened there and when the smoke cleared there was nothing but bones. And she looked at the other man and said, "I have a message. You will return to your camp and prepare a place for me. And I will come in four days and I will bring you this message. I have something to tell your people."

So the man rode home and told everyone in the camp. They instinctively knew what to do; they prepared a lodge and they put sage down because that's what we do to prepare a special altar. They put sage down, everyone gathered, and then she appeared. She came in, and her message to the people was, "I brought you this *Canupa*, this Sacred Pipe. And with this *Canupa* I bring you the laws." There are seven of them. And the people were doing two already. And I think they were doing the others; they just weren't seen that way. So she repeated the other five so we have seven rites that govern our people and seven values that govern our people.

For over twenty-five years, Pansy Hawk Wing has been a pipe carrier in the Lakota Sioux tradition. She follows the ways of her ancestors as they were taught to her people by the White Buffalo Calf Pipe Woman. She picked up the Sacred Pipe because she knew that without a radical change in her life she would die.

"When I first picked up the *Canupa*," she tells me, as we sit at her small round kitchen table drinking water, "I was very definitely spiritually impoverished, spiritually hungry, spiritually without. I picked it up in the beginning because I knew I was dying, spiritually dying. Everything outward looked good, but inward I was dying. I picked it up to save myself, to not die. And I was in it; I was carried along by this momentum. And a few years down the line I realized I was teaching. I never planned that."

I spend a week visiting with Pansy, talking and eating with her, and joining in a sweat lodge in her honor. Pansy is 56 years old, a strong and steady woman with a round head of brown hair sticking up straight and soft around her face like a fuzzy halo or an old fur hat. She has a loud and full laugh, sometimes warm and welcoming, sometimes cutting and clear. She is gentle and generous, and also very strong and cold. After years of commitment to her path and her people she is recognized by men and women alike, both within and beyond her tribe, as a spiritual leader and teacher.

Pansy insists she won't be called a *medicine woman*, explaining that the term originated with Christians who settled the Western territories and oppressed the Lakota people. As she speaks to me I see a look of delight cross her face, and I know a joke is coming. "The only medicine woman I know," she says, "is Dr. Quinn!" We both laugh loudly and I laugh mostly because her eagerness and joy are so contagious. At the end of the week she tells the joke again and we laugh even harder.

Pansy lives on Osage Way,[1] a cul-de-sac off a busy street in northeast Denver. Her small house and garage look like most brick houses in the American suburban landscape, but few houses in working-class America contain and reflect a feeling of being somewhere else entirely. In Pansy's house I feel as though I am on a different Osage Way, where the sage is not just a street sign, but a living sign, permeating every corner of the house, bringing with it the scent of another way of life.

Pansy lives with a roommate, a quiet middle-aged man who served in Vietnam and goes with Pansy to Lakota ceremonies. Their living room is filled with Lakota ritual art—including a stuffed coyote and hawk and Native American patterned blankets. The CD player in the small kitchen plays songs that combine new-age music with traditional Native American chanting, and candles and sage mix on the kitchen table with the day's mail.

On one hand the suburban ordinariness of Pansy's living situation seems inharmonious with being a Lakota teacher, and also reflects the tragic homelessness of Native Americans in our contemporary culture. On the other hand it reflects a different kind of homelessness—the essential other-worldliness of genuine spirituality. Meeting with Pansy here shows me that what is real can exist in every part of the world, even on a little cul-de-sac at the edge of a big city, across from Walgreens and the corner gas station. In her house I feel the richness of who she is and what she helps bring into life, a richness against which every other kind of wealth can only be seen as meaningless.

Every day for almost a week we sit together in her small kitchen and I am drawn into her stories and teachings by her sincerity and humor and also by the atmosphere around us. One night she invites me for dinner with three other friends of hers, all women who take part in ceremonies with Pansy, all of whom I meet again later in a sweat lodge. During dinner, as well as every other time I meet with Pansy, I am moved by her openness and joy, as well as by her steely sense of duty to what is real.

There is always a fullness in the house, a feeling of softness and containment. At times when I am with Pansy I become tired and lose my train of thought, the energy of the house pulling me somewhere else, and then we just laugh together. Throughout our meetings she shows me how to be in two places at once, how to sit with her but also let myself be taken by the energy that is alive around us. I come to understand that the full and sometimes dis-orienting atmosphere reflects an access to the spirit world, what she calls "the other side." She herself is always in both the ordinary and the spirit world, and during our time together I am given the opportunity to be with her in this sacred space where the two worlds meet.

As our week together progresses I come to understand more about Pansy's unique role in the spirituality of her own culture, and her role in the wider context of helping bring a feminine power and energy into the world. But in our first meetings Pansy introduces me to the essential aspects of the Lakota tradition.

BEING IN RELATION

"The way of the Sacred Pipe is the way of instinctual truth, the way of honesty, the way that allows the natural flow of things," Pansy says slowly. The Great Spirit, or Great Mystery, is literally translated as "that which moves in all things," indicating a spirit or energy that exists both beyond and within all of creation. Pansy tells me that human beings have the opportunity to be aware of this natural flow of energy, to relate to it and allow it to go where it needs to go. In many ways this is a simple truth, a simple path.

"It's bringing people back to the basics," she explains. "It's bringing people back to our basic doctrine that says, 'All of my relatives'; that says, 'I am in relation to all things around me.' That's the concept we are teaching: How do I build that relationship? How do I maintain that relationship? Not only with people, but with nature, and with the elements, and with our ancestors, and with the stars."

The way Pansy speaks and acts makes it clear that the truth of being in relation with all things is not an obscure or abstract concept. Rather it is a fact, a simple and basic aspect of life. "You just breathe in and out," she says quietly. "You walk when you need to, sit when you need to. You drink when you need to, sleep when you need to. You learn how to go with the natural flow of things. The way the water flows, the way the air moves, the way the sun shines. To learn how to go with that, to just be in that, and not have to bend the rays, and not have to change things, like dam the water, log jam the water; to go with the flow."

Pansy tells me that while it is a simple path, it is also a dangerous and demanding path, requiring constant attention and commitment. "The path of the Sacred Pipe is so narrow," she explains, "because there is ignorance around us at all times: not knowing yourself, not knowing your spirit, not knowing why you do things. Ignorance is our greatest enemy. We have to face it in ourselves—the weaknesses and the frailty of our humanness.

"This is a way of life," she says with seriousness and deep sincerity. "You're going to have to change things in your life. That's what pipe carriers have decided to do, change their whole way of life. It's not a religion, not just a period of time where they can pray, then the rest of the time go back to where they were. It requires a lot of change. It requires a sense of responsibility, a sense of community, a sense of obligation to do certain things. It's a very basic, very primal way of living your life.

"In the beginning," she continues, "one of the things we learn is you walk on the earth as if you're wearing moccasins—to not be loud. Walking quietly on this path. You become aware of that—you walk differently, you become slower." You must move more slowly, more carefully, because the path requires you "to go inward and rely on your own self-discipline, basic human instincts, basic human truths." These are not taught, are not discovered through a rule-book, but are found only when you take responsibility for your life and use discipline to always be attentive, to listen to what you know and feel inside.

"The White Buffalo Calf Pipe Woman who brought the Sacred Pipe to the Lakota people embodies all of the qualities that we are trying to reach on our individual paths," Pansy says. "Walking in harmony, walking in balance, understanding about wisdom—the difference between what I can know and what I can't—understanding about health, our responsibilities there, being mentally healthy, emotionally healthy, physically healthy. Understanding about kindness and generosity, and ownership of things in its rightful place—not to get off-balance on acquiring things. And understanding that we need to continue in this life to purify ourselves, we need to continue to present ourselves to the spirits by acknowledging that we are the two-legged who need understanding, who need wisdom, and need to learn to care about others, care about ourselves. Knowing whether or not we have the capacity to nurture and how we can do that. And knowing our limitations as human beings. Having the goal to walk in harmony. And as I understand it the Sacred Calf Pipe Woman is one who reached that place. She's the goal. And as we work on ourselves continually we get more of a glimpse of how she arrived there. The teachings come from her, and they are taught to us through the directions."

THE SEVEN DIRECTIONS AND THE OTHER SIDE

Pansy tells me that the rhythms and patterns of creation reflect the ways the divine comes into life. According to Lakota tradition the Great Spirit comes into manifestation through seven directions—Grandfather, Grandmother, North, South, East, West, and the seventh direction which is one's own center, one's own path to the spirit world. Grandfather is the heavens above, Grandmother is the earth below, and the remaining directions form a map or axis on the plane between heaven and earth. The directions reflect the natural flow of life, the natural way the divine creates and recreates the world.

One can look to the directions in order to be conscious of how the Great Spirit is revealing itself here on earth. All directions are included; each has a role to play in the process of creation and in the process of our own transformation. "To the West we seek wisdom," Pansy explains. "To the North we walk a path of seeking health, of balancing mind, body, and spirit. The East represents kindness and generosity to ourselves and to others. To the South is purification. The spirits in that direction are keepers of the purification ceremonies."

Grandfather and Grandmother represent the ways of masculine and feminine energy. They are always in balance with each other, always equally important. "Grandfather is when you step beyond what you think your limitations are," Pansy explains. "When you take the risk, when you go beyond. Grandfather also reflects unconditional love, limitless and transcendent love, love beyond all form."

Grandmother is reflected and embodied through the ways of the earth, the ways of the animals and all of nature. "The values of Grandmother are nurturing, to emotionally, spiritually, and physically feed people. We understand the power or essence of Grandmother by turning inward, by being quiet and listening, by walking slowly.

"And the seventh direction is that which you will find when you live all six. That is your center, your path, your path to the spirit world. The word for the seventh direction means, 'You walk in strength and quietness with all things around you.'" The seventh direction is our way of participating in how Spirit comes into the world. But it is only one of seven directions and understanding this helps a person be humble and in proper relation to the larger process of divine manifestation.

Pansy explains to me that the White Buffalo Calf Pipe Woman brought seven rites to the Lakota people to help realize the values of the directions. And help from the four realms of spirits is always available. "You will have an ancestor for every direction," she describes. "You will also have an animal for every direction, you will also have an element for every direction, you will also have the heavens for every direction. For each of the seven directions one will possibly have help from one or some of the four spirit realms, depending on how much time one spends practicing the sacred rites."

The spirit helpers are always available to help us, always near, but we must access "the other side" in order to receive their help. Every rite or ceremony is designed to create sacred space, the space that opens us to the other side and allows us to receive the guidance we need to realize the values of the seven directions.

The helpers, or guides, exist in the spirit realm. Even the animals and elements which actually exist here on earth also exist as spirit guides on the other side. One might have a relationship with an herb, for example, but one is not relating just to the herb as a physical object, but also to the spirit of the herb, the energy or life of the herb, which can work with a person and help that person on his or her journey.

The spirit realms all exist between heaven and earth, between the Grandfather and Grandmother. "So there's no idea that there's heaven up there and you have to leave here to go there," Pansy says, pointing with one arm upward. "The spirits are in between the two. We are in between the two. We don't have to leave here to go there. Nor do we have to be *here* and forget about *there*. Everything is between heaven and earth.

"The idea of the other side is that there is peace there, there is balance there," she continues, speaking softly. "It's the place you arrive at when you are in ceremony. Each time we go into ceremony, or sacred space, we go to the other side. The idea of being on earth is that this is a journey, this is a path. We can go to the other side in order to assist the journey. Your spirit helpers are there; your relatives are there. Here we experience pain, and joy, and loss. But on the other side is harmony."

BETWEEN THE HUMAN WORLD AND SPIRIT WORLDS

On anyone's path, there is a point of intersection at which the individual's journey crosses the line where the spirits move. Pansy tells me that in Lakota ceremonies, this intersection is represented by the point where the East and West axis crosses the North and South axis. On one's own path, one moves from South to North, and the spirits move from East to West. In the center, one rests in both worlds, neither completely here nor completely there, but in both this world and the spirit world. This is sacred space.

"There is that place you arrive at in ceremony," Pansy says, "that goes on continually there. And all your relatives are there. Everything is similar to here, but on the other side."

Pansy is continually at this center point. She is in constant communication with the other side; she is a bridge between the worlds. I see this in her steadiness, in the way she is always listening somewhere else, in the way she seems to always know more than she says and so easily forgets what it was she did say. She is in the moment, the real moment, the moment in which she embodies the paradox of existence and non-existence, where she seems to be totally present and yet absent at the same time. Here and not here, listening and acting, waiting and participating, she offers constant and direct access to a timeless and peaceful world.

From her place of stillness, the distinctions between here and there, between human and spirit, fall away. She lives within the flow, turning inward to know what is needed in every moment. It was not always this way. When asked if she remembers what it was like for her twenty-five years ago, she answers with sadness, "Oh yeah, oh yeah, I'll never forget. It was like always looking for something, always searching for something. It's like within grasp and you lose it; if you look again, it's within grasp and you lose it again. When today, whatever that thing is you're reaching out for permeates your whole being.

"At the beginning, I remember attending a Sun Dance, being in the circle, and looking up to the hill to the West. And I saw that the trees were dancing. I was thinking, 'Wow!' I was really awed by that. I said to myself, 'Those trees are dancing!' I watched them, and then I put my focus on the sacred tree that was in the middle of the arbor, and I had this overwhelming sense of being home. I'd come home. I knew without any doubt, I didn't have to wonder if it was time. I knew that I was home."

During those early years on the path, she found herself sometimes in the flow, and sometimes out of the flow. It took discipline and focus to bring herself back to where she needed to be. "There were times in my journey where I felt like I was carried by Spirit, and other times where I had to say, 'There is nothing or no one who will come between me and my *Canupa*. This is my life.' And that was a conscious decision I had to make. Almost like a *mantra*. I had to keep saying, 'This is who I am.'"

She was never aware of the exact moment she became permanently situated in both worlds, living in sacred space. "I didn't know I was getting there," she says. "I didn't know that's where I was going. I had glimpses of it along the way, and those glimpses got longer. And then one day it's permeating your whole being. And you just know that.

"I'll never forget the search," she continues, "and I think that's what helps me reach the women I work with. I'll never forget what it was like. I'll never forget that place where it was dark, that place where you're constantly searching for something. And if you grab it, it just falls through your fingers. It's a lonely place."

I ask her if she is ever lonely now, and she tells me that while she knows she is always alone, she is never lonely. In her complete aloneness she is connected to everything she needs.

"If someone watched me without me knowing it they might think I was crazy!" she says, laughing. "Because I'm always walking around talking to myself, talking and responding. I suppose it is a little different!"

I say to her, "But you're not really talking to yourself, are you?" And she shakes her head emphatically. "No!" she says with a big knowing smile, and laughs even harder.

"Well, sometimes a song will come to me," she tells me eagerly, "and I'll just blare it out. And there is always a message in the song, and you have to pay attention to what it is telling you. I have noises that I hear, and I have to listen. Or taking a drink of water, it's like, 'OK, here's healing, allow the water to move through you.' It's like a whole different way of relating to things around you.

"One of the healing elements of water is in the full moon, so you set out a glass of water and let the energy of the moon come into that. When it snows, you say, 'Thank you for cleansing the earth.' When it rains, the earth needs to be fed. When the wind comes, the wind is taking the negative energy and moving it on. The wind is medicine for people. You see a tree limb waving, and I go, 'Oh, the spirits are talking!' Sometimes you listen to that and a song comes to you, and you have to sing! I just follow my instincts; I just follow my inner voice saying this is what I need to do. It's like when you think about a friend and you call them and they were just thinking about you. It's like that all the time now."

While Pansy is continually in sacred space, there is a flux in the intensity of the space. There are times when more is asked of her and times of less demand. "It's like the difference between being in a room alone and suddenly being in a room of ten people, and you're in relation to all of them." Pansy laughs now as she continues, "The only effort I've put into it is trying to remember people's names!"

A LAKOTA SIOUX IN AN ANGLO-CHRISTIAN WORLD

Pansy tells me that the Anglo-Christian influence on the Lakota people has been so destructive and insidious that even within her own culture she has, at times, felt like an outsider. She struggles to maintain and offer the pure teachings of her ancestors in a culture that has largely forgotten those ancient ways and has, instead, consciously and unconsciously allowed Christian indoctrination to influence its spirituality. Here, again, she has learned to walk in two worlds, recognizing the distinctions between them, and working to infuse one with the other.

"Anyone who questions whether or not to be a *Canupa* carrier," Pansy insists, "one of the things I would say to you early on is first you need to understand that Christianity has infiltrated our basic foundation. You need to know that. So what our society has become is a small replica of Christianity where men are the leaders; men are the mediators. Here are the lowly people and here are the spirits," she says, gesturing with one hand at her waist, the other above her head.

"Our spirituality went underground because from the 1800's on there was a heavy-duty emphasis on taking the Indian out of the Indian. One of the areas the Christians were afraid of was our spirituality. People of my parents' generation and older were sort of brainwashed into thinking that this is pagan and blasphemy against the church. And our ways were not going to work. And the Christians have taken the ceremonies and almost ridiculed them to the point that a lot of our people, those who followed the *Canupa*, went underground and were not openly and proudly announced as members of the Sacred Pipe. In that way, the Christian movement was successful."

The romanticization of the Lakota people and other native traditions in the West today is misguided because, as Pansy explains, much of what exists today as Lakota spirituality is greatly contaminated by Christian indoctrination. The idea that contemporary Native American spiritual systems as they exist today might provide a direct link to something pure, uninfluenced by Christianity, is largely wishful thinking.

Pansy explains with a certain sadness in her eyes that the two most destructive ways Christianity has influenced Lakota spirituality are, first, through separating the people from the Great Spirit by placing a mediator in between, and, second, through debasing the role women play in both the ceremonies and the culture. The creation of a transcendent and separate Divinity and the debasement of women and feminine wisdom are two interrelated aspects of patriarchal values that serve to disconnect people from their basic intuitive connection to Spirit.

"Before Christianity came, our spirituality was balanced," she says. "You had a direct connection to the Great Spirit; it encouraged harmony and cooperation and it was a nurturing way. Our spirituality always balanced risk-taking with waiting and listening, balanced going out with staying back. In our tradition, we led by following. But when Christianity came, it put a mediator between the people and the Great Spirit, it put a transcendent spirit in a place no one could reach. So we had to develop a warrior tradition, a drive to go beyond, to keep reaching. And so women and what is intuitive and inward and nurturing were not allowed into the ceremonies."

A WOMAN IN A WARRIOR TRADITION

One night Pansy cooks spaghetti for a small group of her friends and me. Everybody brings something—garlic bread, drinks, dessert. We talk for hours about the ways the ceremonies seem biased against women, and the struggles these women face as they live their spirituality in a tradition that is dominated by masculine attitudes and approaches. They all have a strength and commitment towards their path, and seem to rely deeply on Pansy's guidance, grateful and joyful that she is a respected leader in their community. One of these women is Pansy's daughter, who is being trained by Pansy to lead her own ceremonies.

The next day, Pansy and I talk more about what it has been like for her to be a woman pipe carrier. She tells me that from the time she picked up the *Canupa*, she was aware of being a woman in what had become a masculine tradition. It was often difficult for her, but she never let it hold her back. And later she began to understand her role as a woman teacher, and her role in the larger resurgence of the Lakota ways.

In the early years, desperate for spiritual teachings, Pansy traveled from one ceremony to another, watching and learning. When she herself began to lead and teach, she continued to observe different male teachers and the way they participated in their ceremonies. "In the beginning, I was so hungry! When I heard there was a ceremony going on I made tracks there, I made my presence there, any chance I got I went there."

She tells me that a man would not have been able to travel so freely between ceremonies. "I've learned to take advantage of the fact that I'm a woman in one way." She continues, "As a woman I can move around freely from one ceremony to another. I can participate in his ceremony, then his ceremony, then his ceremony. And no one thinks a thing of it. There's an unwritten law against one man mixing his medicine with another's. But I'm a woman, and I go! I go to this ceremony, then the next week I go to that one. So I know how they do things over there, and over there. And I can say, 'Oh, I want some of that, some of that, and none of that.' And I can kind of interpret their ceremonies into mine. Meanwhile all the men are isolated!" With this Pansy shakes her head and laughs. "I can infiltrate into their territory, and no one says anything. They welcome me, and honor me, but because I'm a woman they don't think anything of me being there!"

It has not always been easy being a woman in a spiritual tradition that has, at least in the last one hundred years, been largely led by men. It was common that men question her sincerity as well as her capacity to lead ceremonies. Pansy kept learning, kept leading ceremonies, and persevered.

"When men approach me, questioning my ability, I just look at them like this," she says, turning to me, wide-eyed and a bit terrifying. "I just look at them and say, 'You tell me you honor women!'" She laughs her big and knowing laugh, and rocks back in her chair. "I say, 'A woman brought us the Sacred Pipe! Grandfather and Grandmother are equal!' I just say to them, 'You tell me you honor women!'" She laughs some more.

"There were times I felt very ostracized and unsupported," she says quietly now. "It's been a lonely world to walk through that. But in the last seven or eight years that has changed. I now feel I have the respect of the men. The support of the men."

Establishing herself as a leader or intercessor with her people and gaining the respect of her male counterparts is only the personal axis of her journey. Where her personal path intersects with the path of her people is a place of greater challenges and responsibilities. Here she recognizes the role she has to play within her tradition—to bring women back to the ceremonies and facilitate the re-emergence of the feminine aspects of the ways of her ancestors.

THE GHOST DANCE

In the late 1890's, the Lakota and other Plains Indian tribes were suffering greatly as the white people continued their efforts to control the western states and their resources. The Ghost Dance was introduced as a regenerative ceremony that would help usher in a new world—a world in which the buffalo would return to the Plains, and the land and its resources would once again be available to the native people. Additionally, the Ghost Dance was believed to render participants invisible, and so protect them against the U.S. cavalry.

But the Ghost Dance did not succeed in helping its participants become invincible to the white man's bullets, and it constellated more fear and aggression from the white people who were threatened by the large numbers of natives gathering in ceremony. The U.S. soldiers slaughtered hundreds of Lakota Sioux men, women, and children during one Ghost Dance ceremony at Wounded Knee. The Ghost Dance was the Plains people's last effort to muster resources against the U.S. cavalry, but as Pansy describes, "It was probably their death song; they ended up getting more people killed in the process, because the government was afraid of the assembly of any numbers."

Almost exactly one hundred years later, Pansy had a vision. "We were in a circle," she tells me quietly, "dancing in a ceremony. And I was leading the women, which is what I'd done for years, so it didn't seem unnatural. We were dancing, but I was noticing that we were dancing to a beat I didn't know at first. And I thought, 'What are we doing?' And I looked to the side, and I saw the women dancing, and I recognized the dancing. And I said to myself, 'We're doing the Ghost Dance.' And I asked myself, 'Why are we doing the Ghost Dance?' And I was scared.

"In reality, the women dance to my right, and the men dance to the left, forming a circle. And in the vision I assumed that the men would be there, on my left. And I got to the north side, and I turned to look at what the men were doing, but there were no men there. And I felt the meaning of that—I understood that we were all near death again, as we were a hundred years ago, and I understood that the men had no part to play in saving us from destruction. I looked to the sacred tree in the center and started yelling an animal yell as loud as I could."

The original Ghost Dance was the last effort to stave off decimation of the Lakota by the white people. In her vision, it was revealed to Pansy that the second decimation of her people was at hand unless women and their specific form of power become the dominant force in the ceremonies. She understood that without the leadership of women, without the power and wisdom of feminine ways, the spiritual life of her people would be destroyed.

The vision shocked and deeply disturbed Pansy. "When I had that vision," she explains, "it was similar to how you feel when you hear that a flood has destroyed a town of so many people. An earthquake killed thousands of people. It's that kind of real. It's like you know that it's true; that's just the way it is. You feel the futility of everything and you feel totally helpless. And I think it's in that place of helplessness that the spirit comes out and you get a new breath of air and are ready to go on.

"The Sacred Pipe has grown in leaps and bounds in the last thirty years," Pansy continues. "Thirty years ago the government allowed us to practice our spirituality. And men have come in hordes and taken the ceremonies all over the world. What's happened, though, is they have lost sight of the role that the women play in the ceremonies. This is where I see the elements of Christian indoctrination coming in. It's become a medicine man who is the mediator between you and the Great Spirit. And this Ghost Dance vision I had was saying, 'If we continue to go with this idea we are headed for destruction.'

"The Ghost Dance was originally calling up the warriors, calling up the warriors to band together to pray for the spirit. But there was a self-destruction in that process. Because the woman was not included. The warrior was called up without the love and nurturing."

Since this vision, Pansy has taken on the task of bringing more women into the ceremonies, placing women into leadership roles in the ceremonies, and reestablishing what used to be a spirituality that embodied and valued the ways of the feminine. In one sense it is something new; and in another sense it is the redemption of how it used to be.

"Everyone needs to know the story of how the Sacred Pipe came to the people," she insists. "We need to repeat that over and over. It's a mental process where we put Grandfather and Grandmother in the same place, not one above the other." This balance, this perspective of equality, of harmony, is what her people need to go back to.

"Now my work has a real focus," she explains. "And the focus is to bring the role of women back into the ceremonies. I've had twenty-five years of these ceremonies, and I know the ceremonies. As a person I've lived my life to be more balanced. My life is not so full of crisis. It's pretty calm, pretty focused. So people know this, and they have the proof. I've been accepted where I go."

Pansy doesn't restrict her work to women, but also includes men. Her focus remains, however, on bringing what can be called a feminine essence back into what had originally been a more feminine spirituality. "Men and women have both masculine and feminine parts." She explains, "It's just that through the Christian influence the warrior part, the masculine part, has taken over. We're out of balance.

"The women have to come forward," Pansy urges. "I believe they have to say, 'Men, you have destroyed, all but destroyed everything! You've done some things that are destructive not only to yourselves but to your families, to your communities, to the world. And it's time to stop! In the name of the ceremonies you've done these things, and it's not right! Now we are here as the other half, we are here as the other balance. We are doing this!'

"It's the Christian indoctrination that says it's a man who brings spirituality to the people. But it's from within that we have to move! It's very difficult for me to look at a colleague, a spiritual leader, and say, 'You've destroyed, not only in terms of physical and spiritual destruction but in terms of the truth, and in terms of honesty you have not done what the spirit is about.' But I am saying it, and we all have to say it now!"

GOING INWARD

Pansy speaks often to me about the difference between the masculine warrior approach and the ways of the feminine. She stresses the importance of what she understands as a feminine value—the practice of going inward. She explains that going inward is an aspect of the feminine that both men and women need to develop. It is from inside that one listens and connects with the spirits, with the earth, with oneself and others.

"The Warrior is more into acquiring things," she describes, "being the head of a territory, exercising power over external things. Acquiring more land, more horses, more power. This is the focus of the warrior. Going outward. The feminine aspect is you go in and you nurture. You go in and you love, you go in and you bring balance, you go in and you clean—your house or your self.

"When things are in chaos I go in and straighten my house. Internally and externally. I settle things down. This way is stronger. It allows people freedom. The freedom to connect with Spirit, freedom to open the way for however far you want to go, freedom to walk this earth, freedom to have access to safety and nurturing and love. It's more inward, the inward kind of freedom. Freedom to explore the seventh direction—our own individual path, to go into that journey. You need to go inward to make that journey."

It is an outward orientation that tends to create separation, Pansy tells me. Separation between people, or between people and the spirits, or people and the earth. How can you know what the spirits need from you if you are not listening for their instructions? How can you know what the earth is saying to you if you are not listening? From an inward listening one connects to life, feels the connection to all things.

Pansy uses the example of the Sun Dance ceremony to illustrate how certain aspects of the feminine can change the nature and essence of ceremony. The Sun Dance includes days of dancing around a sacred tree and a final act in which men pierce the skin of their chests with pegs that are tied with rope and connected to the center tree. The men dance around the tree and ultimately pull themselves away from the tree so that the pegs tear their skin and release them from the tree, ending the dance. Traditionally, the Sun Dance is a ceremony of renewal in which the piercers receive visions and guidance from the spirit world. Most commonly, men come to the Sun Dance with a warrior attitude as the ceremony calls up great strength and a capacity to transcend pain. But Pansy encourages men to bring a different attitude to the dance.

About the piercings, she explains: "I was taught—and with the men I teach I say—'You dance and you communicate with the tree and the pegs will come off.' The warrior approach is that they run, they do a war hoop, and they pull back and the peg jerks and tears. But I tell them to dance *with* the tree, and it will come off. The dancing does the same thing but I don't think it's the same thing. When you're dancing it helps you go inward, you're building a relationship, you're building a connectedness with the tree, which is the pole, the center of the universe, the Great Spirit. So you're going inward. How can the spirits reach you if you're separate? So I teach people, 'No, don't pull. Don't pull away, don't make yourself separate, dance *with* the tree.'"

It is the absence of a nurturing interconnectedness in the ceremonies that Pansy knows must be changed in order for the spirituality of her people to survive into the future. She understands that what she is offering is not new, but rather how it was, pre-Christian-influence. She explains that the ceremonies and teachings that form the backbone of the tradition naturally include the feminine, and it's just that the people have to honor this aspect.

Pansy offers another example of a feminine orientation in her tradition. "The sweat lodge ceremony takes place in a structure that is a dome-like structure," she says. "The branches are crisscrossed, and the whole concept of that represents the mother's womb. So you in fact return to the mother's womb, reconnect, and are reborn. The sweat lodge structure represents mother earth, the womb of the mother. We spend a great deal of time in this space. Both literally and symbolically.

"Oftentimes in our prayers we say we are standing on the head of Grandmother, in the place where she parts her hair. The whole round earth is Grandmother. Either we are returning to the mother's womb or we are standing on her head, in ceremony and all the time. So the feminine aspect is within every ceremony. But what's happened with the Christian influence is these aspects were lost. It wasn't about going inward, seeking that place inside."

PREPARING THE SPACE

Outer form and structure can help a person go inward by reflecting inner space into consciousness, thereby making it more accessible. Pansy tells me that the more outward, masculine qualities of discipline, commitment, and attention to form and ritual need to be developed to help orient a person inward.

"I find myself bringing back a lot of discipline, a lot of ritual," she explains. "Like the people knowing there was going to be a sacred object coming, like the people knowing they were going to be given a way to do things. And then the White Buffalo Calf Pipe Woman came and she said, 'You will go home and you will do this to prepare a place for me,' and they did. And she also said, 'You will prepare a place in this manner each time you do this.' So she brought a lot of discipline but it was to prepare for a journey inward."

The discipline and ritual used in the ceremony help create the inward space. All the ceremonies create a sacred relationship between ritual and space, between outer form and what will come from the unknown. Both aspects are needed to support each other. But ultimately the goal is to create the sacred space that will help an individual enter the ceremony, enter a place of contact with the other side. The outer form supports and serves the journey inward. Just as the form of the sweat lodge holds the womb-like space inside, so too do all the structures of the Lakota ceremonies hold the door open to sacred space in which what is needed can be born.

In all aspects of daily life, not just in ceremonies, we can create space through clarity and discipline, through focus and a willingness to fight for what is most important. "I teach women that they need these warrior qualities," Pansy explains, "that they need to be disciplined, to take risks, to go farther then they have gone before. This strength protects the inner space, allows and creates the inner space."

It is creating and protecting this empty space that allows for the freedom to walk in the seventh direction. One must remain open to what the Great Spirit needs, and this openness demands not knowing. "You have to give yourself to not knowing," she continues, "like not knowing how it's going to be. Then you can listen, then you can hear, then you can act. That's why it's free."

The day before I left, Pansy and some other leaders in her area had a lodge to discuss certain changes in the political structure of the community. Some of the men wanted to resign their positions as board members. Pansy was shocked. She saw that their own spirituality was in a large degree located in the outer structure of their activities, not within the process of something being born into the world from an inner space. The latter cannot be abandoned, like a job or an old home. "The spirits don't say, 'We've helped enough' and resign!" Pansy says with exasperation. "I explained they may have periods of time when things are difficult, but you can't resign from your spirituality, you can't resign from a way of life."

These members also wanted to apply certain rules that are relevant politically to the way ceremonies are run. Pansy explained to them that they can't apply rules of order to sacred space, that sacred space is inherently free, empty, and undefinable. "They're finding something that pulls them to the ceremonies, and they're trying to put some kind of form that's understandable to them," she says, shaking her head. "And you can't, you can't! They're being pulled to something but they can't stay with that nothingness. There needs to be trust, and I have to tell them, 'It will be OK, your only responsibility is to be present!'

"There are no rules, there is nothing tangible about sacred space," Pansy insists. "The teachings themselves tell you we don't have a lot of rules. There's no blueprint; there's no booklet that explains how to do things. But what it requires is to go inward and rely on your own basic human instincts and basic human truths."

FEMININE POWER

Feminine power, Pansy explains, is the power of the inner space. "Women were given an extra charge by the Great Spirit, the added responsibility of procreation." Women carry the power to create, the instinctual wisdom of inner space, how what is needed can come into the world. Women bring this power and wisdom wherever they go, and they need to bring this power into ceremonies.

"We are given the external structures of all the ceremonies, so we have those. And the feminine power is held within the structure. Each ceremony is unique and has a power all itself. I would call it an intuition. It's like you go in and you listen to yourself, you go in and you do the ceremony and it takes on a whole movement of its own. Each ceremony is not ritualistic. It takes on a whole essence of itself. This essence is the feminine power. Because it is found inward, you have to go inward.

"I know the structure of the ceremony," she tells me. "I know that, but when I go in to do the ceremony I have no idea what direction it's going to go; I know nothing. Even to the songs that will come, even to all of that. Everything is just allowing something to come in. You prepare this place and you allow. It's a very, very new experience every time. You go inside and you allow those things to open out, like a flower. And you don't know what direction this petal's going to go, or where that petal's going to go. That's the mystery, that's the beauty, and it's from within. Just like today—every day is a new experience. That is feminine power. I won't remember much of today," she laughs, "but I'll remember that while it was here it was full."

In the Lakota tradition a leader leads by following. In the sweat lodge the leader is always the last one to enter the lodge, to smoke the *Canupa*, to drink the water, and the last to pray.

"Our way of leading is a combination of very direct and indirect at the same time," Pansy says. "This is the story of the spider and the spider web. If you look at the spider web it is a very light and fine material. And the spider is very heavy. There's a lot of weight there, but the web holds. The Lakota style of leading is similar in that what seems is not what is. It might not look like you're leading. We don't lead by moving people around, telling them what to do. A leader is present in the background. The leading is hidden, like the spider's web, but the job gets done, like the spider being held. Even though you are a leader, you have to continue to work to follow, to listen, to watch, to support those in front of you. In your strength you're leading, but it makes you focus on your skills as a follower.

"Out here in the outer world by myself I feel like unleashed energy," she continues. "I feel a lot of power; I feel a lot of strength, a lot of responsibility. In ceremony it's very focused and very soft at the same time. We have these tasks to do, we're moving, we're walking very softly. My focus is inward, and I don't really know what's going on out there. The power of getting things done in an outer sense is not how it is in sacred space. In sacred space I'll know I need to say something by listening inside, and only when I'm talking do I know what it is I'm saying."

In ceremony, intuition and spontaneity are the ruling factors, and intuition and spontaneity are only possible from a place of space and freedom. Pansy offers an example of this unstructured power. "We show up ten days before the huge Sun Dance starts. At the Sun Dance there's maybe three to four hundred people camped. Ten days before the ceremony nothing is done, nothing is started. We show up and people kind of know what they do best. And they go, and they get it done. There are people who chop wood, there are people who prepare the arbor, there are people who prepare the sweat lodges, people who get the food, people who get the stones. We don't have a manager! We don't have a director! Each component just starts happening, then it sort of comes together.

"About halfway through you can see form taking place. And the arbor where we do the ceremony starts to come together. The women go and pull the cactus so the dancers don't step on the cactus. Minor details, but everything is taken care of. Down to the last detail everything is done. And there is not one person taking reports on how things are going. No one gets fired for not doing their part. None of that kind of external structure works. People from inside out are doing the work.

"One of the things we learn about chaos is from the coyote," Pansy continues. "When there's a lot of activity, the coyote and wolf will pull away from the center and stay on the periphery and when things are OK they may come in. The coyote teaches us that if there's chaos and confusion you have to stay back and watch. You don't jump in it, you stay aware, you stay focused, and you know what's going on, and when the timing is right you move. This awareness is like the web of the spider. It's not direct, it doesn't look powerful, but it spreads itself out where it needs to be."

THE BEAR AND THE TURTLE

Pansy's two main animal helpers are the Bear and the Turtle. They are guides in ceremony and in every aspect of her life. The Bear spirit is a balance of strength and vulnerability. "The bear is this huge animal, a ferocious animal," she tells me. "But inside that bear is a real tender, tender spot, a real tender maternal aspect. Whether it's male or female there's a real tender aspect. In myself that's the balance I seek, and it's the balance I try to teach."

Her other prominent animal helper is the Turtle. "No matter what we do," she says, beginning to chuckle, "we're going to get there as fast as a turtle gets there!" She throws her head back, laughing loudly. Then she calms down a bit, and says smiling, her eyes sparkling, "You just have to accept it!"

She continues, serious now, "There's no microwave that's going to get you there, there's no instant bouillon cube that's going to get you there. There's nothing instant. All of it takes time. And that's the natural way of doing things. Everything takes time to create; everything takes time to happen. And it's not going to go any faster; it's going to take time to get there. That's the lesson of the turtle. You're given seven rites and you have to keep doing them over and over and over. And you'll get there as fast as the turtle gets there.

"Wherever the turtle is, that's where I'm at," she says, looking me straight in the eyes. "There are no goals. I came to terms with that when I picked up the *Canupa*. That was my goal, to carry the Sacred Pipe. I live that goal every day, every moment. It's not in front of me, its not something to achieve in the future, it's here, alive right now."

Towards the end of my visit, Denver is hit by the first big snowstorm of the season. The snow is falling heavily as I set out for a women's sweat lodge across town. I question the safety of driving an hour through the snow in a rental car with no snow tires. But I decide to go, and I eventually arrive at a small house behind a field with a large bonfire burning in the back yard. I try to stay warm near the fire for the hours it takes the stones within to become hot enough to provide the heat for the lodge.

Pansy arrives soon after me, and the others who will take part in the ceremony slowly join us. Pansy's daughter, about thirty years old—Pansy's age when she began leading ceremonies—will lead this sweat lodge which is a cleansing ritual for her mother. Late in the night, when the rocks are finally hot enough, we go into a small shed near the house to change our clothes, and then enter into the darkness of the lodge.

I have never been particularly drawn to ceremonies and rituals. I have never liked to pray out loud, or listen as others prayed. Yet sitting in the dark enclosed space of the lodge, I relax into the heat, grateful for the refuge from the snow and cold which, after a few hours, had begun to feel endless and harsh.

There are seven of us. Pansy's daughter sits towards the opening of the lodge, the last one in. We all wear night-gowns. Mine, borrowed from Pansy's daughter, seems way too big for me. And the longer I am in the lodge, the heavier and more uncomfortable it becomes with my sweat.

It is both an odd and very ordinary group. I met some of the women at Pansy's house earlier in the week. They come from different backgrounds, with varied interests and education, and even different nationalities. All the women seem physically bigger than I am, and in the darkness I feel small and withdrawn in the midst of the round, shadowy figures that fill the space. Our faces are occasionally lit by sparks of burning sage when Pansy's daughter throws the plants onto the rocks, and at times we are all hidden in rising steam when she pours water to increase the heat.

While I feel grateful for being present in the ceremony, I feel little personal connection to the other women, and mostly feel alone and disconnected. I try to remain open to their prayers, and their presence, but I long to feel the amorphous energy that I had sometimes felt together with Pansy in her house, that feeling of drifting away, being taken somewhere soft and peaceful. But instead, I am very alert and aware, and sometimes uncomfortable with the heat.

Pansy's daughter intermittently splashes water and sage onto the glowing rocks, and in the dark quiet of the lodge, as prayers are spoken, I suddenly become aware of something I haven't noticed before. A swirling motion catches my attention, and I see a stream of energy moving slowly around the lodge. It seems to hover in a space just above the earth, at the point where our bodies touch the hard-packed ground. But it is neither part of the ground nor part of the air above the ground. Rather it seems to come from a dimension between the two. The energy is smooth and gentle, and as it flows slowly between us I feel its softness and its strength. More than anything, it seems nurturing, a form of love or generosity. Sitting there, I think its presence has to do with our presence. Not with our personal intentions or interests, but just with the fact that we are together. I watch and feel it flow through the dark space until the ceremony ends.

Later, I thought that this energy had in some form been present with Pansy and me since we first met. We had repeatedly entered sacred space, connected to the other side, and allowed this particular force to flow into our experience. Where she ends and it begins I cannot determine. It seems to be carried within her, and she within it. It is a soft and sweeping power like a storm across a sky, or a dark and wide river, slowly and powerfully making its course. It is gentle and complete, and whispers and beckons, then pulls you back into stillness as soon as you get up to follow. Like Pansy herself, it seems to bring together a nourishing patience with a protective courage. And like Pansy, I feel it will persist—sometimes barely seen—until something new has found its way into the structures of our world.

BLAZE of LIGHT, BLOOD of CREATION

a meeting with

Andrew Harvey

BLAZE of LIGHT,
BLOOD of CREATION

What is a mystic? A mystic is a king or queen of paradox. A mystic knows that death is not death, life is not life, the body is not the body, and the spirit is not the spirit. The mystic knows that he or she is an eternal being in a dying body, and that this is the supreme experience—the experience of transcendence and the experience of immanence, both the experience of the Divine emptiness that is creating and the experience of being the creation.

Do you understand the gift? The gift is death, the gift is time, the gift is pain, the gift is love, the gift is extremity. When you receive the gift full in the blood of the heart you dance as Shiva. You dance as the unborn one, you dance as the Divine one, you dance as the child of the Mother, you dance as Christ did, you dance as the liberated one in the complete divine experience, the complete divine madness, which is to be in unity with everything that lives and dies, that has ever lived or died. That is the supreme experience and that is what is being offered to humankind.

Andrew Harvey, *The Way of Passion*

HOT CHOCOLATE AT THE EDGE OF THE DESERT

 I leave my room at the Hard Rock Hotel in Las Vegas, closing the door on the bright-colored modern furniture and the gigantic poster of Janis Joplin—her head pulled back in rock-and-roll ecstasy, her hair wild and sweaty—which hangs above the bed. I have come to Las Vegas to meet with Andrew Harvey, a highly respected spiritual scholar and teacher, author of thirty books, renowned as passionate, brilliant, unpredictable, and deeply committed to a spiritual vision that can help guide our collective consciousness into a new relationship with the divine. I am eager to meet him and hear more of his views which are grounded in an extensive understanding of the divine feminine, and I am intrigued to find out what kind of modern mystic lives and works in this city of celebration and degradation, extreme need and lavish abandon.

I drive up to Andrew and his husband Eryk's pale pink stucco house, one of what seems like a thousand others just like it in the flat and endless suburban landscape spreading away from the city. He welcomes me with a generous and enthusiastic smile and the proposal to talk in a desert park a few miles away. We climb into my car, which soon fills with the luscious smell of roses—Andrew's perfume choice—and sail beyond the sea of stucco into the explosion of color and emptiness that is the desert at dusk.

We sit and talk on a bench in a roadside pullout, the vast sky spreading out above us in endlessly forming and reforming patterns of blue and white, high cliffs jutting upwards like a splendid warning against the dangers of too much space. The sun sinks slowly behind us, and the dry winter air gets colder by the minute. The visitors who have been pulling into this overlook during the last hour are beginning to thin out and Andrew and I are left mostly alone, his passion and despair mirroring the vivid intensity of the desert.

In Andrew's vision of the Divine Mother, the Mother is enraged. She is enraged at spiritual systems that emphasize transcendence and detachment over a passionate and loving relationship with what is *here*, embodied in the earth and our own humanness. She is enraged that the teachings of the Father have been twisted and misused by patriarchal power systems more intent on maintaining control and domination over the world's precious resources than in doing the real spiritual work of transforming consciousness so it can relate to all of life as the divine reality it is. She is enraged that we are not finding joy and love in our lives, enjoying the gifts She has given us, honoring and embracing our life here with Her. And She is enraged that it is taking so long for Her children to understand that life is precious, that every atom of creation contains the love and light of God, that by ignoring this fundamental truth we are spiraling Her world into irreversible darkness and destruction.

But She is not only enraged. Through Andrew She shows Herself as sweet and loving, and generous in the true sense of the word—creative and regenerative. She is deeply sorrowful as She watches us struggle to realize what is truly available within this world, and also outrageously passionate about sanctifying all the aspects of life that are so easily dismissed as base or crude. For in Andrew Harvey She offers us a way to Her through passion and despair, kindness and outrage. She allows a sometimes deranged entry into a world we are not used to, a world where the distinctions between the sacred and the profane are dissolved in divine love and divine hilarity, where purity and earthiness infuse each other, where eating a peach in conscious gratitude and celebrating its juice running down your chin is as holy as prostrating in silence before a crucified Jesus until your knees bleed. In this world—in Her world as reflected through Andrew—life is a chance to be shipwrecked again and again on an island of holy longing and desire until every last cell of your body and every thought and action of your life is fused into a song of divine joy.

There are times with Andrew when I find myself questioning his passion and his excessiveness—is it really the rage of the Mother, or is it his own? Is he an authentic living representation of the Mother's energy, or is he sometimes just an ordinary man with his own personal agenda and personal desires? But the more time I spend with him, the more irrelevant these questions become. For in Andrew I experience passion and joy that seem to defy definition and limitation, a vision of real freedom that comes from unabashedly being oneself despite what others might think. And, ultimately, an inspiring and refreshing potential in a contemporary spiritual atmosphere that seems sometimes depressingly old and stale, fueled and defined by the conventions that it could be shattering.

And when I sit drinking hot chocolate with him late into the night, in the bar at the edge of the desert, on cowhide lounge chairs under dollar bills that hang from every inch of the ceiling, I feel so much joy that I have to abandon any interest in distinguishing what I suppose is "spiritual" from what I experience as "ordinary." And maybe this is Andrew's greatest gift—he brings such laughter, he encourages a way to live in this world that is so joyful, that one has to ask, who cares about the rest? The freedom in going beyond these opposites, these doubts, these distinctions, is intoxicating. Andrew's humor and inspired irreverence send me, relentlessly, into fits of laughter. His compassionate and desperate longing for humanity to take its next step into divine consciousness draw up a deep and ancient sadness. These swirling realities are the basis of my experience with Andrew, and I'd forego what the experts sell as "enlightenment" to drink his cocktails any day of the week.

THE MASCULINE AND THE FEMININE

As we sit in the desert pullout, looking at the beautiful sandstone cliffs and the vast space surrounding them, I ask Andrew to describe his understanding of masculine and feminine energy, and how they relate with each other both within an individual and in all creation.

"Ramakrishna said it so beautifully," he begins, his enthusiasm shining from his eyes behind his glasses. "He said Brahman (masculine energy) and *Shakti* (feminine energy) are two aspects of the same reality beyond name. The wonderful way of envisioning it is the masculine as the diamond and the *shakti* as the radiance of light. Or, milk and white. Or in an even more beautiful analogy, like the serpent and its wriggle. So, the Mother and the Father are the same thing, but the Mother—and I think this is the most wonderful way of looking at it—She is the love power that arises out of the depths of the silence of transcendence and then expresses itself as the creation and lives in creation. Ramakrishna compared it, dazzlingly, to a spider who spins the entire creation out of herself and then goes and lives in every aspect of the web.

"Of course," he continues, "the love power and the silence are two aspects of the same reality beyond the Mother/Father."

Andrew and I sit watching the cliffs slowly become the canvas for the dance of vermilion and luminous gold orchestrated by the sun's submission to the encroaching dusk. In front of this glowing spectacle of heaven and earth, sky and rock, rays and shadows, Andrew speaks of the roles of the masculine and feminine, insisting that it is the role of the masculine to protect and illuminate the feminine. When he refers to masculine properties, he means the transcendent, detached, clear, and active aspects of the godhead. When he speaks of feminine qualities he means the immanent, creative, life-sustaining, receptive, embodied aspects of the godhead.

"We can't possibly have a sane world," he says, "until we realize that the function of the masculine is to allow itself to be irradiated by the feminine, so that it can truly be a protector and guardian and warrior for those forces that actually ensure the continuance of life. If the masculine doesn't allow this deep and intense permeation by the feminine it very easily becomes psychotic, addicted to transcendence, power, and control, and while pretending to be the guardian of life, actually becomes its secret destroyer.

"There is an image in *Kings* describing Samson, describing the masculine as the lion's mane with a river of honey running through it. To me this is a marvelous example of the fusion, the power, and force and lucidity and resolute courage that belong to the masculine, with the intense sweetness and tenderness and intimate love for all things that belong to the feminine. I believe the whole of reality is a sacred marriage, a marriage between heaven and earth, transcendence and immanence, feminine and masculine, life and death, the body and soul. It's a marriage that's reflected in all of these dimensions, and the task of every human being is to come into their own unique version of the sacred androgyny, to infuse it in the way it's meant to happen in their own personalities—the masculine and feminine within them.

"I see the Christ force as a result of the marriage of the transcendent and immanent, the force that is totally aware of the transcendent, but also totally aware of how much the transcendent loves the immanent, and works to preserve and honor that love with everything it is."

Andrew's voice fills with intensity as he tells me that within most aspects of society, including our spiritual systems, we are out of balance, caught in a masculine dimension, focused on transcendence and devaluing the immanent. His enthusiasm is contagious, and I become eager to hear how one can bring oneself back in balance, and how one can help the world become more balanced.

DESCENDING TRANSCENDENCE

"First you have to realize that everything you have ever been told about the divine is prejudiced by patriarchal distortions that define the divine almost obsessively in transcendent not immanent terms," he says with urgency. "The addiction to transcendence keeps everybody in a coma, tells you your emotions are too much, your desires are absurd and obscene, your passions for justice are naïve. This addiction, in fact, is the ultimate heroin because it keeps you high, self-absorbed, and falsely detached. It's a brilliant way of policing the human race, and the deepest reason why Karl Marx dismissed religion as 'the opiate of the people.'

"Supposing you told people the truth?" he continues, raising his voice. "Suppose you told people that the real use of detachment is only to help you fight for truth and love more purely? It is only so your love can become more intense and focused. What would you have then? You'd have an empowered human race that wouldn't accept anything it didn't know for itself as true!

"Let's get real around here!" Andrew almost yells, and I feel his intensity and eagerness sweep through me. I pull back a bit, and he continues. "Transcendence is the first real knowledge on the path. It's crucial, but then you have to learn about love. Don't you think that Jesus could have made all these transcendent junkies look like twerps?

He could have materialized things, he could do anything because he was in touch with transcendence, but he knew *Her!*

"He knew that the only truth lay in serving and loving every single living thing!" His voice now is shaking with frustration and sadness. "So you have to go down on your hands and knees and kiss every living thing. That's about service. About service and being a slave. It has nothing to do with authority, nothing to do with being enlightened. That's the patriarchal world! She's bringing in a wholly different world in which the last really are the first. And there are no masters who aren't slaves! The last thing Jesus tried to do was break people's projections on him by dressing as a female slave and washing their feet. Of course no one got the meaning of that, because it's too deranging. The Mother's world is too deranging!

"Supposing we see that eternity really is in a grain of sand?" he asks, softly now. "Supposing we see that a cat is a totally holy creature, incredibly wise, and instead of thinking of it as stuck on the lower end of the evolutionary scale, we start talking to the cat, and learning from the cat the secrets of serenity and secrets of divine mischief?

"Supposing we do reverse the whole human craziness and start listening to Her? All of this stuff goes! The whole authority structure goes, the elite goes, the churches go, the mystical systems with their prizes to the boys who play the game go. It all goes! And only *She* is here, radiating love between hearts, between all the hearts of all the creation, and that's what She's trying to bring here. Because from that will come the real harmony, the real community of all human beings.

"And all of the powers that don't want that to be born are trying to appropriate Her for their patriarchal games. That's why all the women gurus are Jehovas in drag, or all the men gurus talking about the Mother can only talk about the sweet aspects of the Mother, never the tremendously tortured or torturing or justice aspects. That's why this realization is such a hard realization to get through, because it is a realization that menaces in the most absolute way everything that we think is holy to reveal a much holier world than anything the transcendent junkies could ever imagine. There is a marvelous story that Ramakrishna tells describing real holiness, holiness that makes no distinctions between above and below:

> A few days after the dedication of the temple at Dakshineswar, a madman came there who was really a sage endowed with the Knowledge of Brahman. He had a bamboo twig in one hand and a potted mango-plant in the other, and was wearing torn shoes. He didn't follow any social conventions. After bathing in the Ganges he didn't perform any religious rites. He ate something that he carried in a corner of his wearing-cloth. Then he entered the Kali temple and chanted hymns to the Deity. The temple trembled... The madman wasn't allowed to eat at the guest-house, but he paid no attention to this slight. He searched for food in the rubbish heap where the dogs were eating crumbs from the discarded leaf-plates. Now and then he pushed the dogs aside to get the crumbs. The dogs didn't mind either. Haladhari followed him and asked: "Who are you? Are you a *purnajnani*? (a perfect knower of Brahman)? The madman whispered, "Shh! Yes, I am a *purnajnani*." Haladhari followed him a great way when he left the garden. After passing the gate he said to Haladhari: "What else shall I say to you? When you no longer make any distinction between the water of this pool and the water of the Ganges, then you will know that you have Perfect Knowledge." Saying this he walked rapidly away.

"You see, Ramakrishna got there! Ramakrishna was there! *Here* I mean!" Andrew says, shaking his head, his voice rising again, the Mother's deranged world shining through. "I think of him as a supreme sign of what I'm talking about. Our addiction to transcendence—to splitting the world in two and rejecting half our experience—is madness!

"I heard this wonderful story about Ramakrishna by a man who walked across India to meet him." Andrew now becomes like a child listening to a bed-time story, big-eyed and sweet and enraptured. "I heard this story from the man's family.

"This man arrived in Ramakrishna's village, and went out to the fields. And what did he see? He saw Ramakrishna lying on the ground talking to some rabbits *in rabbit!* This man asked him what he was doing, and Ramakrishna said, 'Well, I'm telling them that there are some terrible snakes over there and they've got to stop being so naïve because if they go across the field they're going to be bitten by those snakes.' They all nodded their heads and went off. So then Ramakrishna went to the other side of the field and lay down and snakes came out of their holes, and he gave them *hell!* In snake language he told them, 'Look, you're clever, you know those rabbits are stupid over there and you just wait for them to come over and you bite them! And that's got to stop, you've got to have more responsibility about yourself! There are other things to eat!'

"The point being that he wasn't standing up!" Andrew insists. "He was lying on the ground in his *dhoti* talking their language! Was he crazy or are we crazy? If the real mystics are right, then Blake was not lying when he said eternity is in a grain of sand. In the whole universe everything is one of God's names and in God's name everything is reflected. Everything is not some bloody illusion that's going to evaporate, but this fantastic, surreal, *glorious* emanation of divine splendor!"

THE JOY OF LIFE

We sit quietly for a while, mesmerized by the desert sunset that is now alive and dancing all around us, watching the cliffs change color in the evening light. Engulfed in this brilliance, Andrew explains that the simplest way to descend transcendence is by celebrating all that we love here, by accepting everything in our lives as divine. Life and love are how the divine comes to us. That which makes us feel alive, that which awakens our senses, engages and encourages us, is how God comes to us in this world.

"Do you think you are here to suffer and learn a few lessons so as not to be here?" he asks me, pointing out the absurdity of striving for a detached and transcendent relationship with the world. "Or do you think you are here so as to finally arrive here, and be here in the fullness of your real being?

"And the fullness of your real being isn't realized by seeing this world as a place where you can have sex, drugs, and rock-and-roll," he says before adding, with a mischievous smile, "though that's not so bad!" He goes on, serious again, "It's seeing this world as a place in which you can fully realize your divine nature and fully realize your human nature and fully realize the marriage between the two and fully realize the bliss that comes from the marriage between the two.

"Kabir has a line I love: 'More than all else do I cherish at heart that love that makes one to live a limitless life in this world.' To live this limitless life is why we are here. And this limitless life is the child of the marriage I've just described.

"If you believe all these patriarchal religions," he continues, taking up again the absurd reasoning, "they're saying to you that you're on this planet as a terrible school in which you have to go through all these dreary lessons so that you can finally get out of being on this planet and be one with the light. That is such a depressing, such a wearying vision of what we are here for!

"Be honest with yourself! Do you really believe that when you make passionate love with someone you truly love that it's not glorious? Do you really believe that when your heart thrills to the music of, say, Tina Turner you are not having an authentic experience? Do you really believe that when you're eating a peach and savoring every bit of juice in the peach you're not actually doing something miraculous? Do you really believe that your body is given to you as a kind of prison?

"Or is this life, is this body," he continues sweetly, "the most overwhelming opportunity to have an over-whelming array of experiences that can help you really celebrate this existence as the dancing ground of joy, bliss, and illumination?

"And if you're honest with yourself, and if you suddenly just abstract yourself from all the garbage you've been told about being a sinful and imperfect creature, you will, if you look at your own experience, realize that it's actually already been filled with all kinds of illuminations of the joy that is the core of reality. I think that will be a wonderful place to start.

"You see, we're *in* the Mother. The universe is the Mother, life is the Mother, and everything that happens in life is designed to move us into this deeper dimension of love. And knowing this truth increasingly is the great reward of the mystic devotion to the Mother. And really embracing this truth is the courage of that distinct devotion. Then from that can come an overwhelming fearlessness and you can become what the Mother really wants us all to be which is radioactive nuisances! Unbelievable rebels of love!" He looks intently at me as I try to imagine what it means to be a radioactive nuisance. And then he yells, "YES!" as though I had just figured it out.

I am sent into fits of laughter. I see in Andrew what it might look like to be a radioactive nuisance and a rebel of love, and am giddy with possibility of being in a similar state. I ask him how he became so aware of the joy of being here on the earth, especially since his spiritual background included involvement in Buddhism, Hinduism, and Christianity, traditions that so often accentuate transcendent elements.

"Well, I was born in India," he says smiling. "I think being born in India was a tremendous help. Temples are fun; priests are fun with their gold robes and the sweets they give you. And Indians have hilarious sacred holidays like *Holi* where they rush around and shriek and fling paint on everything. And the actual gods are fun. It's great to have an elephant god! Hinduism has at its core a hilarity, a *joie de vivre*, a phenomenal acceptance of the gaiety of the human world. That was a terrific antidote to any Judeo-Christian horror I might have been exposed to.

"I remember my mother telling me at an early age, 'Why would Jesus' first miracle be the turning of water into wine at a wedding if Christ wasn't about joy?' And that's something I got from all of my family. They were not hot on sin. They believed that joy was the source of strength, and so it is!

"The real answer," he continues, "is to start getting people out of their spiritual conditioning and into the real mystical dimension by hook or by crook, because as soon as they're in that dimension what they're going to have is an overwhelming experience of bliss! They're going to have that eruption in the heart that nobody, not even

Rumi, has been able to describe, in which it's clear beyond any shadow of a doubt that the essence of God is a joy and a peace and a bliss beyond any imagining. If you really open your heart to the possibility of a direct encounter with the divine, what you'll discover very very fast is that the divine has nothing to do with all these rules and regulations and glooms and despairs. The divine is *here*, in life, in the world as rapture and the fire of eternal joy."

CREATION SPUN OUT OF TRANSCENDENT LIGHT

I only mind a bit that the air has become very cold, and that the coldness of the bench easily cuts through the thin skirt I chose to wear, not knowing we would be talking out in the desert. I can see that Andrew hasn't noticed the drop in temperature as he eagerly tells me that one of the most important myths to dispel is that the body holds one back from spiritual life.

"If the divine has chosen to be embodied, it's not because the divine is playing some mad game of being embodied so as to get out of being embodied," he laughs. "The divine is embodying itself because it's experiencing another level of rapture through being embodied. Creation is a flaming out of this joy. Everything we are is an expression of this joy, including this body, because it's through the body that we can have the experience of this joy here in creation.

"The body in fact reveals itself as the grail," he continues. "The reason why they couldn't find the grail is because they were looking for the grail in the light. They were actually in the grail! The grail is the cup that holds the blood of the incarnation. What holds the blood of incarnation? The body.

"It's important to understand the body is not your enemy. The body is in fact the condition on which this experience is possible, the way in which you can partake in both aspects of the divine. You see, the divine is transcendent light and the divine is also the creation that is spun out of transcendent light. If we were only transcendent light we would only be able to experience one half of the divine. If we were only matter we would only be able to experience one half of the divine. The fact that we are transcendent and immanent, soul and body, spirit and flesh means in the most *astounding* way that we can in our lives experience the fullness of the godhead. That's what the human experience is really about! God loves us so much that God has given us the full experience of God. Not just the light, not just matter, but the amazing dance between the two.

"And you don't need to be apart from this world in an ashram or a monastery to be or live this dance. Kabir says, 'Why put on the robe of the monk and live aloof from the world in lonely pride? Behold, my heart dances in the delight of a hundred arts and the Creator is well pleased.'

"The real Mother is both transcendent and immanent," he tells me, first waving his hands towards vast space, then pounding the bench, "and is trying to help all people to be birthed simultaneously into the Absolute and the immanent. She is helping us to be in the deathless presence that is beyond both, and to know that the bodies which seem to be taking us to death and limitation and heartbreak and sorrow and loss are in fact the grail from which we can drink this astounding wine—this mixture of the blaze of the eternal light and the blood of creation."

Andrew explains that this coming together of the immanent and transcendent is, in part, an aspect of what is possible now, in the evolution of consciousness. Historically, we have yet to collectively embrace this union.

"This is the teaching of the marriage," he says, "the teaching of the feast. And it's because the human race has chosen either the transcendental or the material that it has missed the fusion and the ecstasy and the real transformation. Because not only in this transformation do you have a total awakening to your transcendent origin—that's just the first step—then you descend from that awakening, with that awakening into the actual details of your life. You include the emotional and physical and you use the light to transform your body and your body's actions and thoughts and emotions consciously so that your body then becomes the living experience, a living instrument of the light."

I ask Andrew how a person comes to use her consciousness to transform her body into an instrument of light. His answer points to a harmony between one's body and the rest of creation, to the oneness of all life, the inclusion of love in the body.

"You use your body as an instrument of divine love," he answers. "Which means you move to the rhythm of divine love, you open to loving all beings in reality. A very simple example would be someone who uses his body to really stroke his cat. When you are aware that you're a divine being in a relationship with another divine being, it transforms the way in which you touch that divine being, speak to that divine being. So by using your body as an instrument of divine tenderness and divine love you gradually infuse it with light and it starts to transform. This isn't poetry, this actually happens."

CRUCIFIXION AND RESURRECTION

The process of transformation includes a variety of stages, taking one beyond transcendence to the final illumination of matter by spirit. "In the real journey, not the fake journey of most modern new-age mystics," Andrew tells me, "several things happen. First, you have to separate the spirit from matter so you really taste and know your transcendent origin. This is perhaps best done through the practices of meditation, prayer, and even contemplation. But that's where most people's diagram ends. People believe they have achieved a very high state, but what they don't understand is that they are actually living in this unconscious dualism which they celebrate as transcendence." This dualism is based on the lived rejection of the immanent, the unconscious disgust of all that one has left behind.

"The next step," he continues, "is the really difficult aspect of the path. Now you have to marry consciously the spirit to matter. In a civilization in which matter was celebrated as divine from the beginning, that marriage would be a great deal easier than it is for us today. What in fact and in practice happens for most of us is that after the recognition of our origins as transcendent spirit, most of us have to go through some immense crucifixion that forces us to embody again." This descent can seem so counterintuitive, and is in fact counter to so much of our spiritual conditioning, that many people have to be forced back to earth through a process of intense suffering.

"In my case what happened was that after years and years of sailing off into the light, the woman I worshiped as the Divine Mother on earth told me to leave the man I was in love with and say that her forces had transformed me into a heterosexual. The blessing of that experience was that it compelled me to accept my sexuality as divine in a way that I hadn't been able to before. I had to decide—Is my attraction to Eryk an inefficient expression of transcendence or is it a further stage along the path?"

Circumstances that bring an individual back into life, into the simple aspects of being, often require a withdrawal of a projection of the divine outside oneself, and the claiming of power, love, or the divine within oneself and within ordinary aspects of life.

"What was happening through my love for Eryk," Andrew continues, "was a radical embodying of the light in my body. Once I really chose my love for him over my infatuation with this spiritual figure, everything became lit up by the flames of our love and I knew that human love was divine! Slowly this came. I had to choose it again and again, and suffer through the loss of what I had thought was 'spiritual.'

"I had always understood in my mind that sexuality was a blessing. But I had to actually experience my sexuality as a tremendous initiation of passion and of love, and experience the healing of the shame and humiliations and the wounds and the body-hatred that had been so stored in me, in order to really accept the divine nature of my own sexuality."

Andrew tells me that at this time in his life he suffered a severe back problem that left him incapacitated physically. "It was as if the Mother just took an axe and felled me, and I think she did that because I had just been floating around, I hadn't really considered my body. And having a terrible backache brought me right back into the core of my body, made me really, really start to look at all the ways in which I had fled my body. And I began to attend to my body, bring myself back to it, and this process became a way to really bless my body. I think you can't heal your body until you've blessed your body, and that long process helped me re-enter my life.

"Loving Eryk helped me re-enter my life," he continues. "Healing my back helped me re-enter my life. Seeing the guru system as a power-brokering of transcendence helped me to realize that the real path was into matter, into life, into social and political action inspired by divine passion. And this totally transfigured me and brought me really into the path of the authentic Mother. The path of the authentic Mother is a path of *tantra* which means the marrying of light to matter, which means not only experiencing the divine in the way you make a cup of tea, the way you stroke your cat, the way you make love to the person who is your sacred partner, but also expressing the divine in creativity and expressing the divine in political and social action.

"To really come back to life, back to the body, back to matter, you have to smash so many of the concepts that have been handed down to you, concepts that have even been enshrined as wisdom," Andrew insists. "And what the Mother sends to help you do this is known in traditional terms as the dark night of the soul. This corresponds mystically to what the Sufis know as *fana* and what Jesus experienced in the crucifixion. This crucifixion, both of the false self and of the false self's dualism and its fear and shame at matter, births the resurrection. And what is the resurrection? It's the transfiguration of matter; it's the birth in matter of the light of the divine.

"That is exactly what happens at the higher levels of the Mother's path. It is a crucifixion, and it happens in terms of your own temperament, in terms of your own life, and actually usually in terms of your own body all at the same time.

"My life was annihilated by death threats," Andrew says, shaking his head at the memory, "by the craziness that reigned around all those people, by the Guru's lying, by my back being out, by Eryk nearly dying of cancer, by a whole holocaust. It was really a crucifixion. By being dismembered I was actually able to be remade in the light of the Mother and re-enter my life... That's what happens."

This process of crucifixion is an aspect of transformation, for rebirth can never occur without death, without the shedding of one's self at whatever stage one is. "All the different props of the self," Andrew goes on, "the emotional, religious, physical, conceptual props, are dissolved in the acid of atrocious suffering. Those props are actually walls against the Real. Walls against an overwhelming experience of divine love which, when all the walls are annihilated, can come in and flood and possess the center of the entire being.

"What Jesus did in the resurrection was give an eternal sign of this rebirth on the childbed of the cross," Andrew continues. "The crucifixion and the dark night are best understood as a kind of maternity bed in which one body, one spirit, and one mind all are broken apart to birth the resurrected consciousness, resurrected mind, and resurrected body. This is known in traditions of alchemy, Taoism, and I think by the Mahayana Buddhists in the Vajrayana path; it's known in the Christian esoteric tradition and it is the fundamental Mother knowledge.

"We are here to have this double birth," he tells me, excited by the idea. "We are here to be born into this extraordinary dimension and then to be reborn, which does not mean going off into transcendence but bringing transcendence *down*. Because the aim of the divine in the human race and the aim of the Mother-Father—and I think it's especially the work of the Mother because I think she is the emanating embodying power—is to birth beings on this planet who then can use this *shakti*, this power, to transform this whole planet and all its institutions, all of its arts, all of its sciences, into burning mirrors of love and justice. That's what we are here for!"

EXTREME EMOTIONS

Andrew and I are sitting now in the gentle and full evening dusk. Hunting birds are barely visible against the dimming sky as they make their last turn before dark, and the cliff's edges melt slowly into the desert landscape beyond. We begin to speak about daily life as the arena for practice, and how to include the intensity of one's desire for Truth into the sometimes banal ordinariness of the day. Andrew assures me that it is not only possible but necessary to focus on life as completely as one focuses on more formal spiritual practices. One place to start is in the transformation of ordinary human desires and emotions. Simple human needs, according to Andrew, are not to be denied, repressed, or relegated to the shadowlands of the anti-spiritual. On the contrary, they are the energy of life and the ground for transformation. And in accordance with his way of turning things entirely upside down, Andrew is the living possibility that the wilder the emotions and the more desperate the needs, the more fuel there is for realization.

"I particularly revere Sufism and esoteric Christianity," he tells me, his excitement growing again, "because they never ever ran away from extreme emotions. They realized that in the extreme emotions, if purified by adoration and by profound clarity, is the living *shakti*.

"If you look at the Hubble telescope's pictures of the birth of super-novas you see a great shout of light with billions and billions of miles of streaking fire coming out of it," he continues, extreme emotions beginning to manifest in his voice.

"Does that seem to express to you that there's an extremity, a gorgeous extremity at the heart of the universe? And that this gorgeous extremity might have something to do with a God who tosses off a few universes before breakfast, and creates fish at the bottom of the Philippine trench that look like they were designed by Fabergé on drugs?!

"This extremity, this fabulous, gorgeous too-muchness is part of the essence of the essence of God, and if you're going to find your way to that power you're going to *have* to bless the extreme emotions inside you. You're going to have to purify them without annihilating the source of them.

"I was helped very much by a crazy friend of mine in Paris," he says, like a child again with a good story to tell, "who is a wild old countess. She was shamelessly angry at everything, and she was so out there, nobody could control her. She would go up to the President and tell him off. She would talk to the so-called great artists of Paris and tell them what rubbish their work was—which it usually was—and she would criticize to their faces the famous film stars. And nobody could control Helene. And one day she was doing her thing at a dinner party and I was there and a man sitting next to her said 'Helene, you are too much' and she turned to him and said, 'Bertrand, you are not *nearly* enough!'"

I'm laughing at Andrew, his story, and his snobby French accent, and he goes on, smiling and big-eyed, "I always remember that! People come to me and say you care too much about the environment, or you care too much about the poor. But if you think I am too much, wait till you see Jesus! And wait until you experience the volcano of the Mother's outrage and the volcano of the Mother's love! Then you'll think that anything I'm showing you is a tiny firefly compared to the Krakatoa of what She really is. So let's get real around here!"

CONSECRATING DESIRES

"You really have to turn towards the values of the heart," Andrew continues as the darkness begins to settle in, wrapping us both in the timeless magic of the desert sky at night. "You have to understand that in emotion and love and passion are tremendous truths. You can find these truths, release them, by dedicating your emotions and your desires

to divine love and divine adoration. This is the key of the
tantra.

"If you have tremendous sexual desire—and most
people do, let's face it—" He stops speaking, turns to me
and says with a mischievous smile, "Thank God!" And
then he looks into the dark sky, throws his arms upward,
and yells loudly, "Thank God!" And we laugh, forgetting
where we were in the conversation.

"Bede Griffith said this so beautifully," he continues,
still laughing. "I got the highest teaching from an eighty-
six-year-old monk sitting under a tree in south India
who told me, 'It's quite clear to me what the answer is.'"
Andrew pinches his face now and speaks in a high-pitched,
ambiguous foreign accent.

"'You certainly can't indulge it! Because look at all
these unhappy people, they've done things I can't even
spell! I didn't know one could do such things! And they're
clearly not happy. And you clearly can't repress it, because
the monks are all crazy! All the monasteries are filled with
absolute lunatics in all religions.'" Andrew's accent reaches
a particularly hilarious pitch, before it evens out back to
his normal voice. "'The only way through is to consecrate
it. Is to offer it.'"

It is Andrew again, speaking to me. "And there's only
one way to do it. I mean, you read these *tantric* manuals and
they're so hilarious because after you've read them you
think it's a form of gymnastics! If you can throw your leg
over this shoulder then you've managed *tantra*. This is such
materialistic horseshit!

"The only way in which to experience *tantra* is to be
profoundly, and wildly, and passionately, and holily in love
with somebody. So that the extreme love will take you into
the dimension of adoration, and then in that dimension of
that extreme love and adoration all the sexual desire that
you *explode* in the relationship will *explode* in the divine

dimension! Because love is divine! And holy love is holiness itself in action. And then desire becomes the *shakti* creating the world. And then sexual meeting becomes the dancing-ground of Shiva and Shakti, the site of consummation of the marriage. Then you realize what Kalidasa, the Hindu Sanskrit poet, meant when he said that the entire universe is wet with the love-juices of the gods and goddesses."

I ask Andrew to say more about divine adoration. "Adoration is the devotion to the divine in all things," he tells me. "That's the clue to the experience of the Mother."

He reminded me that I asked him at the beginning of our conversation how we can really come down from transcendence. "To get back to that question you put at the beginning," he says, smiling at me. "It was asked to Ramakrishna. An old lady came to Ramakrishna and said, 'Look, I know you're supposed to be a great saint, and you've got to give me an answer to this because I'm dying and I've got to know because otherwise I'll die ignorant as a dog. I've never done any meditation because I hate meditation. I can't pray because it bores me to death, all those Sanskrit words. You've got to give me a way of connecting with the divine Mother in the core of my life—otherwise I will hold you personally responsible!'

"And Ramakrishna laughed and laughed and laughed, and said to her the amazing phrase, 'Well, who do you love most?' And she said, 'I love my granddaughter the most.' And he said, 'Well then it's quite simple, you go home and you worship your granddaughter as the divine Mother. You treat her as if she were the divine Mother on earth, and you will have realization.'

"What he was trying to do," Andrew explained, "was to say—Look at your life! What do you really love in your life? Personally, I really loved my cat, and treated her like the divine Mother. She *was* for me the divine Mother!

"In the middle of writing my last book, 'The Direct Path,' I asked for a sign that I wasn't crazy to believe that human beings could have a direct connection with God beyond religions, dogma, and all mediators. And I thought, of course, being me, that there would be lightning that would spell my name in the sky. Or something at least dramatic. And I was very disappointed for a whole evening because nothing was happening. And I walked outside my study and there was Purrball, my tabby, absolutely ir-radiated with divine light. *She* was the sign. It was my cat who was the sign because I loved her! And it is love that gives us the eyes to see the divine world more directly.

"It is so much simpler than we think," Andrew says softly. "The divine Motherhood of God is pure love. And when we love purely we are living in Her. Whatever we love like that, whether it's a rose or a cat or a piece of music or four lines of a poem, we're experiencing a part of that great love which is taking and binding together all of those experiences.

"And it doesn't matter what you love!" He raises his voice again. "You could love a peach! I mean, I love spa-ghetti Bolognese!" We both laugh at his example, and he continues. "It's wonderful! I love it, I really love it! And if I can take the essence of that love and link it to the essences of all the other forms of love, then I'm coming to intuit something of *my* capacity for love and something of the love that is trying to reach me through all these different aspects of life.

"Rumi says it so clearly, 'Everything that you love and enjoy is a ray from the sun of the Beloved.' As you really love and enjoy something, anything, just remember where it's coming from. And in the love and the enjoyment is threaded the intense memory of its source. So you know you are eating the divine. And you feel through that the incredible mercy and blessing of this experience.

"I try to be always conscious that the enjoyment I feel in life is Her, and is Her enjoyment. When you know who you are and whose child you are, all of what we call private ordinary pleasures are seen as unbroken miracles. And I try to live, more and more, in Her dimension of ordinary miracle. The whole of life is threaded with Her miracle.

"And then the difficulty," he says, softly, "is to see Her presence in pain and suffering and death and darkness. But that comes later, through an initiation into heartbreak, and the acceptance of the price of love."

INITIATION INTO HEARTBREAK

When one takes a transcendent stance, and limits life and the world as an illusion, it becomes difficult to engage in the problems of the world and to work to resolve these problems. Passionate engagement in life includes the willingness to experience, deeply, the needs of the world and the suffering within life.

"When I think of somebody who came into the complete consciousness I'm trying to describe I think of St. Francis," Andrew tells me. "And I think of a particular detail. When he was dying it was spring. And he spent a lot of his last energy in this world going out from his deathbed into the little paths around Tuscany, picking the little slugs up from the paths to save their lives. Each of these little slugs kindled in his heart infinite love.

"Don't tell me that he thinks of reality as an illusion! Because he experienced the full mystical initiation, he came to understand that the illusory nature of the world is actually an element of one's own senses, of the limitations of one's senses before they are transformed. He saw that one's senses create the illusion of separation, the illusion that the forms of the world are not real. And he saw that underneath and in all of these forms is light, this whole creation is in fact a creation of the dance of different-colored lights that emanates from the one white light.

"The Upanishads tell us there are three progressive levels of illumination. The first reveals the world as an illusion. The second reveals that only Brahman, the absolute transcendent presence, is real. In the third, the world itself is unveiled as a manifestation of Brahman. So the world, finally, is not an illusion. The world, as the divinized senses experience it, is saturated with divinity—it is absolutely, absolutely divine, super-real, not unreal." Andrew is now yelling again. "If we go on saying this world is an illusion we'll kill the whole planet!"

We sit in the dark stillness. After a moment, he says calmly, "It is essential to know and see and experience that the world is the living manifestation of the glory, the power, the radiance, of the Father-Mother's unbelievable passion and unbelievable love. And when you have experienced the dissolution of the ignorance of the senses, when you have experienced the whole world vanishing into light, and when you have experienced the world reappearing from that light, when you see each single object saturated with light and vibrating with light in every single moment, then what you come into, interwoven into the bliss and wonder, is heartbreak. Because at that moment what you share is the heartbreak of the Mother at what is being done to *Her* body, *Her* world, *Her* children, *Her* reality. *Her!* As a result of ignorance and craziness!

"So, you see the world as totally holy. And when you see the world as totally holy, you see yourself as totally responsible for the protection of every living thing in the world, and of beauty and of joy in the world, so the Mother's truth can play out everywhere.

"A Sufi text I love says, 'When you attain union, you are drawn near, and when you are drawn near you never fall asleep and the rays of sublime heartbreak engulf you.' You see, on the path of the Mother you're being led to the moment where you can be strong and surrendered enough to see the world in its total divine glory and also to feel the infinite pain of the infinite love that has created this glory and is trying to awaken the entire creation to its presence so that creation can become transfigured with its power and divine justice.

"That is a completely different model and we have to get there. And it doesn't deny the nothingness or emptiness. It just includes the very real initiation into heartbreak, and into the tremendous passion and compassion that arise from that heartbreak, and into the living commitment to direct action in the world that is born from that tremendous compassion. That's Jesus' path, that's the Sufi path, that's the Buddha's path, that's St. Francis' path.

"St. Francis was able to talk to the plants because he was able to realize they *weren't* an illusion! They weren't unreal! They were *super*-real! So that his being with them in that state of intense divine humility allowed them to speak to him! It's because we think we're superior and because we've used transcendence as a way of reinforcing this ridiculous arrogance that we don't talk to the plants, that we don't speak to the animals, that we are burning the world and killing the environment.

"We are being led by human history to the moment where either we awaken to this, or we don't. And if we don't awaken we will be talking about transcendence, going on about the sixteen types of emptiness, when the last tree in the last forest is burnt down, and then we will suddenly discover that there's no more bloody oxygen. And at that moment, where *will* our transcendence be?" Tears are forming in Andrew's eyes, and he is now shaking with anger and frustration.

"What set of disasters will it take for us to see that this is why She appears in tears? What more could She do? She's appearing everywhere, She's constantly trying to give us messages, She's erupting in human hearts, She's organizing this huge catastrophe. You would have thought we would have done something about it, but we've done nothing! Nobody's talking about it! The churches aren't talking about it, all these supposed masters are going on about transcendence and how to worship *them*, when we're in the middle of a holocaust that threatens the life of every single living creature! Does that suggest that we are crazy?"

THE PRICE OF LOVE

Andrew's desperation moves me deeply, and I ask him why people won't pay attention, why we don't recognize the impending disaster around us. He tells me that the price is simply too high.

"To face it requires facing that we do not have all the answers, that science, reason, and human wisdom are simply going to prove inadequate to the situation. We're going to have to take an evolutionary leap if we're going to solve it. That's the first reason.

"The second reason is that facing it is like facing, finally, that you may die from the cancer that is ravaging you. It is a terrifying experience full of extreme grief.

"And the third reason is that the only possible response to facing it is dedicating your entire life to transforming the conditions that are creating it.

"This heartbreak is so painful," he continues. "You realize you have to accept the derision, you have to accept the cruelty, you have to accept the upset you're going to feel with the price of real action in the real world. All of it has to be accepted; you have to shoulder it and get on with it.

"People want illumination, they say they do!" he says, shaking his head. "People want divine love, they say they do! But do people really want to see the glory and the agony together? Because if they do, they'll plunge into the fire of transformation and give themselves wholly up to the work that's required now.

"I think everybody who has even the beginnings of this realization understands that if they do this work they are going to have to go against all the churches, they're going to have to go against the transcendence-selling mystical systems, they're going to have to go against the material jamborees of our culture, and they're going to have to go against everything that the human race has been addicted to! And this is terribly scary for most people."

And Andrew explains that we can't do it alone, or within the systems already established. "It's only by connecting directly with the force, the power, and the majesty and the extreme compassion of the Mother that we are going to be given the strength to accept it, to accept the stern terms of the transformation, and to actually start infusing ourselves with the divine so that we can become servants of this transformation. It can happen only through Her because She is the power of the embodiment of the light."

THE DARKNESS OF THE MOTHER

Andrew and I are now sitting in the desert night. The stars are beginning to show themselves—vivid and alive—as they only do in the uninterrupted vastness of wilderness. The black space and the light of the stars seem equally brilliant and engaging. Andrew's face comes in and out of distinction as the occasional headlights of departing park visitors sweep by us. I am growing colder and colder, but still absorbed by Andrew's passionate description of the path of the Mother.

"People fear this vision because it's so fiery and demands so much responsibility and also calls for a frank acceptance of ordeal. But there are so many people thrilled at last to hear people say, 'Look at the facts, look at what's going on, look at how the solutions can't possibly be solutions. Accept that there is a way through, and it's the way of love in action, and that way is a way that depends on honoring the feminine as sacred.' Many people are thrilled when that is voiced.

"Passion is the key," he continues. "Rumi says it so beautifully:

> Passion burns down every branch of exhaustion;
> Passion is the Supreme Elixir and renews all things…
> Run my friends, run far away from all false solutions
> Let Divine passion triumph and rebirth you in yourself.

"It is essential on this path to be naked to the passion and emotion that the death of the planet potentially causes you. It's very important to get at the agony of the Mother, the rage, the suffering of the divine inside us, at what's going on, and to stop buying their version that being realized means being calm and peaceful. That's such a stupid idea! Was Jesus calm and peaceful all the time? No, he got furious at the people selling God at the temple! He raged at the priests at falsifying the relationship between the divine and human beings.

"The Mother is a tigress," Andrew says, fiercely. "A tigress protecting Her children. And sometimes She roars and She can roar with rage, and She can roar with agony, and She can roar with ferocity, and She can roar with terrifying lucidity.

"It's very important not to buy into the dreary, spiritually correct categories of what people describe as 'holy.' I mean, I live in Las Vegas, I'm gay, I have a marriage with a man I absolutely adore and I talk about sexuality being one of the experiences of the radiant empowerment of the Mother. I enjoy Tina Turner, opera, and cabaret singers. I believe enjoyment is a divine gift. I don't believe that I have to stand on one leg at the top of a mountain, or wear standardized clothes, or change my name to 'something Ananda' or any of that garbage! The realization that the Mother's grace feeds me in the core of my ordinary life is enough for me!

"I just encourage everyone out there to be their wildest, deepest, passionate compassionate selves!" he says so enthusiastically that it is hard to imagine any other solution to the problems of the world. "That itself would be a tremendous witness! Some people don't get it, other people are thrilled!

"If you buy this transcendence stuff you have to be totally awake before you can have an opinion on anything, and totally awake means totally calm about the destruction of this illusion. The Mother isn't going to sit around saying, 'It's OK if everything is destroyed and the planet is destroyed and human beings suffer appallingly,' because She is all of those human beings suffering!

"This is another level of awareness! You know why they stress being calm and peaceful as the ultimate?" he asks me. "Because that's the easy part! Then you don't bother about social conditions, you don't bother about the caste system, you don't bother about women being burnt or homosexuals being tortured and crucified. You don't bother about any of that because it's all only an illusion, which means that the power of divine realization can never inspire society to transfigure it! Calm and peace is one half of the godhead, but the other half of the godhead is tremendous passion, tremendous burning outrage at cruelty, and enormous commitment to just action! And that's the Mother!

"And Jesus is such an extraordinary example of this. He is as much Her son as he is the Father's. He lived life! *Not* the life of transcendence. He was offered transcendence and all its powers. He could have dined like the gurus do with all the famous rich people and sold them transcendence over martinis any day of the week!

"But he didn't. He married the masculine and feminine within him, transcendent awareness with the passion for justice of divine love, entered into the world and fought against all forms of oppression and was killed because he was so bloody uncompromising about his vision of how society must be changed. And that to me is the violent, pure, sweet love of the Mother coming through and possessing him and making him. And his whole yoga is the yoga of the transfiguration of matter into spirit through the crucifixion through the Absolute, opening in the depths of his being to the blazing power of divine love."

DETACHMENT AND PASSION

At the end of our visit we have finally moved out of the cold into 'Bonnie Springs,' a desert saloon reminiscent of the old West, with an unlikely pond outside filled with swans, dollar bills hanging from the ceiling, and western music playing from a hidden jukebox. I feel oddly at home with Andrew, sheltered from the desert by the unavoidably peculiar atmosphere of the bar. We drink our hot chocolate sitting on cowhide lounge chairs in front of an open fire, amongst a vague combination of gamblers and cowboys. Here, we speak about the balance between detachment and passion, between transcendence and immanence, between hot and cool spiritual practices.

"We need these technologies of transcendence," Andrew tells me, "as developed so skillfully through Buddhist practices, to purify the mind so we can bring down the light more effectively. I truly honor Buddhism. Buddhism has given us great techniques, and I call them the 'cool techniques.' I use Buddhist forms of meditation, of visualization, walking meditation, sitting meditation, but I use them in conjunction with Sufi heart forms and the Christian sacred heart forms to marry the masculine and the feminine. You need them to cool you down, and you need these other practices to heat you up, inspire you, and get you *thrilled* about life and about compassionate engaged communication with it.

"No one can live a life of dedicated passion without rooting their passion in deep prayer, meditation, and profound contemplation. Because only prayer, meditation, and contemplation can clear away all of those neuroses and obscurations in the psyche that prevent it from being a pure and vibrant instrument of holy passion.

"Look," he says, "detachment is there to make passion more white hot, to purify passion and make it diamond-pure. Someone put it so well when he said, 'Passion is a long patience.' And this is so true. How can there be patience without true detachment? And how can you wait and wait and wait unless you are passionate about what you wait for? Passion not rooted in detachment is useless, will just burn itself out.

"Detachment without passion is death, and passion without detachment is chaos. And passion fed off the silence and peace of detachment will find endless energy. The Mother's boundless fire draws its strength from the boundless silence of the Father. The Mother's boundless ecstasy draws its passion from the endless peace of the Father.

"At every level we are talking about a marriage of opposites. The greatest realization comes from this marriage. Life and death, good and evil, detachment and passion, masculine and feminine, heaven and earth. In marriage, both qualities interpenetrate each other to create the mysterious third that is both and neither.

"From the marriage of passion and detachment," he tells me, looking into the fire, "is born a laser and a passion that is pure as wind. Birthed from passion and detachment is the third—the fire presence of the awakening ones who are at once surreally calm and wildly extravagantly passionate in ways that confuse all categories."

Sipping his hot chocolate, he adds, "Passion is so wonderful. But without discrimination to balance your passion it's like climbing the Eiger in a tutu."

Andrew and I look at each other and burst out laughing at the absurd image, and as at other times during our meeting I let the fun flood through the seriousness of the point. I am grateful to be overwhelmed by laughter again with this extremely joyful and passionate man, and by now I trust that the power and urgency of his vision are not lost within these moments of hilarity, but infused within them.

Andrew insists on paying for the hot chocolate, but I sneak the waitress a bill while he isn't looking. We leave the warmth of the bar and head into the night, driving down mysteriously wide streets, often in the wrong direction, drifting through a sea of pale pink suburban stucco, trailing the scent of wild roses, towards the lights of Las Vegas.

THE STORMING of LOVE

a meeting with

Jackie Crovetto

THE STORMING *of* LOVE

A PLACE TO WASH THE DEAD

 In the cemetery of Wells Cathedral, behind two large sarcophagi, a gaping hole opens into the earth. Blackness pours out from this hole, stark against the green lawn and clear blue sky, and echoes of something swirling and alive arise from inside. Jackie Crovetto tells me that there is water running below, that a spring flows from behind the Cathedral under the cloisters and cemetery, probably used by the monastery years ago. Now, in the silence of the tombs, she suggests that it could be seen as a place to wash the dead, to begin to wash the dead in us all. When I ask her to explain, she says, "The water is like life! The life flowing deep within us. It's the hidden key. We need to let it wash away our old habitual patterns and open us to a spontaneous, heartfelt relationship with our world."

Jackie tells me that at one point the spring water was valued by all the people of the area, just as in the spiritual history of our Western culture there was a time when we valued the purity of that which flowed from the earth. Before our striving towards transcendence drove us continually above and beyond the simplicity of being human and being part of a greater living whole. But now a black iron gate closes the underground passage from the few who actually notice it hidden here between the graves, and one is turned back into the stream of tourism at the Cathedral, to the more obvious and uplifting places of worship.

What flows underneath these graves is a real presence. On the most obvious level it is the presence of pure water, rich cool air, moss and rocks, and the darkness itself that moves through the underground space. Also, as Jackie helps me see, it is a living symbol of a dimension of reality that is usually hidden, a place in the mystery of creation where form has just emerged from formlessness. In Jackie's presence I come more and more to experience what is often referred to as the *Dark Feminine*, this primordial ground from which all life pours—a particular realm of oneness in which the created world flows through barely differentiated energy structures. Chaotic and uncontrollable, teeming and full, this level of life can be as frightening as it is nurturing. It allows for no individuality, no separate identity, and moves through barriers with the power of a hurricane or tidal wave. If we are surrendered within it, this primal level of creation nourishes us with its abundance, and holds us within a web of love and life that links us to the whole of existence.

Jackie points out to me that the iron gate now stands as a symbol of our culture's response to this power and presence. We keep our distance and turn instead to what is more common and comprehensible, what we build with our own hands to reflect our own ideals and interpretations of virtue and devotion. Frightened by the unfamiliarity and total inclusiveness of primordial life, we starve ourselves of its abundance, and isolate ourselves from the sustenance that can only be experienced within its dark mystery.

But our culture needs access to the energy of the Dark Feminine to add fullness to the skeletal structures of our lives. If we accept this energy with awareness, its oneness can consciously connect us with each other and the rest of creation, enrich our detachment and sense of individuality through care and attention for all experience. It can help balance our need for order and our sense of direction with freedom and unpredictability. It can repair the split between ordinary and spiritual life, and nourish us so that we can partake of life fully.

Less than a hundred feet from the fissure behind the tombs is a sign of the deprivation that arises if we deny our connection with this aspect of experience. At the edge of the cemetery throngs of tourists eat at the café and spend money at the gift shop. This corner of the Cathedral is the most densely populated, and seems to Jackie and me to be an example of our unconscious collective starvation. It is as though the fertile darkness living under the earth, and in the depths of our own instinctual nature, cut off from our consciousness, surges through our structures of consumerism. Western culture's fervor for food and material goods is the shadow side of the energy of the Dark Feminine, what happens when it lives through our unconscious.

The Dark Feminine is the ground of all being, an elemental dimension of creation. We cannot cut ourselves off from it because it exists everywhere. But if we deny it a place in our individual and cultural consciousness, if we resist and denigrate it, this energy will continue to manifest in our lives through cycles of starvation and overindulgence and we will be left spinning within collective patterns of desolation and isolation. Its power will nauseate instead of nourish us, devour us and lead us to devour.

Historically, the energy of the Dark Feminine has been imaged by goddesses or deities who guard the processes of life and death, the cycles of the earth, and human fertility. This is a natural, creative, and instinctual energy, like the Greek goddess Baubo who had the power to disorient and evoke humor by revealing her vulva. She is also known as Para Shakti, the un-manifest cosmic force, Kali who laughs at and dances with death, and Durga astride her tiger as she rides to do battle with elemental demons. She is also the triple-headed Hecate who sees all that passes in the world of gods, men, and the dead. Like Sumerian Ereshkigal, these feminine forces often rule the underground, the depths of unconscious being that informs and determines conscious thought and action.

A MYSTERIOUS HUE

Jackie carries the power of this hidden creative energy and, due to her years of meditation and devotion on her Sufi path, it exists in a very pure form. When her ego is out of the way the energy flows through her freely and with great force, giving rise to an environment that clearly reflects the power and effects of this energy. It is an environment of wholeness and inclusion, joy and spontaneity. To step into her world is to lose a sense of separation, to enter into the abundance of oneness. It can seem dark here because there is total immersion, little order or sense of direction. There is the swirling disorientation of love, the joy of complete acceptance, and the constant, demanding attention to the possibilities within total freedom. In her presence, the most effective forms of perception are intuition and relational knowing—the knowing of love, generosity, and need, and the wisdom of the body and the natural world. Depending on how you relate to this energy, it can reflect the power of the devouring goddess or the nourishment of the ideal mother.

I spend more than a week visiting Jackie in Glastonbury, England, where she lives with her husband and the youngest of her three children. Glastonbury is a beautiful old English town set amongst what seems like endless rolling green hills—an ancient site associated with the grail legends, King Arthur, and early Celtic Christianity. Now, it is an odd combination of ancient lore and new-age spiritual indulgence. The narrow streets are lined with shops selling crystals and books on pyramid power and goddess worship. In fact, the week I was there was the beginning of the Goddess Conference, featuring priestess-training seminars and courses in witchcraft. Hippies and spiritual seekers from around the world hang out on the street corners and flood the sacred sites. The land is abundant with natural springs, some offered freely, others bottled and sold for profit. Some springs are capped or neglected; others lie hidden in the undergrowth out in the surrounding fields.

I spend the first half of my visit in a local bed and breakfast on the outskirts of town, walking to Jackie's house in the morning. Often we stay at her house to talk, where guests drop by unannounced to chat or ask Jackie for help interpreting dreams. Other times we visit sacred sites in town, or drink tea with her friends in the local cafés. Midweek, I move into Jackie's sitting room and spend the rest of my visit with her family and another houseguest. She lives in a sweet and small old brick house sandwiched between myths—windows at one end look up to the famous Tor, a high, prominent hill with the tower of St. Michael on the summit, while windows on the other side look across the fields fabled to be the shores of the Isle of Avalon where King Arthur is said to lie sleeping.

Jackie is a voluptuous woman with sparkling blue eyes and sensual features. Her full and open face is almost always partially hidden by an uncontrollable wilderness of curls. She seems to have boundless energy and enthusiasm, and is in a constant state of generosity and joyousness during my visit. She has a deep rich voice, and is a natural storyteller. She often speaks in archaic English, and describes the most intimate personal experience without any hesitation or embarrassment. At times she appears like Medusa—intimidating and protective—frightening when too close. Other times she is like a Venus, sublime and tender, luminous with grace.

Jackie works part-time at a local health clinic, and sometimes gives lectures on dreamwork—a practice of her Naqshbandi Sufi path. She lives an extremely ordinary life focused mostly on her family, yet the structures and order of her outer world are fed with an energy that continually offers new possibilities.

At first it was unsettling for me to be with Jackie. I sometimes felt overwhelmed and disoriented. I was confused and tired by the degree of activity and chaos that naturally move within and around her. When we spoke about this chaos, I was surprised to find that it was only I who experienced the energy as chaotic. Jackie and those close to her experience it as spontaneity, a generous freedom. While I sometimes felt exhausted, I saw others feeling nourished.

Not only was the chaos confusing for me, but the particular kind of chaos was generally unfamiliar. The energy Jackie carries is very instinctual, and I am not particularly aware of this aspect of myself. For example, I often found myself in the situation of being over-fed. I would sit down at a meal with Jackie and friends or family not feeling particularly hungry. But before I knew it I had eaten four courses—starting with a delicious array of breads and cheeses and ending with irresistible pie! This happened many times despite reminders to myself to make sure it didn't happen again. At the end of my trip Jackie and I just laughed at this sign of how the energy of the Dark Feminine can on the one hand nourish one completely, and on the other hand over-feed in a flurry of courses too tempting and disorienting to keep track of.

With Jackie, my familiar ways of thinking and organizing my life—particularly at the instinctual level, which included how I eat and sleep and the simple rhythms of the day—just didn't stand a chance against this very natural force that easily swept away my independence, rationality, and sense of control. Even my tape recorder didn't work during our interviews. One day I sat down to listen to the three hours of tape I had recorded earlier, only to find them all blank.

Not that they would have been helpful, as Jackie could talk for hours and hours, seemingly never answering my questions. Eager and enthusiastic, she would answer what I thought was a simple and direct question with a half-hour story, taking place in some other time or country, that left me totally bewildered. There was a point, as we were sitting together by the Abbot's fishpond at Glastonbury Abbey looking at a collection of glowing water lilies resting on the smooth black water, when we were both at a complete loss as to how we would ever communicate with each other. I kept asking the same questions again and again, and she would answer them in many ways, each time trying something new, hoping to get the message across. We would both be left dazed at the end of the day, not sure how to continue.

By about mid-week I threw out my tape recorder and notepad and made the commitment to just be with Jackie. To follow her through the day, instead of trying to keep my own schedule, to allow the continual spontaneity of her life to determine my activities, and to really just *be* with her without trying to understand her. I was determined to let her talk and talk, having faith that at some point I would hear what needed to be heard.

I realized that even the structure of this chapter had to adapt to her way of being and expressing herself. Rather than try to organize or explain her thoughts and ideas, I let the chapter accommodate her. Each section begins with Jackie's dreams, one of the most direct ways to reveal and express her experience. Dreams are an important way for her to relate to life—they offer her entry into a deeper part of herself, and into a deeper reality beyond the usual forms of this world.

Jackie lives in a symbolic world, where signs continually point her towards deeper involvement with whatever situation she is in. Eventually, all signs point to the beyond, into the nothingness that she knows as her Beloved, and she experiences life as a continual call into divine surrender to this love.

As the days wore on, and even through the months after my trip to England in which I worked on this chapter, Jackie and the events of our time together seemed to take on more profound meaning, as though I was being shown how Jackie herself experiences the world. I could begin to relate to life at a more symbolic level, in which situations reflected deeper meanings and opportunities. From this perspective, I began to experience what is hidden beyond the disorientation and incomprehensibility of the energy that flows through her. I saw that the darkness of the Dark Feminine lies in the *experience* of this energy. From one perspective this energy is dark and confusing. From another perspective it is something altogether different.

When I stopped resisting the energy I refer to as the Dark Feminine, I saw that, in fact, it hides within itself a substance of light and love, fine like a single ray of sun that threads through every living thing with a power that is unrelenting and imperishable. This power is not destructive but truly creative. Its oneness is not binding but freeing like an infinity of possibilities. Its abundance is not heavy or overwhelming, but sensual and joyful, fundamentally enlivening. Its energy is not really dark, but more like a mysterious hue, only visible at a certain time of the day while most people are too busy to look out their windows, or under a certain cover of trees where no one sits any more.

Yes, to be with the Dark Feminine is to sacrifice part of oneself to disorientation and chaos, raw power and powerlessness. But it is also to be nourished by a deep level of life, to be given insight into how the world is fed and formed by a hidden light of oneness. I don't think one can really directly know this energy, because it seems beyond our usual ways of perceiving, but one can sense when it is allowed to enter the structures of one's mind, the contours of one's day. It brings with it the scent of what lies beneath, and permeates life with the joy of the unknown, with the hint of something incomprehensible watching, laughing, at the borders of the ordinary. If we welcome it, we can—like Jackie—be drawn into a deeper and deeper relationship with life, love, and the divine.

LIVING WITH CHAOS

I am in a house; water has flowed in though it is not flooded. Looking down into the water I can see ancient foundations going down in layers to the Roman times and before. I watch as a huge old salmon rises slowly up to the surface. In his life he has encompassed the whole world, always returning to this, his birthplace and source, to breed and now perhaps to die—if such as he could ever die, as he seemed to possess a timeless eternal quality.

Lifting his head clear of the water, he wordlessly communicates to me the whole history of the earth, the history of everything in creation. It has nothing to do with what we learn at school, for I have no sense of order or facts or specific events. Rather, it feels as though I have stepped into an ocean of wonders, with ebbs and flows, cycles of being and becoming, and a sense of the profound mystery that lies behind all.

Jackie's house is very open. Everyone seems welcome here, to talk for an hour or visit for the entire afternoon. Some come for a few nights, and stay for half a year. People, mostly women, sit in the living room, which opens to the kitchen, and talk for hours about daily life, dreams, children, work, or whatever comes to mind. People come and go, joining in for as long as they want, fixing tea or helping themselves to lunch or dinner. The activity is strikingly ordinary, and it is often not evident to me why these people come, or what they receive. Yet Jackie's living room and kitchen seem always filled with friends and visitors who return again and again for what is offered here.

Jackie's family, her husband and daughter who live with her, provide constancy in the milieu, and mingle with whoever else is there. When she is not at her part-time job or giving lectures on dreamwork, Jackie is busy cooking, feeding, cleaning, and talking. She tells me that sometimes there are days when it is quiet, when she is silent and alone. But I don't witness this in my week with her. On the contrary, whether it is someone yelling from a café window for us to join her for coffee, or a spontaneous invitation for lunch the next day, Jackie's life seems entirely unpredictable and chaotic.

"There is a simple spontaneity," she explains, "a way of saying 'Yes' to whatever life puts in my path each day. So, when I am asked by someone to plan weeks ahead, to set a time and date for something, I add—in some form—the injunction 'God willing.' Because how can I know in advance whether I will be able to go, or what will need my attention that day, or what else I might be asked to take responsibility for at the time?"

When I sit in Jackie's house amongst a group of people, I can see that some are able to align themselves with the dynamic energy that is present. They contribute with stories, dreams, or insights, which reflect immediate involvement and openness. They can allow the richness of the environment to breathe life into their ideas and stories; they offer something vital, something that sparkles and excites. In stark contrast, others' words and actions sound tired, feel musty and old. The others are too frightened or inattentive to respond to the demands of the moment; their contributions are left behind, lost from what is real, left out of the interplay between the created and uncreated.

When I talk to Jackie about this, she says that she also sees this happening. "I am very aware of when people are not able to step into the river. Often, the person just isn't listening, isn't receptive to what is going on. She may hear words, but she isn't really open.

"I sit here with people, and they will tell a dream, or tell a story, and then someone comes in the door who contributes something, and suddenly something is happening, people are coming together in a certain way. And there is no way to plan that. It happens organically, things just unfold. And these moments are usually completely unexpected. People somehow perceive that there is space for them here, and they open into that space which is full of possibility. Then there is freedom to respond. All life can respond. But one needs to be open, to be listening, in order to receive what is available.

"Listening is an essential aspect of the feminine," she says. "It refers to a dynamic receptivity to the life going on around us, an awareness of our own interconnectedness, and our responsibility to be open to what comes to us. True listening is a tangible experience of this state, an opportunity gifted to us in every moment throughout life but one we choose largely to ignore. Often instead of listening, the ego has us preoccupied with what we ourselves are going to say next. Too busy even to notice what is going on around us!

"I see, also, that some people are more in touch with their capacity to *play*," she continues. "When we all sit around talking, there is an element of play, a way that we move freely from one person to the next in a state of spontaneity and generosity. Some people can lose themselves in the moment, the experience, just be it. They can interact, play with new ideas, new images, new events. They see something as if for the first time, through different eyes or from a different perspective.

"But it's not *safe*," she says, laughing. "Some people just want to stay on the outside, watching, assessing, and criticizing. All nice and safe with no real engagement. Life is flowing but they aren't flowing with it!"

When I point out to Jackie that sometimes I experience what she calls 'life' as chaos, she laughs again. "Well," she says, "I think what we can experience as chaos is simply a resistance to life. This resistance is pitted against the Self—our own essence—which is unknowable, beyond our understanding. We are afraid of that unknowing, so we resist. The power and energy engendered by this resistance flies about and gets projected out as chaos.

"I simply relate to what is going on as moments of pregnant possibility," she goes on, still smiling. "A bowl full of ingredients being stirred by a spoon in an unseen hand. One can fall in the mix and be swirled about, become disoriented. But the unseen agency stirs love into the mixture and that is the thread to follow at all times. And this love has an element of endless space. In order to participate in life at a very deep level, we need to be aware of this space. And we all have the responsibility to be caretakers for that space—which is the receptive silence, the stillness, the blackness, which is where this transcendence comes in."

The inner stillness Jackie refers to is a space at the core of life and at the core of one's own connection to all that life brings. It is like a golden silence at the center of the thread that weaves us all together in an interrelated whole. Jackie explains that one can find this core of love and silence by surrendering to life. By letting go of the need to control life, to stay separate from life, and letting what seems chaotic come into the rigid framework of our experience.

She told me a story of a recent lecture she gave on working with dreams. "I had written a short paper to present, and made copies for people, but I suddenly felt it to be too dry and limited. So I decided to just trust that something would come. I started to speak, and suddenly I could not think at all—as though my mind was turned off. I was left with just a detached consciousness, and also an anxiety at being in this state in front of professional people!

"But something in me just accepted the situation, to just sit there like an idiot. I didn't try to fight or fumble for words. Something in me just went into the silence. I really don't know what happened next. But slowly I became aware that someone had told a dream, and other people were dynamically interacting—completely involved. And I understood that the divine had found a doorway into the gathering!"

In her absence, in the space created by the absence of a controlling mind or ego, something completely alive and spontaneous could come into being. This is how it can happen with her. Jackie, in a place of stillness, allows a dynamic and seemingly chaotic interplay of people and events around her.

She tells me that unformed and uncontrolled life is always present beneath the ordered structures of our experience. It is a natural resource of great potential that waits for the chance to live through us. Allowing chaos draws up the power of the hidden into light, and in turn offers the world conscious entry into a wilderness of oneness and freedom. Surrendering to this level of life allows one to experience the love that flows at its core.

"Love lies at the core of my being, and enters all my days," she says. "To the eyes of others maybe it has appeared that I have done crazy things, at times thrown opportunities away or all caution to the winds. But over time the lover learns to be at home in the chaos of emotions and the storming of strong passions. For to be in love is to live in love, is to be vitally *alive*. Every moment is born anew; everything has significance and meaning. But to live out of this passion, a passion that is usually associated solely with sexual expression, makes the more restrained individuals amongst us shrink away in fear, stand back from life. For what they sense is a real power; what they sense is our true nature. But this is love, love beyond all our understanding. Love that knows no bounds, that flows through the created and uncreated world, that brings emptiness into form, and brings the freedom of death into each moment."

DANCING WITH DEATH

I am walking along a green mountain pass. There seem to be a guide and several other people in our party. We are just walking, taking a pleasant Sunday afternoon stroll, when suddenly without warning I step into a deep bog that lies across the path, and I start sinking fast. There appears to be a moment of choice; I can either struggle to keep my head above the water, thrash about and shout, or just accept that I am sinking and that I am going to drown. For a moment I see my husband and daughter and all the people I love. All the loved ones who hold me to life. I see how death is part of life and how, in such an instance as this, it unexpectedly comes to the fore. I wonder why anyone would be shocked, since death is always present in every moment. I know that at some point in my life that I will have to let go of them all, so why not today?

I let go. It is so easy. I breathe in the fluid, not resisting it as it fills my mouth and lungs. Dying is so simple I am almost amused by the thought that anyone could be afraid of something so natural! Then I am aware that I have become a detached observer watching my own responses to death and that this is just another distraction. I am forgetting to remember God, I am so wrapped up in this process.

Remembrance changes everything and something happens that cannot be put into words, because the mind was not there in its limited separation.

Jackie tells me that just as chaos and stillness balance and allow for each other, so are death and life both included within the oneness that is the core of existence. Everything that we experience has arisen from and will return to a ground of being. I see from being with her that both aspects—becoming and ceasing—are included and lived. It seems that every moment is like new for her. The space left open after the death of the last moment allows the next moment to be completely present. I see in her the joy that arises in this freedom, and acceptance of what is offered in that newness. In this way, absence and presence work together.

One day Jackie and I go out into her garden and harvest some glowing yellow squash. Vegetables—squash, carrots, chard—seem to pour out of the earth in excess. She hasn't spent much time here in the last weeks, and exclaims as we walk along the path, "My garden grows abundant in my neglect!" I am struck by the obvious symbol of how her life flourishes through the inclusion and acceptance of absence, and how those around her are fed by this flourishing.

"Our culture lives largely in denial of death," Jackie tells me while we cook dinner in her small kitchen. "We have all this violence on TV and it is one-dimensional, external entertainment. But we can bring the reality of death here, into our lives!

"Look," she says emphatically, "if I was told I had three months to live I would spend all that time with the ones I love. So why shouldn't I live that way now? If you really bring in the reality of death, would you treat other people and yourself the same way you do now? Would you have made the same choices and decisions that you made today or that you are planning for tomorrow? When I listen to the news and hear about the rise of some dictator, or the power struggles and atrocities we all at some time get embroiled in, I always seem to be left with the one thought 'Why have we forgotten that we are mortal? Why have we forgotten that on the day we die all that we have grasped after, all that we have sought to control and have power over, will be as sand flowing through our fingers?'

"Many cultures have understood that one has to face death, know death, and include death," she goes on to say. "This is the basis of the warrior tradition for men—they had to go to battle and face death in order to mature into manhood. At seventeen, my son chose to go into the army. This wasn't out of a lust to commit legalized mayhem and violence but to test his courage and fortitude, and learn self-discipline. Alongside maybe was the ideal that some things are worth fighting for and protecting. Whether you think such idealism is misdirected or näive is to completely miss the point. As a society we are failing to understand and provide for this primal need of our young men.

"Women usually don't have to go anywhere," she says as she adds spices to the soup we are cooking. "We have a deep instinctual understanding of death, and how life and death exist in the same moment. We experience it in how we give birth, which is to stand on the very threshold where we cross into life and death, and through the cycles of our bodies, and the cycles within our daily lives. We know that life includes death, and we can live from this place of oneness!

"In tribal cultures people used to be so aware of death that they knew when their life was drawing to an end. The old people would simply say that they were close to death and there would be a parting celebration or they would go off somewhere private to die. They were connected to wholeness; they knew when it was time to go. And they went without fear!"

Jackie explains that only from the space that includes both life and death can one live within a state of conscious remembrance of God. Here in the space and openness is the connection that aligns us with what is Real; everything in the created world becomes a sign pointing to the beyond.

"When we are faced with imminent death," she says, still stirring the soup, "remembrance of the divine spontaneously arises from deep within us. If you knew that you were going to be killed at noon today, everything would be vital, each blade of grass a wonder. All awesome beauty and terror, everything would carry the name of God.

"Why should this be? Because everything we have held on to has suddenly been stripped away. We are shocked out of our comfortable perceptions, made naked, stripped down to our essential being, and at that point we rediscover that we are His.

"At such moments we stand at the isthmus, the interface between the sea of life and the sea of death. At the point where the unmanifest comes into manifestation, the place where past, present, and future all arise together outside time. At this place we encounter an awareness of the primordial covenant between creation and its Lord, the covenant in which the uncreated mankind was asked, 'Am I not your Lord?' and mankind replied, 'Yes, we witness it,' which lies impressed within the heart. Awareness of this covenant gives rise to remembrance, a remembrance that is actually His remembrance of us. This becomes accessible and apparent because everything else is lost.

"In my own experience, if I stay with an awareness of death, His remembrance cannot but become a tangible presence throughout the day.

"At the times when I have got caught up in life I go and stand under a starry sky. Immediately a sense of proportion is re-established, for what am I and my troubles in the larger scheme of things? I am less than a grain of sand or dust alongside that infinitude of space. This vastness marks not my coming or my going. I was not caught up in life's difficulties before I was born and when I am dead they will have passed away too. So why not look beyond those troubles, which are so insignificant, to what is real?"

Jackie points out that it is not easy to become comfortable with death, to embrace absence as much as presence. Real freedom comes with a price, and this is the willingness to accept one's own non-existence, which can be terrifying.

"When I fell in love with my husband, Mario," she says, "I was totally and utterly in love. You know—that *seizure* of being overtaken by love. And then one morning,

I just woke up in this stillness, complete stillness. I realized I was totally, utterly 'other' than him, totally alone. And that was devastating because in my heart I knew that that intoxication, that seizure, that love was real. And yet, I was alone. As though he didn't exist at all, as though there was no one with whom I was in love, and vice versa! I, of course, was equally absent from him! I was devastated, I could hardly think about it. And it felt such a risk to talk about it, to say it, in part because I thought it meant I had failed in my love for Mario.

"In my immature notions of romantic love, I had felt certain that if I were to find the right man, my soul mate, I would be completely fulfilled! And there I was madly in love, and yet somewhere still utterly alone, filled with this nameless longing. It was a devastating realization, one that tortured and baffled me until I met Mrs. Tweedie, our Sufi teacher, and this longing was explained. I learned how there is a place in every heart that none can touch save Him, our one true Beloved. I knew then that this was a heart-ache only He could cure.

"Sometimes we will only know something by how we are shut out from it. We only know it by missing it. That is why now, in our world, we have a great opportunity because we feel the absence of the divine. We are all hungry for it. In life, in our society, there's the hunger because of the absence. And somehow the potential is now here because that absence is the potential of total presence."

We sit at her large dining table; the setting sun is shining its last rays softly against Jackie's face, shining gently into her wild curls. "When I talk about this union," she says quietly, "this union of life and death, presence and absence, it sounds like something special. But really it is something so simple, something to do with the simplicity of being. Like the space between every breath. It's always here."

THE POWER OF BEING

> I see the stark image of a huge snake. A great black worm from the earth's birthing. The sort that tales and legends describe as laying waste to entire kingdoms. A snake whose body encircles the oceans of the globe, each coil capable of whipping up a storm's fury. An unwary glance at such a creature would prove fatal, one drop of its blood bring searing pain and death.
>
> This creature is before me, and I know it is a reminder and a warning against falling into heedlessness and complacency, but also as a wordless appeal. It could overwhelm me in an instant, could consume me utterly. Yet it rises before me and I am to approach it—have a direct encounter, a rare opportunity to look it full in the face.

One afternoon in her living room, drinking tea and eating biscuits from the local bakery, Jackie and I talk about power and the Dark Feminine. She tells me the dream above, and says, "When I think back on this dream, I see that this worm was merely before me. It was in no way menacing or threatening. But this is my own and our general conditioning that when we encounter such raw power we respond primarily in terms of it having power over us. Measuring it with reference only to a possible destructive potential.

"We start imagining what would happen if such power were to be unleashed, how it would engulf us, and all our insecurities and fears start rising unbidden. This is the usual response to the energy of the Dark Feminine. We approach it with the largely unconscious expectation that something of us will be annihilated.

"But it is simply power, the power that makes up the very fabric and web of life that weaves together all our hopes and days. Can one endow a volcano with malevolent design and intent when a village built too close to its rim is engulfed in rivers of fire? Our rational selves would answer 'of course not!' But in some hidden part of our primal being it seems we do! We blame the earth for its inability to be controlled. We blame ourselves for our inability to control our instincts, our appetites. This blame gets in the way of really relating to the energy of life, to seeing what comes from it when we accept it and live it consciously.

"The power of the feminine is the power of being," she continues. "It is power that just is, inherent in the substance of life itself, present in every moment all around us. We hold it in our own bodies. But our culture is to do with competition and struggle for gain and so power is only understood and responded to in terms of what it could do to us. Harm, hinder, or help us subdue others. We need to see this terrible error! All life is under the tyranny engendered by this false perception!"

I ask Jackie to talk a bit about the shadow side of this energy—what happens when it lives through women unconsciously. I remind her that fear of this energy is not entirely groundless, that it can do damage when women are not aware of it, when they allow it to come through their own personal needs or limitations.

"Ah!" she says with excitement, putting down her biscuit. "The webs of collusion and entrapment! Two arms of the withholding, ensnaring, fearful, frightful feminine. When the web is woven not out of the fabric of life but out of the woman's own shadow self, out of her caprice and that which she does not want to face, her own icy controlling nature, then you get the power dynamics of the Dark Feminine.

"You see, this creative feminine energy is itself part of the energy of oneness. And if it pours out into the world through a woman's own immaturity it becomes a great ensnaring web. It is prone to annihilate, to control, to take over. Such a web of fixed perceptions is a shield from experiencing life in the raw and, as such, cuts one off from life's ever-changing horizons.

"If you stay close to a woman who lets this energy feed her own shadow you will be drawn to collude with her version of reality or at least never challenge the reality that she spins about herself. She will, by passive manipulation, emotional blackmail, or some such ploy, demand your total acceptance of her distorted reality, or you are out! Occasionally she will agree with a different perspective that another offers, and then just seconds, days, or weeks later the old pattern is firmly back in place. I have noticed that the web she weaves is very fixed; the same story will be told to you again and again.

"Women have the ability to become frozen in their own fantasies, trapped in their own interpretations. And they use symbols and signs to reinforce their interpretations. Then it can seem as though all creation is working for them, against you.

"But it is not real!" Jackie insists. "As we know, the intrinsic nature of the symbolic and the imaginal realm is *like* life; it is fluid and changeable. But in this frozen place the individual no longer trusts herself to be open to life; she tries to control life by fixing her version of reality and imposing it on life and others to keep everything within the confines of that terribly constricted and limited frame. A frame that reinforces her own position of power, her own security.

"But seen for what it truly is, it is pitiful and pathetic. Spun out of self-delusion and usually in response to the pain of some crisis or traumatic life event. The causative incidents are often violent in nature or violent in their effect on the whole system, physical, emotional, mental. Often perceived as a shocking betrayal by another or by life itself. The key note, I feel, is that the woman always has someone or something to blame and out of this blame comes the very substance that serves to hold such a web so firmly in place.

"Some women caught in such games and dynamics are ruthless in maintaining their webs and will go to any lengths, often applying circuitous and devious means, and they don't seem to care what turmoil they create in the lives of those around them! Often sly and indirect, they are skilled at assessing people, their weaknesses and vulnerabilities, and with facility can set up bewildering situations all around them. They behave like this because the pain of their isolation blinds them to all other suffering. The feminine is primarily concerned with relationship, so this isolated, cold, and frozen stance is against her core nature as a woman."

Jackie confirms that to be on the receiving end of such behavior can be very baffling and evoke feelings of deep fear. "One has to detach in order to see the pattern of the web, and also what lies behind it. And once one sees that, the weaver then becomes a sad figure who evokes compassion.

"It is also helpful to see the part we play," she reminds me. "When we are embroiled in such situations, the first step must be to recognize where we have got caught, maybe in some collusion through a fear of rejection or because 'their story' or reality initially sounded so plausible and we have been completely taken in or are simply just baffled by the mixed messages, etc. The trouble is these webs are sticky and they find the bit of us that is unsure and vulnerable.

"But we can become aware of our own vulnerability, our own insecurities, and then turn our vulnerability to the only real source of what we need—the divine, He who through His infinite grace and mercy provides all. This way we re-orient ourselves to life itself, instead of remaining caught in this web of illusion and power games. But this takes attentiveness and a willingness to always look to what is real; otherwise we will be forever caught in our own or others' winding fantasies."

PASSION AND ATTENTION

A brick building like an old kiln or oven is now a living space. As I go in an owl flies out. There are a man and his wife inside. I am shown a photo that is supposed to be me but I have the man's face.

I notice that the man now has a very long thin erect penis. So long it looks like a wand, the caduceus of Mercury, symbol of healing. He moves to enter me but at first I can feel nothing. He doesn't reject, ridicule, or comfort me but remains watching, as I shed the roles of wife, mother, etc., and come to know myself for what I am in essence: Lover.

This time he enters me and I am aware that his penis had to be that long in order to reach me. He enters me and I surrender totally and utterly to this penetration that moves deeper and deeper until finally entering every cell of my body. In this dynamic state of receptivity it is as if Pure Spirit is entering Matter. Love entering Being. Love that is He, the Beloved, the Sun at the very center of each and every cell and atom in creation, and I am experiencing through my body how each cell and atom praises God's glory and is infused with the power of His love. Something utterly tremendous, beyond description and yet tangible in the wonder of this our living world if we but choose to see it!

Jackie's passion is like a laser that focuses her deepest love with fierce attention. Her passion and focus for what is real bring direction through the chaos, allowing what is circular to spiral into deeper experiences and understanding.

"Women sometimes come to me in states of confusion," she says, while we make up the futon in the sitting room where I will sleep for a few nights. "They are overwhelmed and on the edge of despair. They are usually doing too much! Juggling children and partners with careers and the need to cook and keep fit and buy groceries. I ask them one simple question: if everything else is stripped away what do you really want? What do you long and yearn for? If we can stay true to our inner aspirations, whether it be to write that novel, climb a mountain, or raise your children, it will bring focus and light into all the dark places. Joseph Campbell calls this 'following your bliss'; the Sufis call this following the golden thread. It is the longing in the heart, which at its essence is the longing for what is Real, for Him whom you love."

For many women this focus is not goal-oriented. It doesn't always mean one goes out into the world with effort and searching to find what one longs for. In Jackie it is as if this concentration exists as an inner reality. As though there is a substance in her heart that always orients her precisely in the right direction. Her role is to have faith in this inner state, and to stay constantly attentive to outer signs that can direct her into the world. This is a state of being, not a goal-oriented expedition. It is an inner state of dynamic receptivity to the power that is love.

"In me there is a 'Yes!'" Jackie says, smiling widely, now sitting on the futon. "This inner 'Yes' is always present. There is a total faith and clarity in this 'Yes.' Faith that it will be fulfilled somewhere, sometime. There is no 'pushing' energy inside me, nothing that goes outward towards a goal, as if to achieve something. I hold this 'Yes' within, and a part of me is totally focused on it, totally present."

I ask Jackie what this "Yes" is, and she says, "It is the 'Yes' to God, the 'Yes' to service, the 'Yes' to love, the soul's 'Yes' to the life God has given me. And my life is how this 'Yes' comes more and more into the outer world, into the light of day.

"It is as though everything inside me is a process of unfolding," she continues. "This unfolding is hidden deep inside, like a seed. It happens in the darkness, a deep inner hidden process. But there is also a focus, an attentiveness, so that the light of consciousness balances the darkness. They work together within and also outside. Without the focus I would just be a drifter or a dreamer, I would be completely unbalanced. This focus is always attentive to signs in the outer world to reflect the inner process and allow me to participate in it."

Soon after meeting her, I realized that Jackie lives almost entirely in a symbolic world, a world of images reflecting the reality within her. Her inner world is a complete commitment to God, and to love. Yet this commitment lives like a wild energy deeply hidden. She needs the outer world to help her locate herself in life, to help bring the inner and the outer into a creative process of deeper unfolding. It is as though she only knows herself reflected through the signs around her. Therefore she is always attentive to outer symbols which are crucial to reflecting what is needed in the moment. Her whole world is alive with information and guidance; all of life helps her see where she is, and what is needed from her.

Some of the disorientation I felt with Jackie had to do with my sense that she related to me not so much as an individual person but more as a sign to be read. It is as if Jackie sometimes understood me as a reflection of something else, something with which I was not entirely familiar. When I tell her this, she says, excitedly, "Yes! A reflection of the divine!"

"I am always watching, always attentive to what goes on around me," she goes on, "for He reveals Himself anew in each moment. For example, when someone comes to me needing help with a dream, or even just to visit, I notice everything—what they talk of first, how they move about the room, the body language, what they choose to say and leave unsaid, the repeated phrase that pops up an hour later. The pun or slip of the tongue, whether the atmosphere in the room is calm or if the phone keeps ringing. I look to see what archetypes are at play; I seek the mythos of that individual's life where the divine enters in.

"I guess what I am trying to say is that I approach the whole of life as another might only approach a dream or a poem or music. Everything has meaning, reflects something potentially relevant to the moment. And if someone comes to me, over time I see the cycles and spirals of their life, the joys and the difficulties weaving out into a rich tapestry as they journey back to the Source.

"I remember thinking one day about the responsibility of being a parent. I am here to teach my children about life, and if I were to fail in everything but one practical lesson, what would that lesson be? I discovered it was the hope that they would always be able to put themselves in someone else's shoes, always to ask what had led that person to behave in that way, however much it hurt to be on the receiving end of the blow or sneer. And what I was really striving for here was to help them stay connected to the wide realms of the imagination. To be able to come to know and expand their understanding of the mystery behind all life through their imagination.

"If we look closely, everything is born out of our imagination, all our ideas and projects, hopes and fears, the design of our cars, our particular self-image, our dress-style, our homes, and our relationships. Through our imaginations we can aspire to reach the divine, discover what the heart sees: His face everywhere."

The world of the Dark Feminine is an imaginal world, where everything reflects upon something else, where symbols turn one around and around, like clues in an endless treasure hunt. The danger is when the imaginal world only reflects back upon itself, never revealing what lies beyond. In this case the darkness and disorientation of the feminine can be incestuous and self-absorbed instead of nourishing and empowering. As I sit with Jackie and the people in her house, I see some women circle endlessly, without the direction or creativity brought in by love or passion. Their conversations can seem dry and lifeless, ideas and thoughts cut off from real power, cut off from the heart. What they offer seems self-affirming and limited.

"Yes," Jackie says. "The inner passion has to be there or one is caught, lifeless, drifting, in a sea of worthless signs that point in all directions that lead you nowhere. To stay true to the love inside is what brings the outer its purpose. And to pay attention to the outer is what helps the inner unfold into life. Both contribute. But it takes a fearlessness to stay true to the inner 'Yes,' to what is essential to your being. It might be different for everybody, but for everybody it takes courage and willingness to stay with what you know is true, and it takes courage to read the signs as they are, not as you want them to be! When we see the signs as answering our own desire, they lead us round and round till we tire of ourselves. Then maybe we can start to see symbols as the signs of God. Everything is a reflection of God, everything points to the Beyond of the Beyond!"

UNFOLDING INTO LIFE

I look through an open door into a room. What strikes me is the sheer number of books lining every wall. I very much want to meet the man who lives here, and I enter in. The man arrives and there is an instant recognition. He is a stranger but I respond as if we are old friends. The atmosphere is electric for I can see the same regard in his eyes. The room beyond has a double bed in it and as a very natural course of events we end up on it.

After making love I start to dance for him. I am already naked but as I dance it is as if a veil falls revealing a mystery that is in turn veiled. And again as I move another veil falls to reveal a yet deeper level of this mystery that is itself veiled and so on. This veiling and unveiling of the mystery of the divine feminine. While I dance the man stands silent and motionless, never taking his eyes from me.

His presence is terribly important because in this dynamic he is shown something of this mystery and I come to experience the mystery, and the joy inherent in it. It is at my core, within my own body.

As the great Sufi, Bhai Sahib, says, "In the whole of creation there are only two: the lover and the Beloved." The man then expresses some of his fear of how the world will find me changed, the stiff poise and decorum replaced by something vital and dynamic which will make many uncomfortable. How the world fears a natural being, fears Nature.

In Jackie's world of symbols and signs, one of the most important elements is masculine energy that comes through the agency of an actual man—father, teacher, priest, friend, husband—in relationships both casual and intimate. Jackie tells me that throughout her life she has become more and more conscious of herself through her relationships with men. This is always a process of love for her, in which the depths of her being are penetrated and brought into consciousness, the outer expression of herself drawn up from the depths of inner mystery.

"The one constant in my life from my earliest recollections is the longing to go Home," she tells me one day as we sit quietly in her garden. "To our True Home. When I was a child, the story of Jacob's ladder moved my heart and fired my imagination. As I lay on my bed at night I would start to climb the stairway to heaven. I only had to put one foot on the bottom rung to arrive at the first heaven, and I knew that if I could only come to the seventh heaven I would come into the presence of God, throned in all His glory and majesty.

"I got as far as the third great stair when a man stood before me and I knew him to be Jesus. He beckoned me to him, and in that gentle presence I could unburden my heart. I was so baffled as a child to be in a world of so much suffering and hypocrisy and contradictory behavior masquerading under the label of love. Many nights I would find this ladder. This figure of Jesus was always there in the first heaven.

"The world of my parents passed these events off as fantasies, just dreams, so I learnt to hide this inner life from their ridicule. But for me, it was so real to just be in the presence of that silent unconditional acceptance. It was sustenance I have never forgotten.

"I learnt at some point that this body is transitory, and that it will die. Still a child, maybe six years old, I would lie in bed and instead of the ladder I found myself moving through a long tunnel at the end of which was a great light. I knew that light was Home. And I longed to go there. My aching heart drew me on up the tunnel towards the light. But each time a figure would appear. He wore simple gray apparel, and my eyes could not take in his features. Many years later I learnt this man was Bhai Sahib, the teacher of my teacher. As a child, I heard his voice within my heart, and gently he would say that I must return to life and the world, that the time was not yet for me to go Home. I would plead to be allowed to go on towards the light, telling him that the pain of separation was too much, the world too harsh. I would cry and cry. But it was always the same. He would, with so much compassion and tenderness, lead me back. I returned again and again, night after night, for many years.

"Gradually this figure impressed upon me that life is given for a purpose and our task is to find that purpose and do the task appointed us. He reminded me that something within me had agreed to this purpose. He couldn't tell me what that was. But he did say it involved being in the right place at the right time to say the right thing, and I needed to be fully engaged in life to fulfill this purpose. He told me that I need to have some part that always stands back and watches. First, so I notice things, and second so that I can bear the pain of being in a world that has forgotten God. And most important, to be in some small part the eyes and ears of God.

"But I was just a child, and that child, born with a need for love and approval, started to twist her true nature so that she might fit in with what made others comfortable. Gradually she learnt to keep her soul-life hidden, locked within. But the thread was always there and the few expressions it found were in such things as dance and singing and a profound joy in the beauty of nature, and this was enough to keep the spark of longing from becoming entirely covered up and hidden to sight."

I asked Jackie to tell me more about the role men played in her process of coming to know herself more deeply. And she told me of her grandfather.

"My paternal grandfather was a stern Victorian; he was what they called at the time a 'self-made man.' He had all the arrogance and insecurities that come when one attributes all one achieves to his own endeavors and not to the grace of God. His four sons lived in fear of his disapproval, which might cut them off from his largesse. When the family was summoned to pay him a visit the atmosphere was electric with tension.

"On arrival, all the grandchildren had to line up to be presented to 'Poppa.' The form, as we had been drilled, was to sit on his knee and when he asked 'Who do you love best?' we were to answer, 'You Poppa!' If we did so, we would be given spending money that to us was rich rewards!

"I went through this ordeal once, but the second time I was even more unhappy, and hid the money away and couldn't touch it.

"On the third occasion, I sat with the question hanging in the air, my heart full of a fearful dread. A terror seized me. Grandfather asked why I was crying and in the anguish of my heart I told him that the one I loved best was not he but God!

"And at that moment, this love, this eternal love that lived inside me, became more fully conscious. And from that moment on, our relationship grew. I think I was the only one who wasn't afraid of him. We would go on long walks together. He would talk on and on. And I doubt he had any awareness of the receptivity of his listener but I listened intently as he talked of the Middle East, and the mystic traditions of the three great religions of the Book. And he would recite poetry to me, verses where the rose garden is an allegory of the soul, and my heart listened hungrily. At night he would come and sing me to sleep, songs which communicated such love and longing in his tortured soul.

"Then it all changed. I was never sent to stay in my grandfather's house again, unless my parents were staying as well. I was no longer put in a room of my own but back in with my brothers. Nothing was said, and again I don't think it was very conscious why any of these changes were made. With hindsight I guess that our intimacy made others uncomfortable; there was a charge in it, the charge of Life that got equated with something erotic, therefore sexual, and not quite right. A similar response I have encountered again and again from those who fear the soul's life. Well, I never heard my grandfather sing again. But he gave me entry into a deep part of myself that I had not yet been conscious of.

"And my own father was a powerful figure. He was a warm, generous, fun-loving person and I loved him dearly. He was one of the few who could enter my imaginal world. He was happy to come into the fields at dusk and watch for the little people. He would take us to visit ruined castles and bring them alive with old stories and legends. He was away often, and on his return he would talk of all the dragons he had slayed and maidens he had rescued.

"He would take me out under a starry sky and explain what we knew of the universe, which laid bare the Mystery, and we would stand there together on the brink of the unknowable.

"So through his agency I never lost connection to the imaginal realm. And he set me free. He had a father's plans, a life mapped out, good career and education and socially advantageous marriage. Yet he always said that when I was eighteen I would be my own person; I would be free. And he let me go when I decided at that age to follow my heart far from him.

"You see," she tells me, "for me, love is distilled from concrete expression. From lived relationships especially with men, never in isolation. The masculine evokes a response and I, as a woman, in dark stillness, silently attentive, await the call, which initiates the dance, which spirals deeper and deeper into love, in all its myriad forms and expressions.

"So for me there was always this process of love which involved a masculine presence, or an actual man. When I grew up, I projected this love into romantic relationships, as so many of us do. For many women, romantic love is often our first taste of divine intoxication. But this is a great paradox—that a man offers us a taste of divine love, and yet he is just a man! Can you hold that paradox? That through this person you touch some deep core of the Mystery and yet he doesn't change his socks! Can you stay with those conflicts and still stay true to love? And not just today, but day after day, year after year?

"Loving another human being is such a magnificent test and trial. For even as you love him completely, you will never be fulfilled! Because there is always the emptiness inside that belongs only to God, that only God can enter. So time after time we are drawn into love only to be left with nothing!

"Look, if you watch a couple in the beginning of love, you see how they can be so very selfish, their love so exclusively theirs. The world exists, but only for them alone; the rest of the world can go hang. We have all behaved like that, claiming love for ourselves when we are born to be the vehicles of divine love in the world.

"But as time passes the real tests begin. Can you love him for love's sake, not your own? Can you love him through everything, through not getting what you want, through the rejections and the insecurities, and the selfish demands? Or can you consent to the suffering of unrequited love? When you love and you should not, can you consent to a relationship that does not give you what you want, but instead tortures you with the flame of passion that rages within unabated? It would be so much easier to say 'No!'

"If you stand in this paradox you put yourself into the fire, the fire that burns away this lower nature. For every time you feel that human impulse to reach out for what you want—what every cell of you wants—what you find is the emptiness that has always been there. Then you are tested. You are confronted with your own desires and all your attachments to this world. You want, want, want, and yet the reality is that you will not get what you want. Not from the man on whom you project your desires. And so you can be angry, you can be hurt, you can be rejected, you can stay in all that still binds you and keeps you from His embrace, He who is the King of Love. Or, you can give in, and let go, and love without wanting anything, and in doing so wait patiently for what He wants you to have!

"If you stay in the fire, true to Love, true to the deepest longing of your heart, a strange alchemy happens. Your expressions of love deepen and become more inclusive; an unfettered love starts to permeate all your relationships; your love becomes more and more selfless. This is mature love, love that wants nothing for yourself, love that is not confined to you and your lover. It is the real love that burns away the 'you' so that love can move through you into the world.

"The 'Yes!' in your heart consents to this process, to everything this process includes. And the suffering can be tremendous, the 'not getting' sometimes more than you think you can bear. But this 'Yes!' will suffer anything in the name of love, all for His sake! And one day you understand that there is really only one relationship. And it is nearer when it is truly absent.

"Eventually this storming of love, the agony and torment, becomes your most precious possession, the sweetest thing that you would never wish to relinquish. The hunger is somehow like being present at a great feast, the pain full of a baffling tenderness. His absence becomes full of His presence, the longing His 'HERE I AM!'"

UNBOUNDED LOVE

I experience the vast ocean of love, deep within my being.

I have found the place where the Ocean of Love enters Life and I stand on its shore.

It is as if I stand at the very edge of the created universe, at the threshold, where life is called into being. I see how this ocean of love just flows into the whole of its creation, never diminishing. If we could be but empty it would flow through us and out into our lives but we get in the way, through our desires.

Instead of being conduits, we seek to channel this ocean into the places we choose: this relationship, my job, that project. I see how the love still manages to seep through despite all the obstacles that we erect to impede it, but in our meddling our experience of love and life is somehow diminished. And I see how *this* is the reason why we are never truly satisfied with our lot. We sense that something is always missing or lost but rarely do we come to see that it is only ourselves and our attitudes that are to blame for standing in the way of love.

It is within the heart that I discover the shores of this ocean and I seem to stand at a midpoint, as a fulcrum, for there is as much space without in the created universe as there is within the human heart.

I know that to dive into this ocean, "where all swimming ends in drowning," is to surrender to the power that is love.

One day, sitting outside in her garden, looking across the endless green fields encircling Glastonbury, Jackie tells me she has always been in love. "By the grace of God I came into this world full of remembrance," she says.

"From my earliest years my heart has ached with a longing to return home, to our True Home. If I look back, I see that I have always been in love and this love has had many expressions, and through its ever-changing hues I come to know my Lord.

"I don't fear being engulfed by the flames of love; I live within them. I am a lover. Something in me cries 'Yes! Yes! Yes! Yes!' to love, however painful and bewildering to the little 'me,' for the little 'me' is lost in this battle. This love has me and draws me ever closer.

"This love is the single thread weaving through my life and all our lives. This love is the one power in the universe, calling into being and holding together the very fabric of creation.

"This is not a concept of how things are, but a lived *reality!*" she insists, looking at me as though something inside her is on fire. "I stand at the place where this love flows into creation. Where the command '*Be!*' arises. It is there within the human heart—yours and mine!

"This love is the black void between the stars, and the space between atoms. This love permeates every cell of my being and every cell of yours. This love is the roaring lion of your true nature!

"God is love! It is not a cliché, but such a truth! God is love and my love is miserable and small by comparison.

I have done what some would label mad things in the name of love. I risked everything that I held dear time and time again, but what has been offered up is pitiful next to the Grace I have been given.

"We all suffer the torments of human love, the jealousies and betrayals. Its twisted and distorted expressions, weighed down with our values, judgments, and conditions. And many come to build a wall around their hearts. But my longing is a raw open wound that nothing can shut out. What my heart seeks lies beyond all this. And yet here in life I find the school for love. In this schooling my heart has never betrayed me, though it has certainly led me at times in fear and trembling because of what it has demanded—to gradually learn to want nothing, to be nothing, to become empty. For then only the Beloved exists and the emptiness rings with His presence.

"This 'Yes' cries out still for the love to be increased, never diminished. This 'Yes' challenges life to produce enough love to act as the driving force to take me Home. And it is in life that this happens. This was the instruction I was given as a child by the figure in gray—to be in life. 'Be involved in life,' he said, and this is where I have found exactly what is needed.

"Love is the entrance to oneness, to the underlying connections of all things. The oneness is visible behind all the apparent duality in life. Somehow in life there have to be two, whether the other is a tree, a piece of music, two aspects within an individual, whether between a man and a woman or a woman and a woman, whatever combination. It can be a cathedral's lofty heights or your cancer, anything! But it is in a conscious participation within this relationship that something gets ignited out of which the transcendent can be glimpsed—out of the two comes an experience of the One."

For Jackie, it is the consciousness of the heart that unites her with creation, that allows her to experience God wherever she looks. When the heart is turned towards what is Real, all of life reflects the relationship, through love, of the individual to the many. "This is why," she says, "I keep repeating Bhai Sahib's lines: 'In the whole of creation there are only two, the lover and the Beloved.'

"One night I was shown a doorway," she says gently, "beyond which was everyone who had ever touched my life, every forgotten playmate and school friend, every shopkeeper, even every stranger I had glanced at in passing on the street. It didn't matter if I knew them for ten years or ten seconds, everyone was there, and they were all still held within the eternal moment of the heart, for the heart does not forget what touches it. Even if you live with someone and then part in animosity, the love remains, though the expression has changed. It is still there some-where hidden. Love is the one constant in life for it comes from the beyond, from the eternal."

THE STILL CENTER

> Three wise women are helping me to understand dreams.
> They ask me where I am now living.
> I reply that I have left the house of my mother and they rejoined,
> "And now you are living in the house of the King!"

In the tumult of life, in the swirling currents of love pouring into the light of form, within the endless cycles of cooking, cleaning, going to work, caring for her family, and helping people to learn how to interpret their dreams, Jackie lives from a place of stillness, situated in the center of everything that flurries around her. On an outer level, the center is her home, the place where she spends most of her time, where her family lives, where visitors come and return to. But like all things in her world, the outer place of stillness reflects an inner stillness, a place where Jackie is truly at home.

"What happens when we stay in one place?" she asks me, as we sit at the dining room table, one of my favorite places to talk. "What happens when we allow ourselves to stop looking, stop running away? Throughout history women have been situated in the home, providing nourishment for their families, offering a source and foundation for the life that emanates from them and encircles them. It is a natural instinct to root oneself, as well as a profound opportunity to experience the abundance of surrender.

"When my teacher, Mrs. Tweedie, sent me home to my children and my husband the first time I met her, I was completely confused. Somewhere I just couldn't comprehend why, having just found the only place that I had ever felt that I truly belonged, I was immediately being sent away. With hindsight I can now see that this was absolutely right, how it had to be, all the lessons I need to learn playing out in the daily round of meals and washing up, the joys and frustrations. It was a gift, the most precious gift. I felt, and still feel, what a privilege that was, and still is! And I want to acknowledge my husband's part in this, his support, and I don't mean just financial, that has enabled me to remain at home. Home was where I needed to be in order to learn how to *Be*, through being grounded in the ordinary things of life.

"I have noticed," she continues, "that women, mythic or actual, saints and others, are often associated with place: The oracle at Delphi; Circe with her Isle; St. Teresa of Avila;

St. Catherine of Siena; Mother Theresa of Calcutta. Our Lady of this place and that, Mrs. Tweedie in her London flat.

"I have found my place, the ground of being, and I have found it by simply being at home. And paradoxically I have found that my place is also the 'Placeless' that Rumi speaks of. What I have learned, gained, been offered through staying at home! Well, I wouldn't have chosen to do it any other way. I no longer feel the tug to be anywhere else.

"I find it deeply sad that other women don't allow this for themselves, don't give themselves this gift! To be with their children as they grow up, to be with the ones they love, to always remain rooted in the center of their lives. It is all here! It all springs up here! Women used to understand this. Why has it been forgotten? If a woman wants to work, that's fine, but why are we creating a society where a woman has less and less choice about whether she goes out to work or not? One income is often no longer enough. And often the woman is the only one now who can find work!

"As we run around our lives," she goes on to say, "there is no longer the time just to stop. To have a good old gossip. The derivation of this word is quite revealing—it literally means 'God's speak,' 'to speak of God,' for it was a term used to denote the function of a Godparent at baptism. There is so little time to just be together and gradually reveal the whole of ourselves. We end up with lives full of people who remain strangers. The shoulder to cry on now has to be bought in the therapy hour."

One morning Jackie and I eat scones in her living room and talk about England's weather and the dampness that plagues many of her neighborhood houses. Hers is not damp, she says, and when I ask her why, she replies, "There is a void under my house!"

I understand that though there is an actual space below her floorboards that keeps the dampness of the earth from entering, Jackie is speaking of the presence of a real void, a place of complete emptiness at the center of where she calls *home*. It is an emptiness that receives the divine; it is the place where light enters the darkness, where love answers the call of longing.

"I used to experience more of the chaos," she says, "more of the sense of being lost. But I saw that it was born from my need for control, my fears and my resistance to life. More and more I experience my nature as a still center, the ground of being, a place of absolute silence where I stand completely naked. I don't know if this could have happened if I hadn't allowed myself to stay in one place in the outer sense, to suffer my restlessness and resist moving. But in staying here, in resting in my outer life and in my inner life, I could trace my restlessness, my longing, back to its source, the real Source, the source of all life."

LIFE

I went to visit the Mothers, three ancient women, and asked how I might serve them or learn from them. I was instructed to fetch water from the well. I was sent three times.

The first time it felt like an order or a duty and the work was hard, for I had to pull the bucket up by hand from a very great depth and I labored hard and long, maybe for years.

The second time there was a winding device so the task was somewhat easier.

The third time as the bucket rose, the water level rose up with it. This water greeted me and told me to drink, something I hadn't done till now. Indeed, I was very thirsty and hadn't known it until that moment.

The water sprinkled playfully over me as I drank, showering me as if in blessing.

I felt such joy and humility, and thanked the water for this gift.

The Mothers said I was ready to leave now, and smiled.

One day Jackie and I sit amongst the ruins of Glastonbury Abbey—ancient structures of worship reaching up from the earth, few floors, few ceilings, mostly arches and remnants of walls standing in contrast to bright green grass, white clouds, birds, and sky. Despite the many visitors to this sacred site we seem to be wrapped in a light, protective stillness. As we sit there talking, the voices of those around us fade away, and it is as though we are completely alone on the soft, bright grass. Alone with the birds above, and the trees that reach over the Abbey walls from the street, and the one or two willows near us with their long light branches gesturing in the breeze.

In the stillness that seems to be given, I begin to sense that everything around us is communicating both to each other and to us. One leaf speaking with the leaf next to it, and as well to the leaves across the Abbey grounds, and also to us. Everything is alive with a delicate light, everything whispering in a barely hidden softness. All the noises of the ordinary world fade to reveal this secret communication.

I say to Jackie that suddenly everything has changed, that suddenly everything is alive. I sit with her in wonder. She looks back at me and says, "This is how it is." And I understand that she is right. This is what life *is*. This is how life, trees, grass, clouds, sky, and all the whispering leaves really *are*. I understand, as well, that Jackie experiences life like this all the time. That my one moment of 'seeing' life is how she *lives* in this world, moment to moment.

I feel a sudden sadness, and say to her that it seems everything around me is sad. She explains that this is my sadness at not knowing creation for what it is. For living without knowing this simple, nurturing oneness that is life itself.

Jackie and I sit in the Abbey ruins for what seems a very long time, but there is no sense of time. Then a security guard insists we leave because the grounds are being closed. We are the last to go, and the guard locks the gate behind us.

Sitting in her living room later, with the sunset throwing splashes of deep orange across the carpet, Jackie explains that people do not usually associate this lightness, this knowing, communicating oneness with the Dark Feminine. But it is at the core of feminine creativity.

"When one uses the phrase 'Dark Feminine,'" she says, "people's immediate associations are with the dark devouring aspects, the witchy, the thrall of death, an overwhelming powerlessness and despair. But this is her face when we have not given her respect, and the face we might only choose to see until such time that we come to acknowledge our frail mortality, our own vulnerability before powers of creation. Until we fully acknowledge and accept this gift of life that we have been given and at last really begin to live!

"You see, all of life is in service to a seeking of the divine. An artist—he doesn't just know the divine through how he relates to his work, he knows the divine as well through how others relate to his work. And it's the same with the Great Artist. He has the whole of creation. Each of us in the unfolding of our lives is responding to that creation and He is known through His creation. Transcendence comes in when we ourselves open to life.

"Participating in life is a spontaneous and flowing dynamic of whatever is going on in any one moment. In a conversation with someone I might articulate an insight; I can put it in words, or a short sentence. But if someone the next day says, 'What did you say?' it's gone! Because it was in the moment. And I'm often not conscious that I'm even making a statement at the time.

"For me, life is made up in the moments, there's an awareness in the moment that whatever we are in relation to at that point, whether it is the washing up or whether we have just picked up a pen to write with, or been jostled around on a bus or are with the one we love, it's all the bubbling spring rising up. And somehow in our present life we only experience that at odd moments. The 'special moments.' But that's how life is always.

"We had that moment in the Abbey, but then we were escorted and shut out. Like a symbol of, 'Yes, you can touch it,' and, 'Yes, there's a hunger for it.' But because there's a hunger for it we're being made to pay for it. That was such a painful experience for me. I was being escorted out from this place of being. A place that is available to all of us all the time, and yet we act like it is something that can be restricted. We even charge money for it!

"People have to have their own experience of life. We were being shown how this experience gets shut out, and it is up to us to take that experience out—out of that restricted area—into every moment. It is not limited. The transcendent comes in every instant! We are being asked to know this now, to know that the transcendent is *here*, in every moment!

"As this man was shutting the gate behind us," Jackie continues, "I was also perceiving the pressure of time. But what is real is beyond time, because it has to do with the whole of life, of whole moments, moments to moments. Time as a concept to me is strangely ludicrous.

"Have I only just met you?" she asks suddenly, looking directly into my eyes. "Or have you been here forever?

"When you leave here, it doesn't matter," she says now softly. "We will always be in relation. You will always be there within. So even if we fail here utterly, if I fail to communicate to you how life is for me, how God comes into my life, the commitment is not lost. The question has been asked and heard and is held deep within silence and unknowing, and if an answer is needed, over time something will crack open and the pearl will come out.

"What we are doing here, as we talk, as we sit together, is putting grit in the oyster. What we are enacting is a problem or difficulty in our culture—people connecting with each other, with themselves. There is such hunger, such longing for just being. And our constraints of time, of protecting ourselves, of holding on to what we have and what we are, come in and kill the opportunity. The antidote is to trust, to give ourselves to life, to recognize we are in love, and to want nothing for ourselves. This is a state of being, it is our birthright, it is available to us all. And now more than ever it is present!"

THE OPEN DOOR

> Humanity is in what seems to be a large space with some sort of domed ceiling. All those present are standing still, silently waiting. The place reminds me of an observatory but there is no telescope. We are the observers, the watchers. After but a few moments the dome above us starts to open; this is not a mechanical movement but more organic, fluid like a veil of mist rolling away. An opening is revealed, a black square, a portal.
>
> The gate is now open.
>
> It is such a simple event, strangely reminiscent of the cervix drawing back over the head of a foetus so that a birth can take place.
>
> What is revealed? What has been drawn aside?

What is apparent through this doorway? What is moving through? It just is, like the space between the stars or the depths of one's own being. As if it had always been, for there is in essence a simple familiarity, like the beating of one's own heart but with the sense that what is now accessible is something that was previously shut off from our day-world minds, sight, and senses.

I am now lucid within the dream, watching the figure of myself standing directly under this portal. I am talking aloud and expounding the relationship of the collective unconscious to number as the primary archetype:

THE NUMBER ONE: The Primordial Originator, the One from which all comes. Allah, the Lord our God, the Divine Lord of creation. God indivisible.

TWO: The world of opposites and polarities, man/woman, day/night, spirit/matter, this manifest realm of separation, dynamic potentiality, creative tension.

THREE: What is born from the two and out of the realm of free will and choice, changeable, fluid possibilities, perceived as exciting but also unstable and therefore frightening. The world of humanity as it is today.

FOUR: This world, the square, this portal, what will be born into this world of matter when the three reunites with the One. When God is again visible and worshiped within His creation, when matter is again perceived as sacred.

ZERO: Then follows the reflection that when numerical systems did not contain the concept of zero, the divine presence was always totally tangible within creation. With the inclusion of zero, something happened here in the West on the level of the collective.

For with the zero has come all our technical sophistication. But the zero in the depths of the psyche has come to stand for an absence and negation of the divine and of nature. On the collective level God is dead or reduced to a gray-haired old man in a cloud, sitting on the Sistine Chapel ceiling. Number one became synonymous with the puny individual human ego, whose only concern is for looking after 'number one.' What has also been lost is zero being seen to represent the transcendent reality, the void, the beyond of the beyond. But the glyph '0' needs to be seen not as empty but as a circle representing wholeness, 'God as the center of the circle whose circumference is everywhere.'

The ONE must be seen in conjunction with the ZERO. That is: each individual's relationship to the Divine is held alongside the utterly unimaginable Transcendent Reality.

Then, 1 and 0, the yin and yang, masculine and feminine principles can again be in balance within the human heart.

There was somehow no coincidence that the primary language of computers is based on these core archetypes, and I awoke with this last statement.

"The world has been so much in conflict," Jackie tells me after showing me this dream. "Through polarized positions, a 'tyranny of certitude,' as a wonderful Palestinian put it, holds sway. But there is a new energy that is coming down, as in my dream of the open door. It is an energy that indicates we can hold polarity without conflict. Usually the ability to do so requires so much inner work! But it is possible now without so much work. It is possible for us all to play our part."

I ask Jackie to explain what she means by conflict, and she says, "Well, conflicts between nations, or conflicts between political parties, or conflicts between men and women, between different ideas or ways. Usually we live in a world of conflict. One person wants something, and another wants something else, so one person has to give up. One person wins, the other loses. It's a mind-set we can fall into.

"But there is a new energy coming into the world which suggests these conflicts need not follow the old outworn patterns, those old responses that so often resulted in aggressive behavior and violence. We can live with these polarized situations, but in a different way. We can all need different things, but nobody has to lose. If we can just let go of the absolute certainty that we are always right. Let go, regardless of whether this is a personal, political, or religious position, and step instead into a place of 'unknowing,' which has nothing to do with backing down, appearing weak, or admitting defeat. We need to acknowledge our needs and fears and then step away from them for a while in order to provide a space for something else to come in. This state of unknowing is then offered up to that ineffable something which is beyond us all, like a prayer. And life will respond; life will provide the light by which to see the new doors as they open.

"The East and West, masculine and feminine, transcendent and immanent, the opposites can meet in a new way, without polarization. We can value multiplicity, validate multiplicity.

"I see this new possibility coming with a sense of wonder, curiosity, and such joy. We are waking up to— 'Wait a minute, this is an adventure!' It will enable us to step more fully into other people's shoes, to see how they see! To rediscover and validate our common humanity. To see that the Holy Land isn't *here* or *there*, that it doesn't belong exclusively to the Jewish or Arab people, but that all the land is holy, for all the earth is God's land.

"Many people I know are experiencing this possibility in their dreams, and in their lives. A friend had an experience in meditation. In the vision, he referred to a specific place as 'the Cup.' It was in Jerusalem between the Dome of the Rock and the Al-Aqsah Mosque. First of all, a fountain of light emanated from the Cup, rising heavenwards. Then the flow of light reversed itself, pouring out of the sky into the Cup, entering the ground, spreading a silver light through the earth. The light continued to spread, covering the whole of Israel, the West Bank in one direction and reaching the Mediterranean Sea in the other, still moving outward.

"The same week I met an observant Jew and his friend, a Palestinian Muslim. They work together in Israel bringing different groups together. Every Friday they sit with people of any faith and pray at this very spot. They sit in an attitude of unknowing, and to bear witness to the unfolding events.

"The silver light can not be stopped," she goes on to say definitively, "because it flows through matter, through the space between the molecules of matter. This light is a new healing energy flowing out everywhere. It is a groundswell of change.

"Look at the situation in the Middle East. It is the center of conflict at the moment. So much conflict. The men are fighting each other to the death. Suicide bombers, terrorists. In those countries people have had enough, and their voices are starting to be heard. They are saying we don't know what the answer is but we want the killing to stop. If I hurt another I hurt myself too, and we don't want to pass this situation on to our children.

"This light cannot be stopped because it flows through anything that could possibly be used to try to impede its progress. It is so subversive because in essence it is the power of true prayer, the hearts of people responding to the Light of God visible within His creation. The great Sufi Najm al-Din Kubra explains:

> There are lights which ascend and lights that descend. The ascending lights are the lights of the heart. The descending lights are those of the Throne. Creatural being (the lower self, the ego) is the veil between the Throne and the heart.
>
> When this veil is rent a door to the Throne opens within the heart, like springs towards like. Light rises towards light and light comes down and it is Light upon Light.
>
> Each time the heart sighs for the Throne the Throne sighs for the heart so they come to meet... Each time a light rises up from you, a light comes down towards you, and each time a flame rises from you, a corresponding flame comes down towards you.[1]

"With September 11, there was such a shock. But then tremendous love arose. Many people I spoke to felt deep compassion for the victims' families but also for the people who did the bombing. For their families, and in recognition that their terrible actions must have been born out of a great desperation and delusion.

"The world has changed. We stand on a knife-edge, but such shocking events are also a wake-up call, a call to recognize the opportunities and need for change. And behind all, something new is flowing into the world that carries with it a quality of joy in such contradiction to the daily news. A spontaneously arising joy.

"I experience it myself when I give talks now. We come together as a group of people. We are usually a group of strangers. We don't know each other; we don't necessarily have anything in common. But somehow because we are focused on something beyond ourselves, a veil is lifted. And then people connect to this energy, to something dynamic and alive. It's as if there is really something new! And anyone can feel it."

I ask Jackie, as I have asked others in this book, how people can recognize or align themselves with this new possibility, this new energy. She says, "The most important thing is to not be looking for anything for yourself. This new energy comes into groups, through people being attentive to their community, to something beyond themselves. This is my experience. Something alive is coming through relationships, through how we look to and care about each other. Something to do with life itself, and the love and joy at the core of our being, where new meaning is revealing itself. And this meaning is of course to do with what is real, with our hunger for what is real. And we are all hungry for *That!* We all want to go home to the Source, to return to what is Real. But what if it is right here? What if we don't have to go anywhere? We can just look in a new way, and then we will see."

HIS FRAGRANCE

> I enter a room where a couple who are soon to marry are sitting. They are so passive and still, I ask them what they are doing. They tell me that they are watching the washing dry. My ordinary day-world mind is rather taken aback at this, taking this remark as a statement of utter boredom. Then I see how wonderful it is—the work of washing has been done and now that everything is clean it just needs to be left to dry. All one has to do now is to wait and allow

this natural transformation to take place, a process well worth watching!

We listen to Wagner's "Tristan and Iseult." There is one piece where they are alone together. Iseult sings and Tristan responds and then she sings again. At first they are tentative and coy, but gradually they become more confident until finally their voices merge in a crescendo of intense passion. I experience this climax as something very physical; it is as if the fluid part of my brain turns one hundred and eighty degrees, resulting in a loss of horizon, and I fall to the floor.

Hot air blows in through the French windows. Some petals caught on the current of air dance and tumble as they move closer to where I lie. I catch them, and the fragrance of rose stays lingering on the air as the fragments melt into dust in my hand.

The room is both known and familiar, but at the same time has expanded into vast desert terrain; I seem to be lying exposed under the searing midday sun of the hottest place on earth.

I watch a desiccated shrub, tossed by this hot wind, blown hither and thither, subject to its will. His will. I sense that I need to stay here 'drying' until nothing remains. Just held between His two fingers, nothing but dust, dust at His feet, nothing left, only a fragrance. His fragrance.

THE TWENTY-TWO TARAS

a meeting with

Ani Tenzin Palmo

THE TWENTY-TWO TARAS

Homage to Tara, swift and fearless
With eyes like a flash of lightning
Lotus-born in an ocean of tears
Of Chenresig, protector of the three worlds.

Homage to you whose face is like
One hundred autumn moons gathered together
And blazes with the dazzling light
Of a thousand stars assembled.[1]

THE DELIGHTFUL GROVE

Throughout the evening in Tashi Jong, stray dogs fight and howl, monks speed away and come home on their motor bikes, and the smells of smoke, cows, and night-blooming jasmine take their turns drifting through the windows of the monastery guest-house where I try to sleep. Hours from now *puja*[2] chants—first from the nuns, then the monks—will lift through the darkness like an early sun, and the Tibetan refugee community will wake for another day of business. The heavy Indian heat and the shelter of the surrounding hills create a stillness in this valley, and I lie awake for hours, wrapped in the warmth of the night.

I have come to Tashi Jong in northern India to visit with Ani Tenzin Palmo, a British-born nun of the Drukpa Kargyu line of Tibetan Buddhism, renowned for her twelve-year retreat in a cave in the Indian Himalayas. Now she is establishing a sister nunnery to Khampagar monastery, the monastery of her guru Khamtrul Rinpoche, originally located in Kham, eastern Tibet. Before he died, Khamtrul Rinpoche requested she build his nunnery and in 1992 she began plans to create Dongyu Gatsal Ling (Delightful Grove of the True Lineage). The nunnery will offer young women of the Himalayan border regions of India and Tibet a unique opportunity to practice and study the *Dharma*[3] under the guidance of the Rinpoches and yogis from Tashi Jong and Ani Tenzin Palmo herself.

Education in Tibetan and English language, monastic discipline, Buddhist philosophy, and rituals of the Drukpa Kargyu lineage, will provide these nuns—who have now reached twenty-two[4] in number—with a rare opportunity for spiritual accomplishment. Additionally, a small number of nuns will be offered *togdenma* training. One aim of the nunnery is to revive the tradition of female yoginis, or *togdenmas*, that at one point flourished in Tibet, mostly thriving high in the Himalayas, but in recent history has all but disappeared. This training includes long retreats—lasting years—involving ancient practices designed to completely transform the body and consciousness of the practitioner.

I arrive at Khampagar Monastery on the second day of a four-day traditional Tibetan picnic. As I climb the steps of the monastery courtyard where the picnic is taking place, I feel as though I am entering another century. Tibetan teenagers of the community perform traditional songs and dances in full costume, and monks of all ages in their maroon robes and shaved heads listen and watch, or play in the background. The young Khamtrul Rinpoche, now twenty-one years old, sits on a small throne under a colorful tent. Choegyal Rinpoche and Dorzong Rinpoche, close disciples of the previous Khamtrul Rinpoche, who live part of the year at Khampagar, sit cross-legged on lower benches near to him. Across the courtyard, reclined on a bench, head in hand in a traditional yogic pose, long hair wrapped in a large bun on the top of his head, lies a resident *togden*—one of the *yogis* who will eventually transmit meditation practices to the nuns. On a small Tibetan carpet on the grass behind the Rinpoches sits Ani Tenzin Palmo, a slight and focused Western woman in traditional Tibetan monastic clothing, relaxed and smiling as she watches the dance.

I wanted to interview Ani Tenzin Palmo as soon as I read about her twelve-year retreat and her project to establish a nunnery that would allow young women to take part in the ancient *togdenma* training. I was inspired by her courage, discipline, and complete commitment to realization as well as by the possibility that she could encourage and nurture these qualities in other women.

These twenty-two young nuns are being given unique ingredients for their spiritual training. They live in a secluded and protected environment and are offered the guidance of the local Rinpoches and *togdens*, and Ani Tenzin Palmo, a highly respected teacher herself. They sit at the juncture where an ancient science of spiritual transformation meets the resources of contemporary study and practice, the juncture where Buddhism of the East meets Buddhism of the West. With these resources and opportunities, the girls of Dongyu Gatsal Ling seem likely to achieve spiritual maturity in a time when accomplished practitioners and teachers are direly needed. "They are seeds, small seeds," explains Choegyal Rinpoche. "Ani Tenzin Palmo is like the gardener, giving them water and sunlight. And they will flower."

Accomplished women teachers and practitioners, especially, are needed at this time in the history of Buddhism to offer a new balance within a spiritual system that has largely been guided by male teachers. "The Rinpoches are so pleased when they hear the nun's *puja* chants in the morning," Ani Tenzin Palmo explains. "It is as though something which has been missing for a long time is finally here." Choegyal Rinpoche agrees. "Males have certain energy and females have certain energy; they can balance each other and support each other. All the lamas want the nuns to develop; we are so happy to see this."

Because of their link to the West, the achievements of these young nuns could spread far beyond the borders of India, and offer Western Buddhism a new perspective on the potentials of monasticism. Buddhist monasticism in general and nunneries in particular have not found fertile soil in the West and, historically, nunneries in the East have often suffered from poor resources, mediocre leadership, and lack of educational opportunities. It is therefore reassuring to be faced with the predicted success of the young nuns at Dongyu Gatsal Ling. Only time will tell if the nunnery will succeed, but I can't help feeling that something exciting is being planted here in this Delightful Grove. "Yes, I am like the gardener," Ani Tenzin Palmo tells me, with a knowing smile, "but we have great little seeds!"

WOMEN AND MONASTICISM

Meditation and study are cornerstones of the Tibetan Buddhist path, and Tibetan Buddhism has always emphasized long retreats that support in-depth practice. The great Tibetan Buddhist saints were generally ascetics, often going into cave retreats for many years. Long periods of meditation and other practices—such as visualizations and mantra recitations—help one still the mind and open oneself to higher levels of consciousness which one stabilizes through continued attention. Ultimately, one stabilizes one's experience of the true nature of mind and all reality. The mind's true nature is fundamentally empty, devoid of independent nature. And yet it contains a light or wisdom often referred to as luminosity. Empty, luminous, and always giving rise to compassion that connects all beings in an interdependent whole, absolute reality—or *bodhicitta*—is present in every sentient being and every aspect of life. Realizing this essential truth is a state of freedom, freedom from the world of cause and effect, freedom from the suffering inherent in a perspective of duality.

One needs a great deal of time to stabilize one's experience of reality; therefore most Tibetan Buddhists view retreat situations as essential to the process. Even today, it is standard within many Tibetan Buddhist schools that one goes into seclusion for three years to undertake meditation, study, and yogic practices. In this context, monasticism has always been highly regarded, as it is a life of retreat, allowing complete focus on practice and study without worldly distractions.

Tibetan Buddhism's emphasis on retreat appeals to many Westerners. But it also leaves lay people who have families and full-time professions a bit at a loss for how to progress. Many women, especially, can feel that time away from ordinary life denies them something essential. Women with families, professional lives, a strong sense of social or political responsibility, or who relate to life through their sexuality and physicality, want a way to practice Buddhism while remaining involved with and sustained by these aspects of life. Long, isolated retreats that disconnect one from one's outer physical experience, and ascetic practices such as fasting or restricting one's sexuality, simply don't work for many women, often leaving them drained, unhealthy, and feeling dissociated from the ordinary world.

Partially in response to these needs, a recent trend has evolved in the West towards applying Buddhist teachings to everyday life where most people find themselves most of the time. Additionally, we are seeing many efforts towards integrating the *Dharma* into Western psychology, the conventional framework for understanding and relating to oneself and one's experience.

Ani Tenzin Palmo is the only monastic in this book, and as such goes a bit against the grain. But she and Dongyu Gatsal Ling offer an alternative to current trends in Western Buddhism and even in the wider spiritual climate for women, because they are preparing to offer women a way to live the *Dharma* with complete commitment and support *within* their tradition. This path does not seek to integrate Buddhist teachings with Western cultural norms or psychological science. This is a path of renunciation, in which ordinary relationships and elements of worldly life are not included. Personal and psychological needs are mostly viewed as irrelevant; service to others is the constant focus. It is a spiritual path including ancient practices that turn one continually inward, transforming one's mental and perceptual capacities as the ground for transforming one's relationship with all existence. It is a path of complete commitment, potentially drawing every element of one's life into a stream of devotion to the truth and service to all beings.

For some women, a path of renunciation is the most appropriate way to live their commitment to the truth. For these women, the demands of daily life within a materialistic culture based primarily on greed and self-interest are deterrents to spiritual development. Not every woman needs to live out her instinctual nature through having children or being in a romantic relationship. Some might need to live within a different kind of rhythm and movement, one that could seem unnatural to others. A way of being reflecting directness and focus that propels one forward instead of allowing the more circular movements of the natural rhythms of family or professional life. Ani Tenzin Palmo and the nunnery provide an example of this kind of path, one grounded in an uncompromising focus and discipline and a constant attention to a goal, balanced and guided by deep devotion to one's spiritual teacher and compassion for all beings.

Spiritual groups have always existed, providing a particular kind of container and momentum for spiritual evolution. Ideally, monasticism allows for the energy and power of one's commitment to the *Dharma* to flow unrestricted into every moment of the day, every aspect of one's experience. Like a protective structure, it contains and reflects the energy of the path, and allows that energy to nourish those within.

I sense from watching the nuns of Dongyu Gatsal Ling and talking with them briefly that they are being nourished by a particular quality of life and love that arises when a group of people come together with one common goal— in this case, the sole intention to realize the truth for the sake of others. And maybe this is a sign pointing to the real potentials of monasticism for women, in which complete devotion to the *Dharma* is itself a continual source of joy and vitality, as though one's commitment to the truth contains a spiritual substance that is essentially life-affirming. In this case, monasticism doesn't cut one off from life; rather it allows direct access to the deepest sustenance of life.

I spend almost two weeks in Tashi Jong meeting with Ani Tenzin Palmo, talking to her staff, and visiting with the nuns. There is no mistaking that these young nuns are adolescent girls, and reflect qualities—brightness, wildness, and enthusiasm—of most adolescent girls. Yet they have the opportunity to take a certain confidence and inherent wisdom into adulthood without having to pass through a socialization process that is so often, particularly in the West, damaging for girls. They will be given the opportunity to carry what is inherent in women through adolescence without the impacts of contemporary cultural norms, and with the continual guidance and focus of what is real according to the teachings of the Buddha.

BALANCE

Ani Tenzin Palmo's small room is located just next to the nunnery office, in a building at the entrance of Khampagar monastery. While we talk, Ani Tenzin Palmo sits on her bed, a small wood frame cushioned by a thick maroon Tibetan carpet patterned with a leaping golden dragon. I sit across from her on a chair next to a small shrine featuring a beautiful gold statue of the Buddha and a statue of Vajrayogini—queen of the female deities called *dakinis*. On the wall in front of me, to the right of Ani Tenzin Palmo, hangs a traditional Tibetan painting of Green Tara, the female Buddha of Compassion.

Next door the business of the office continues, while nuns come in to try on their new shirts, just made (but not well, it seems) by a local tailor. Monks, nuns, and inhabitants of Tashi Jong pass outside her room, and the mid-day heat enters through her window with the sounds of the passers-by.

Ani Tenzin Palmo has a serious and focused demeanor, with a strong, straight nose, a half-inch of gray hair, and cold, sparkling blue eyes that look like ponds of frozen light. Often while we talk she moves instantly from coldness to warmth, as though something completely unrelenting gives way to sudden softness and generosity. I like talking with her very much, as she always gets right to the point with cutting clarity that inspires quick thinking and instant response.

Before we begin talking about Buddhist monasticism in general and her nunnery in particular, I ask her if she finds any value in delineating between female qualities and male qualities as an aspect of training a group of women. I ask this question because many people interviewed for this book highlight the differences between the spiritual needs of men and the spiritual needs of women, and emphasize that spiritual training should reflect these differences.

Ani Tenzin Palmo, in contrast, makes it clear that she sees little difference in teaching the *Dharma* to women as compared to men. She herself has little sense of being a "woman," even laughing, seemingly bewildered, at the fact that she has been born with a female body. I find her perspective refreshing as it emphasizes the similarities rather than the differences in spiritual training.

"The *Dharma* is equally relevant for everybody," she says matter-of-factly. "There is no difference in the teachings or practices for men and women, because men have feminine characteristics and women have masculine characteristics. The whole person is transformed. Later during the yogic training there might be practices more suited to a woman's body. But in general the nuns will get training that monks and other practitioners would get.

"You can call certain things feminine principles," she continues, "and certain things masculine principles, but you can call them anything you want, can't you? Calling qualities 'masculine' or 'feminine' is fine, as long as one is very conscious that males also have very much the feminine, and females have very much the masculine within them. Many men are extremely sensitive and intuitive, and many women are as tough as old leather! Men also have intuition and wisdom, and women also are very practical.

"The problem is that if you start polarizing masculine and feminine people will think that men are like this and women are like that, which is not what we are dealing with. I think that each individual needs to be balanced. And that is what we are doing here. The girls are already very practical, so what they need is to develop their meditative side and their intellectual side."

On an absolute level, Ani Tenzin Palmo explains that Tibetan Buddhism delineates emptiness as a feminine principle, and compassion or skillful means as a masculine principle. "With the girls we are working to balance the wisdom side—the understanding of the emptiness of reality—with the skillful means side—the ability to bring that wisdom into the world, into your everyday life."

I ask Ani Tenzin Palmo to explain why emptiness is considered feminine. "I think it's the idea of spaciousness," she answers. "The feminine side is something open, inclusive, intuitive. The teachings convey the idea that the perfection of wisdom—the understanding of emptiness—is the mother of all Buddhas. Wisdom gives birth to Buddhas. Without wisdom there are no Buddhas. I guess it's like saying babies are born from the emptiness of the womb that includes everything but is empty. Likewise, that emptiness, that spacious quality, includes everything but within itself is not a thing."

The emptiness that is the absolute nature of reality endures through all time. Yet the Buddhas who come into this particular time and place will pass away. In that sense, feminine nature allows or gives rise to the capacity for compassionate or skillful action in the world.

"Any understanding of the nature of reality automatically arouses great compassion because you see how we create so much suffering for ourselves and others when we don't see the essential emptiness of things. The more clearly we see things, the more we can realize our own predicament and the predicament of all other beings. Then naturally great compassion arises, genuine compassion, because you see what the problem is. Emptiness and compassion are two sides of the same coin, working together. Without the realization of emptiness, compassion can just be an emotion, another way to be caught up in illusion. Helping someone based on one's emotional reactions or needs is not real compassionate action, or skillful means. Even emotion can be a bondage unless you realize the emptiness that is its intrinsic nature. With an understanding of emptiness comes detachment, which is also a basis for compassionate action. You are not acting for yourself, but for others."

I ask if there is anything at all her nuns need in order to succeed that might be different than what young monks need. At first she seems unable to cite any specific needs women have, but then she points to an issue that has been given a lot of attention in women's developmental psychology in the West—the issue of confidence.

"All women need in order to be successful at what they want to do is confidence and courage," she says. "That is all they need.

"We have told the girls basically there was nothing they couldn't do!" she continues, offering a simple solution to this problem. "We told them that we are here to provide possibilities so they could study *Dharma*, so they could really practice *Dharma*, that we really hoped in the future some of them would be teachers, some would become meditators, that they would begin to develop their true *Dharma* potential, and that this was the opportunity to really go for it, and we all believed in them.

"We told them that they were the founding members of Dongyu Gatsal Ling. They were the roots, and the roots had to be very strong: if the roots were strong the tree would grow well. We told them we had great confidence that Tara had sent these girls and that these were going to be very strong roots. And they see this, they see that the Rinpoches support them, they understand they have the full support of the community here."

A PATH OF RENUNCIATION

Ani Tenzin Palmo and I find common ground in our enthusiasm for monasticism, agreeing that it offers a rare opportunity to completely devote oneself to the *Dharma*. "I think it was the Buddha's intention that in order to attain liberation you have to give it all you've got," she says. "And of course one can do that in lay life but it's extremely difficult. And therefore the Buddha created the monastic *Sangha*, the community of monks and nuns. The Buddha spent much of his energy and wisdom on not only trying to create the *Sangha* but on seeing that it function in a harmonious manner. And for the last two-thousand-five-hundred years down to the present day it has continued and flourished in many countries basically without inter-ruption. There must be a reason for that."

I ask Ani Tenzin Palmo what the reason might be. She answers, "One is of course that the monastic *Sangha* are people who have renounced worldly life. This means they've renounced family relationships, marriage, parenting, and careers. In that way they have renounced the normal attach-ments and distractions of our lives. And then they have devoted all their energies to the spiritual path. At least hopefully," she says, smiling. "This gives them not only direction but ample time. And I think you need to give your practice and study a lot of time.

"In some ways there is something very special in being a monk or a nun. Practically everybody on the *Dharma* path at some point or other thinks, 'Can I be a monk or a nun?'

That idea comes from a recognition that monasticism is a way to completely give yourself to the *Dharma*—to give yourself all the time, twenty-four hours a day."

I point out that taking vows doesn't mean that a person's attachments disappear, and that sometimes taking vows includes a denial or repression of attachments, which is a problem. She agrees, saying, "That's true, but taking vows does mean that the *Dharma* will be at the center of your life. And it's easier to deal with attachments when you are not in an intimate relationship, or believe that relationships are going to bring you love and happiness.

"Nowadays, there is this incredible adulation of the three poisons: passion, aggression, and prejudice. Romantic relationships, family relationships—well, the whole of lay life—are based on attachment and involvement. Your whole happiness is invested, really, in family and relationships. Especially for women, but not just for women. And that's what monasticism is freeing you from. You don't have to deal with it anymore. That whole section of life just drops. Emotionally you're very free. You still have emotions; you still love your friends; you still have devotion to your guru. But it's not sticky. You're not expecting them to give you anything back.

"These girls are together, they love each other, they support each other, they're very harmonious, but it's not a needy thing. It's a supportive thing. Most of them have looked around at their parents or their sisters or their aunts and said, 'Forget it; that's not what I want! I want to do something more worthwhile.' Spiritually speaking, they see that other life as a dead end, which it is. They want to really do something else with their lives. My feeling is if you give them a life that is fulfilling, a life where they can study, practice, do *pujas*, can have a real community feeling together, they will feel fulfilled. Why would they want to leave that? For what?

"In the West it's different, because women have more options, they are more free than they used to be. But nonetheless, if you're a single woman, if you're not careful you're still going to get caught up in relationships, in the dream that somehow everything's going to be perfect in the right relationship." Ani Tenzin Palmo pauses, and then shakes her head, saying, "What that does to your mind!

"Monks and nuns devote themselves to something else. As a lay practitioner, even if you have glimpses in practice of the nature of mind, if you see for a moment what is real, still you go back into life and the emotions take over. There's a reason we call it 'falling in love.' When you're falling you can't stop yourself. Down you go!"

We laugh together, and then she says, seriously, "I think our girls are really, really lucky. They are on their way to freedom."

THE *SANGHA* AT DONGYU GATSAL LING

A moment passes, and I ask Ani Tenzin Palmo to speak a bit about the importance of the monastic *Sangha*. Particularly, I am interested in how she is establishing the *Sangha* at Dongyu Gatsal Ling, and the principles upon which it is being founded.

"The Buddha again and again praised good companionship," she says. "There is one *sutra* where Ananda says he thinks that on the whole, good companionship is at least one half of the spiritual path. The Buddha says, 'No, it's the whole of the spiritual path.'

"In a well-run nunnery or monastery the people around you are also faced in the same direction. You're all flowing together because spiritual life is like swimming upstream and it's very difficult to swim upstream all by yourself when everybody else is going down the currents. It's very difficult not to be pulled down with that whole momentum, but to keep the direction and energy required to swim upstream."

To help create such an environment for Dongyu Gatsal Ling, Ani Tenzin Palmo used specific guidelines to form her group. First, she required that the girls really want to be nuns. "Traditionally, children are offered to the monastery or nunnery by their parents," she explains. "But I didn't want that. I wanted that the girls should make this choice for themselves, that it should be their own decision." In this way, the community is established with individuals who are committed to being nuns. In the East, this is quite unusual for a monastic *Sangha*, for, as she explains, the monastery system is very much a part of a larger social system that is not always directly related to pursuit of the *Dharma*. In contrast, Ani Tenzin Palmo plans that the nuns undergo a rigorous practice and study program. She requires that they "not only study and have the theory but at the same time have the experiential qualities which come from meditation and practices, so the two should be in balance. For that, you need someone who is willing to put a lot into it, who doesn't just want to become a nun so she can get security."

In fact, a few of the girls had to insist that being a nun was what they really wanted. "One girl had to outrun young men riding yaks who wanted her for their wife," she tells me, clearly impressed. "Another girl's father was so against her decision to become a nun that he promised her a motor scooter if she would stay at home. So she ran away!"

Another guideline is that the girls have received some secular education so that they are skilled at learning. "The important thing is not that they have learned a lot in school, but that they know how to learn," Ani Tenzin Palmo explains.

The last, and possibly most important, requirement for the girls was that they all have "a certain spark, a real spark of intelligence," as Ani Tenzin Palmo describes it. This spark, along with the desire to be a nun, would drive and support the girls through their practice.

The girls are intelligent, devoted to each other and to Ani Tenzin Palmo, devoted to the profession of being nuns and teachers, and committed to their own practice and studies. Their day begins early, the nuns having all agreed to wake up at 4:30 to chant and meditate before breakfast. Most of the rest of the day they do ordinary chores, practice, and study. They have some exercise time, and one day I was able to play frisbee with them for an hour.

When I speak with the nuns or watch them go about their chores, I am struck by how much they embody these qualities that Ani Tenzin Palmo has worked to find. Like many ordinary young girls, they have a grace and a natural camaraderie that are beautiful to see. Whether they were carrying water to the nunnery, welcoming a new nun to the community, or out for a walk in the evening, I felt as though I was watching a dance troupe or a sports team, or an extended family around a holiday dinner. Within any grouping of these young women there is a communal way of moving that suggests unspoken connections and hidden communication of which even they might not be aware. A slight pull on another's robes, a push of enthusiasm sending someone off on an errand, a quick and encouraging glance, a finger linking with someone else's finger swinging gently back and forth: the girls are constantly in contact, providing a continual undercurrent of information exchange that forges them as a unit. I was able to have short interviews with some of the nuns, and despite language difficulties they seemed unusually bright and surprisingly composed.

THE WESTERN *SANGHA*

Ani Tenzin Palmo and I now talk about monasticism in the West. I ask her to address some of the possible reasons why monasticism has never really emerged as a strong force in Western Buddhism. She suggests some of the difficulties rest in misconceptions or misunderstandings about the monastic *Sangha*. She speaks about the Buddhist practice of taking refuge, saying one issue in Western Buddhism is that the element of taking refuge in the *Sangha* is rarely seen to be as important as the other aspects of refuge. Also, she suggests that the lay and monastic communities in the West have never fully taken on the appropriate relationship to each other.

'Taking refuge' refers to a formal commitment one makes at the beginning of the path that one also repeats during practice sessions. It is a commitment that deepens throughout one's life, and means one accepts that the Buddha, the teachings of the Buddha, and the community of Buddhists are the only sanctuary in the world, the only source of truth and freedom. One must embrace all three jewels—the Buddha, *Dharma*, and *Sangha*—as the source of liberation.

"In the West," Ani Tenzin Palmo continues, "You tend to have this situation where people can really take refuge in the Buddha and in the *Dharma*, but not in the *Sangha*. In Buddhist countries people do appreciate that without the monastic *Sangha*, especially without the monks, there would be no *Dharma*, because the monastic *Sangha* were traditionally the professionals. They were the ones who, having renounced family life and outside professions, had all the time to devote to their practice and in that way have been keeping the *Dharma* alive."

She pauses for a moment and then repeats with more emphasis, "Alive!" and pauses again. "For two-thousand-five-hundred years!" She shakes her head, as though she sees something precious being unrecognized. "So that in anyone's country there are genuinely enlightened beings who have devoted their lives to bringing the *Dharma* to fruition, not just stuck in their heads but in their whole beings. They embody the *Dharma*. This is not really appreciated.

"Especially nowadays in the Western *Sangha*, there is a preconception that when people get ordained they are not getting ordained to devote their lives to the *Dharma*, but to run away from things that are happening in their lives. So there is a lack of appreciation as well as respect. And I find it sad that this is almost encouraged by certain *lamas*, not towards their own Tibetan *Sanghas* but towards the Western *Sanghas*."

I ask what she means by this, and she says, "Many *lamas* don't encourage their lay practitioners to support their monks and nuns, motivate them, take care of them. Traditionally the lay people support their monastic *Sangha*. Part of the *Sangha's* responsibility is to be an example—to benefit and help the lay people. It's reciprocal; it's as the Buddha intended. And of course Westerners would be happy to support the *Sangha* if they were spurred on to. The *lamas* encourage them to help look after the monasteries in Nepal or India or Tibet, but they don't encourage them to appreciate the *Sanghas* from their own country.

"Here in Tashi Jong, people love their monks, they really care about the monastery, they look up to the monastery. So the monks on their side try to be good monks; they try to do everything as well as possible to repay the love and devotion of the lay people. So both sides gain. The problem in the West is that most Western *Sanghas* don't receive that kind of approbation and encouragement to do their best, because people are looking to Tibetan *lamas* or the glamorous and exotic Tibetan monks. But their own people might have many more qualities and much more understanding of the *Dharma*. That's what's very sad, this lack of appreciation of their own!"

Ani Tenzin Palmo tells me that the situation of monastic *Sanghas* not receiving support and respect from the lay community exacerbates the Western tendencies towards individualism and competition. Individualism is already one strike against Westerners' successfully establishing monasteries that depend on working together harmoniously.

"On the psychological and emotional side the Western *Sangha* is not getting support," she goes on to say. "And of course on the financial side they're often not getting support. It makes it very difficult for them! And in that kind of environment where it's 'every man for himself,' of course when they come together there will be difficulties and clashes.

"Living in harmony is a part of living in the monastic *Sangha*. In the West, people take ordination usually when they are already fully formed, already very set with their personalities, prominent in what used to be their sphere, and very individualistic. So when they come to take ordination, they are taking ordination in the Buddha and in the *Dharma* but not really in the *Sangha*. And so although they are ordained, and even if they live together, it's often very difficult for them to stay in harmony."

Western culture supports those who stand out and succeed at all costs. And yet a deep commitment to living with others, a sincere interest in forgoing personal needs for the harmony of a group, and the recognition that every *Sangha* member is essentially a Buddha have always been part of Buddhism. Ani Tenzin Palmo and I turn again to her own nunnery for an example of how a harmonious community can function.

"Our girls come from village backgrounds; they're usually part of a large family. And in Asia, as in the West previously, it is a great virtue to live in harmony with many people. Learning how to live with others in an accommodating manner which at the same time gives each enough individual space is regarded as very important. In the West, this sense of 'every man for himself'—you're out there on your own, and you're going to make it—is so prevalent. Interacting and being in harmony are much less encouraged. It makes it very difficult for people to learn how to live together. Westerners simply don't learn that other people are every bit as important as yourself, and that giving away to other people is the way to acquire positive qualities and genuine happiness."

Ani Tenzin Palmo tells me that the nuns are very industrious and work with a strong sense of group pride. She says that as soon as the nuns arrived, they immediately set up cooking and cleaning rotas. And when they were told that the Khampagar Rinpoches were coming to visit their temporary quarters, they assigned themselves into groups and began preparations, never having to be told. "We never had to tell them what to do—who will clean this, who will prepare that. They just worked it out themselves. It was really nice to see. It all just happened amongst themselves. They seem to get along beautifully together. We don't have to teach them!"

While they do run into a bit of trouble now and again, the nuns seem willing to do as they are told. "When they first came, they were all chewing gum," Ani Tenzin Palmo says, smiling and shaking her head. "Especially the Nepali girls. And we told them it just wasn't suitable for nuns—it looks horrible, and it's bad for the teeth. So we told them to stop. And so they stopped. No one argued; no one glared at me or talked back to me or came up with excuses. They just stopped!"

Ani Tenzin Palmo sensed my skepticism at how well-behaved the nuns seem, and assured me that most of the girls are genuinely well-balanced, and have few psychological or personal problems. Her remedy for any personal issues or disruptions that might arise is simply more *Dharma*. She tells me that the solution to one Tibetan girl's nightmares was a blessing by Dorzong Rinpoche.

"There is some psychological trauma," she says. "But we'll deal with it by trying to give them a happy and calm environment and help them study and practice and go on. Eventually they'll work it out. All we can do is give them lots and lots of *Dharma*, take them to meet *lamas*, help them practice and study, and hope that will be like a balm that eventually will heal the wound. And of course our hope is that through practice and study the girls will really have tamed their minds, and this will have lasting results."

The enthusiasm and commitment embodied in the nuns are a wonderful alternative to the individualism and social difficulties that can disrupt monastic *Sanghas* in the West. Why don't Westerners really embrace this aspect of taking refuge and work hard to live together harmoniously? Because, as Ani Tenzin Palmo explains, we are not taught to respect the *Sangha*. "Who do we honor and respect? The *Tulkus*, the *Geshes*, not each other! And that's so sad. It's so sad!"

GARDENING OR *SAMADHI*[5]

Ani Tenzin Palmo and I try to talk in her small room while monks outside the window whoop and holler as they load hay onto a truck for delivery to the barn at the other end of the monastery. At least one of the monks wears a cowboy hat, giving the escapade a certain ridiculous air. We laugh at the image of this boy in his robes, his shaved head, and the cowboy hat as he struggles under the hay, and shut her window against the noise. Our discussion now turns to the recent emphasis in Western Buddhism on applying the *Dharma* to everyday life.

One aspect of this movement seems timely and important—namely, bringing a balance to one's life by integrating all of one's experience into the *Dharma*, thereby undermining the split between practice and life that can plague so many lay Buddhists.

"We need a balance," Ani Tenzin Palmo says. "My feeling is that in *Dharma* circles, mostly in the West but sometimes in the East, there has been this tendency to think that *Dharma* practice means studying religious books or listening to talks, going to the temple, or sitting in meditation or saying *mantras* and so forth. And sweeping and cooking and cleaning and scrubbing the toilets etc., are just worldly mundane activities. Everybody wants to sit on their cushions saying *mantras* but nobody wants to get out there and take care of the ordinary business of life. And that creates this split.

"How many do we know who resent their work, and dream, 'If only I could go off into retreat I could become a great whatever, and this is my obstacle?' Instead of realizing, 'That isn't what's happening; I don't have the *karma* to do that right now, and these are my opportunities to practice, this is where I'm going to practice generosity and patience and loving kindness and compassion and understanding.' All these qualities are right in front of you! Otherwise you make the *Dharma* irrelevant and you end up with a lot of frustrated people all dreaming of being great yogis and just resenting what's happening right in front of them here and now.

"The important thing is to realize that everything we do—if we do it with a quality of service and also of awareness—everything is *Dharma* activity. The Zen practitioners have understood this very well, and incorporated clean-ing and sweeping and all these mundane activities into practice. The point is to integrate it all with an awareness and presence so there is not one moment you are not using as part of the spiritual path."

She tells me the story of Mary and Martha from the Bible to illustrate the split in Western thought between contemplation and worldly life, and to offer an alternative balance between the two.

"In the Bible," she begins, "Jesus is invited to lunch by two sisters, Mary and Martha. Martha is busy organizing the servants, getting everything prepared and the table laid, making sure everything is as it should be. Mary, instead of helping her, is sitting at Jesus' feet. At one point Martha turns around and says, 'Look, Jesus, tell Mary to get up and help. She's just sitting there being lazy.' Jesus says, 'What you're doing there is really good Martha, but Mary has the better part.'

"There is the sense," Ani Tenzin Palmo continues, "that contemplating the goodness of Jesus in his presence was more important than being busy. Just being there in the moment in his presence was more important than running around organizing and doing all these things, even though if they'd both been sitting there no one would have eaten!

"But still, the appreciation of that was the demarca-tion of the contemplative orders and the active orders in Catholic monasticism. Now traditionally, the Marys, the contemplative orders that were continuing the presence of the divine and also praying for the world, were regarded as having the better part. But after the so-called 'enlight-enment' in Europe, the contemplatives were misunder-stood and regarded as selfish and lazy because they weren't producing anything that you could see. While the Marthas, the active orders, the teachers and the nurses and so forth, were regarded as exemplary. And so what happened in

Catholicism is that the inner mystical tradition that was the life force, the stream within the church, basically dried up. You were left with everybody being ever so busy, but there was no inner experience anymore.

"The perfection is to have a Mary/Martha—to be Mary in Martha's part and to be Martha in Mary's part. To integrate the two."

I ask why it is said, then, that Mary has the better part. "Because," she answers with a tone of certainty, "it's very hard to be a Mary/Martha until you have really sat and practiced one-pointedly."

This brings up my own resistance to the current trend to integrate Buddhism into everyday life and even into Western psychology. It seems that the number of so-called Buddhist retreats emphasizing gardening or daily chores is growing. But does one really want to be in the garden, or does one want to be in *samadhi*? To suggest that one can be in *samadhi* while working in the garden seems a bit naïve to me, unless one has been practicing seriously for many years and attained a particularly high state of consciousness.

I tell Ani Tenzin Palmo that I wonder if the emphasis on everyday life might be a way to avoid committed practice. She agrees, somewhat, affirming that without long and serious practice, most easily gained in retreat situations, 'everyday life' will most likely not provide the most nourishing material for realization. Rather, practitioners need time in retreat in order to realize and stabilize higher states; only then will post-meditation experience be transformed.

She suggests that the current trend for Buddhists to emphasize everyday life might be another aspect of the split between practice and ordinary life we have been talking about. It is simply the pendulum swinging away from formal practice, after years of swinging towards it. "Renunciation took off when Buddhism came from the

East in the sixties," she tells me. "Westerners got so enthusiastic, and threw themselves into practice. Many people
wanted to turn to the *Dharma* and thought that this meant
turning away from ordinary life. Some of the Western
teachers who are now bringing the *Dharma* into everyday
life have already been monks. They went to the monasteries,
wore robes. But while they had many great experiences
they didn't have the realization. They thought their experiences were realizations—they thought they had really
gotten somewhere when they were obviously just beginning.

"I think they should have kept going. But they didn't.
Why not? Because as soon as they came out of retreat, as
soon as they came back to dealing with everyday life, they
couldn't cope. All their anger and frustration and resent-
ment hadn't really been dealt with. It had been repressed,
or laid low; but it was still there, latent. This is also true, that
you can be in an environment that is not challenging and
you think you've dealt with emotional ignorance when
you haven't. So they came out of retreat and they went to
psychiatrists!"

I ask what happened next. Did these practitioners then
believe that monasticism had failed them? Did they buy
into the view that monasticism is a reaction to psychological problems, a turning away from issues that really should
be resolved in some other way? She agreed, "The pressures
are great to think that if you're a monk somehow you're
missing out on something, or running away from something. And many people who disrobed believed that. I
mean, you *are* turning away from things. You're turning
upstream instead of going downstream. There's no doubt
about that—that's the point! To get a real stability in your
practice takes time. It really takes time. You have to really
stick with it through the disappointments."

I feel genuine sadness in Ani Tenzin Palmo as we discuss the current emphasis on everyday life in Western *Dharma* circles, and the underlying backlash against monasticism. We talk about this trend, and about how it influences her teaching. She says with some frustration, "What are you going to do? You're talking to an audience in which ninety-nine point nine percent are lay people who don't want to hear about monasticism. What are you going to say to them? Are you going to say, 'Well, frankly, forget about it—unless you want to spend twenty years of your life in retreat!' You can't do that, even though there is some truth in that. But there is also some truth in the fact that if you really get yourself together, and really use your everyday life and your family and your children and all that as a way of really expressing *Dharma* principles, then you'll live a much happier, more meaningful life."

I ask if she feels that this new trend is really driven mostly by audience demand. She says, "Well, yes, in part. Teachers have traditionally stressed long retreats and time set aside for in-depth study and practice. But practically speaking that's just not possible for many practitioners in the West. People interested in the *Dharma* now are mostly people with families, careers, social lives, and so forth. So the time which they can actually devote to formal study and practice is minimal compared to someone who has renounced the world and can go on long retreats, or who can give ten, twelve, or twenty years to intense study. Therefore the dynamic of the presentation of the *Dharma* has to be adapted to the current circumstances because it's a very different kind of person who nowadays is interested in the *Dharma* in the West."

Based on the Benedictine model, the nuns of Dongyu Gatsal Ling will partake equally in practice, work, and study, thus integrating the *Dharma* into every corner of their world. And this seems to be one of the benefits of monasticism, that one can live in an environment that subtly and not so subtly continually confirms one's commitment to realization and a life of service. In this way, monasticism provides a particular and very practical opportunity for an individual to live with a sense of balance and wholeness that comes from devoting all of oneself to one thing.

"There will be times when the nuns are in strict retreat," Ani Tenzin Palmo explains, "but the emphasis will be on incorporating work periods and practice periods. There will be times of intense practice periods, when that's all they will do; then maybe after they've done that they'll come out and they will be the ones who run the office and things, and the various tasks that have to be done serving others, and give the others the chance to go into retreat."

I ask Ani Tenzin Palmo how it can be that time in retreat, time in deep meditation, can really affect outer life. I wonder how this split is repaired through closing one's eyes and dissolving into the emptiness that is the true nature of our mind and all experience. She tells me with assurance, as though speaking of the most natural process, "Yes, you go into practice, you dissolve into emptiness. But when you come out you appear as a deity, you see all beings as deities in the mandala, all sounds are *mantras*, the whole environment is a pure land. All experiences are included, nothing is left out, everything partakes. All of reality is transformed!"

LIVING THE *DHARMA*

Ani Tenzin Palmo and I now begin to talk about another issue facing Western practitioners—another split that manifests in their practice and in their lives. This is the split between the mind and the heart, and the emphasis on intellectual rather than felt understanding which comes from the heart. The best way to address this obstacle is to make sure that one's practice and all of one's life are permeated and driven by devotion and the living energy of the *Dharma*—to really *live* the wisdom and love of the tradition.

"We are so totally caught up in our heads," Ani Tenzin Palmo tells me. "Especially Westerners—thinking, conceptualizing, analyzing, and so forth. The mind is going click click click click. Even when we meditate we still maintain this dichotomy between the observer and the observed. We are still locked in these patterns of dualism.

"People in the West 'get it' so quickly," she continues. "They pick up on a certain aspect of the meaning of the teachings so easily! Their minds are so bright, so attuned to intellectual understanding. The *lamas* say, 'Oh it's so easy teaching Westerners because they immediately get the point.' Yes they do, with the head they get the point brilliantly. But nothing changes in the heart!

"For Westerners the challenge is to use the *Dharma,* not just to memorize the recipes and the menu and know all about how to cook and have that all down pat, but to really eat the food, digest it. Intellectual understanding is the first step, but you need to really practice in order to get experiences. From the experiences you get realizations, and in the realization you become it. In the West we are fooled into thinking that since we know *about*, we know. If you know all the answers intellectually, it can actually act as a barrier. You're not eating, you're just busy staring at the menu.

"If you don't meditate skillfully," she continues, "you just stay in your head. Sometimes it's tricky to recognize the difference between feeding the ego and making ego more and more transparent. If you practice in the wrong way it solidifies the ego. Going for refuge, taking *Bodhisattva* vows[6], doing guru devotion[7] are intended to undercut the ego. If you do it from your heart it works, but if it's just rote it solidifies the ego.

"The problem is that most people, even when they meditate, even when they're doing practices to engender generosity or devotion such as practices of loving kindness[8] and practices to generate *bodhicitta*,[9] are still in that gap before the subject and object become one. It's something to do with the intellect and thought; it's not really touching the heart. The thing is to bring the meditation down into the heart. This is much more difficult for Westerners because our training is in the head. Tibetans don't even think about it!"

From spending time with the nuns it is clear to me that the *Dharma* is expressed through their hearts, and alive in their whole being. Speaking with them about why they want to be nuns is quite difficult, as they are not yet facile with expressing what is obviously so much a part of who they are. But when I ask one young girl what her favorite aspect of practice is and she tells me, 'I love silent meditation,' softly, quietly, with an almost unsettling intimacy, I feel the strength of her devotion.

As Ani Tenzin Palmo explains, the girls will have to go in the opposite direction from Westerners, bringing into conscious awareness what comes naturally for them; they will have to bring something up into the head, instead of down to the heart. But the heart is the location of real transformation. She reiterates the importance of generating love in the heart during practice, a process that takes one out of the ego and places one in a relationship of service to all beings.

"How do you start meditating?" Ani Tenzin Palmo asks. "You start by going through the lineage and generating the reason for doing the practice—your reason is not in order to advance the ego but in order to benefit others. Then you do a form of guru devotion and bring the guru into yourself, into the heart. *Then* you start the practice!"

Why is it so difficult for adult Westerners to accept that love and devotion are essential in practice and in life? These young nuns don't seem to have trouble with it. Love is such a disturbing word to most practitioners in the West that they are relieved to be able to talk about *bodhicitta*—the absolute essence of all life that includes an essential element of love—which has an exotic and distant ring to it. But guru devotion, love of the *Dharma*, and the need to serve others are the lifeblood of Buddhism. The inner communion that takes place in the heart but which expands to include every part of oneself and every aspect of experience is the living stream within any mystical tradition.

I ask Ani Tenzin Palmo if it's possible to realize emptiness without the arising of *bodhicitta*, without awakening the heart. I have in mind the image of the stereotypical detached, ascetic monk or nun who can achieve states of peace or tranquility in practice but can't seem to relate to others or life with genuine compassion or real presence. Ani Tenzin Palmo seems to recognize this stereotype, and answers, "A genuine realization of emptiness has to be down here," she says, gesturing to her heart. "Any genuine realization by its very nature is beyond concept and thought. It's when that whole thought-pattern drops away, and that has nothing to do with the brain.

"Genuine realization," she continues, "in contradistinction to a very subtle intellectual realization, will automatically engage an inner transformation. As Choegyal Rinpoche once said, 'First you have an intellectual understanding, then you have a taste of it, then you become it.' Then there's no duality between the thinker and the actual realization. This is a state of being. And the idea is if you have a genuine realization, by its very nature compassion will arise. That is why when the Buddha attained his great realization he didn't have to meditate on *bodhicitta* afterwards!"

On the last day of the picnic, I asked Dorzong Rinpoche to comment about love and the importance of generating *bodhicitta* in practice. He said, so simply and profoundly, "A warm heart is like life, like food and air and water for the body."

THE YOUNG *DAKINIS*

One day, sitting in her small room, I ask Ani Tenzin Palmo to talk about the *dakinis*, the female deities who assist individuals in their pursuit of the truth, the deities who helped her on her twelve-year retreat. I can't help but feel they are a part of what is happening here in this nunnery, and that the *dakinis* are themselves an example of the potentials of monasticism, an example of total and complete devotion and commitment to the *Dharma*. A wild, life-sustaining energy full of drive and courage, passion and power.

"*Dakinis* exist on many levels," she tells me. "They represent, first, that drive to enlightenment. Whatever we wish to accomplish in the world, if we don't have energy and drive to accomplish it we are not going to reach the goal. That deep inner passion for enlightenment is represented by the *dakinis*. Why are they shown usually naked and abandoned? Because it is an all-or-nothing situation. Unless you really want it, you're not going to get it! It's a one-hundred-and-ten percent commitment, and that's represented by this very wild figure who is completely throwing off all taboos and inhibitions and going for it with everything she's got.

"In ancient India, *dakinis* also meant these women who hung around in the cremation grounds. They were often lower-caste women, kind of yogini characters—living amongst death, understanding the impermanence of this world.

"Lahoul, where I was on retreat, is said to be the 'land of the *dakinis*.' Here, again, there were two aspects. On one level all Lahouli women are said to be *dakinis*, which is very possible because they are very strong ladies, much stronger than the men. A powerful force!

"But on another level there are certain sacred places which are considered to be pure lands, where *dakinis* gather on an astral level. I certainly felt it in Lahoul. Whenever I prayed to the *dakinis* there was instant help. They were a very strong force. I would ask them for something, and it happened. There was a kind of surety that yes, they would take care of it. And they would!

"The idea in the Tibetan way of perception is that the *dakinis* play the role of removing obstacles and creating auspicious circumstances for practitioners. So that in a situation where somebody wants to practice, the *dakinis* are there to help things along. And they are also considered to be messengers. Often in the life stories of great yogis like Milarepa *dakinis* would appear to give them messages— telling them what to do next or where to go or so forth."

I ask if there is a reason that *dakinis* are female. She says, "There are *dakas,* male *dakinis*." She pauses and continues, "But they are less important," and we laugh a bit. When I ask her why the *dakas* are less important, she says, smiling, "Well, they are there, but somehow the women seem to be more active. They are the ones who really get things done.

"I always admire that Vajrayogini, queen of the *dakinis*, carries her old man, Heruka, in her staff"—she points to the wild golden figure on her shrine to my left who carries a staff in her left hand. "She carries him around with her and when she wants him he can manifest.

"So," she says seriously, returning to the real point, "Vajrayogini stands out by herself."

Then Ani Tenzin Palmo states what I have felt from the time I arrived. "I really regard these girls as having been sent by Tara," she says. "They're just so good! They're young, eager, enthusiastic, and they really want to learn, they really want to practice—they have the aspiration, they want to be good nuns and later on be able to benefit others. This whole project is in the hands of Tara. And the *dakinis* are all out there doing what *dakinis* do."

One evening during my last days in Tashi Jong, just as it was getting dark, I walked the straight road that runs from the Tibetan community past the Indian farm houses, joining with the main road a mile away. Coming towards me was a group of nuns heading back to the nunnery for the night. Bundled together, joyful and laughing, they stopped to say hello. We spoke a bit, as best we could with our language differences. Then I saw it—a girl blowing a bubble. Gum! The forbidden indulgence, and they all were chewing it! The nuns were not as obedient as they appeared. Those chosen, perhaps, by Tara herself to become accomplished meditators, teachers, and yoginis have a streak of ordinary wildness, a strain of adolescent disobedience. Maybe it will disappear, through devotion and discipline, through the process of growing up into women and teachers. But maybe not. Perhaps Tara was very particular in her choice of girls, maybe she had an idea for something else, a way that something free and untamable can be included within an undeterred stream of devotion—a new kind of nun for a new kind of monasticism.

WOMEN'S WAYS of LIVING

a meeting with

Sobonfu Somé

WOMEN'S WAYS of LIVING

"Women are on the front lines.
Women have always been the first to
see what is coming."

Sobonfu Somé

UNDULATIONS AHEAD

 I am overwhelmed by the smells of blossoms and fruit trees as I drive into Sobonfu Somé's neighborhood in Sacramento, California. It is a hot spring day and everything is in bloom. Fruit trees, roses, flowers, and shrubs seem all to give off the scent of gentle and exotic beauty. As I pull up to her house to park my car, I am slowed by asphalt bumps on the wide street. On the right I see a warning to drivers, "Undulations Ahead," and I am intrigued by the strangely feminine version of the "Speed Bump" signs with which I'm familiar. I feel slightly lulled by the luscious scents and the suggestion of an undulating ride as I walk towards Sobonfu's cottage where we have planned our first meeting.

Sobonfu answers the door in traditional African dress—a purple-and-white floral wrap and head scarf. She is a beautiful woman, and draped in purple she echoes all the exotic softness I felt outside. But as I shake her hand I am struck by an entirely different force. She greets me with such strength and directness that I immediately become alert.

Her handshake reflects the direct immediacy of our initial contact. A month or so earlier I saw Sobonfu's picture in a catalogue just in a moment when I was asking myself where I could find the next person to interview for this book. When I saw her picture and the description of the course she was teaching—"Reclaiming the Indigenous Feminine, Women's Initiations and Rituals"—I knew I had found the right person. After talking to me for less than five minutes on the phone, she let me know she would work with me. I was surprised that she didn't need to meet me or hear much about this book in order to make that decision. As I shake her hand, standing at the threshold of her cottage, I am aware of a similar feeling, a power and directness that are at once natural and simple and yet shockingly unusual.

Her small cottage is filled with the tools of any business-woman—a computer, file cabinets, books, and papers—and also with African art and photographs of Africa and people I assume are from her village. I sit on a comfortable couch in front of a fireplace in a warm and bright room. Light pours in from the giant window that looks out to the backyard, and Sobonfu brings two glasses and a pitcher of water to drink.

I visit Sobonfu twice in her home, and I also attend a weekend workshop with her, one in a series of workshops for women called "The Circle of Women." During our meetings and also at the retreat, I experience Sobonfu as a combination of complexities. She seems always to be very still and also very active, both visible and hidden. She appears ordinary, simple, and direct. Yet as we work together I become aware that her stillness and simplicity are balanced by many extraordinary qualities and skills, including extreme courage and perseverance, deep passion and commitment, and the ability to exist in many worlds beyond this one.

In the "Circle of Women" retreat, she lets her co-leader do almost all of the talking and give most of the directions for the events during the weekend, while she stays relaxed and quiet in the background. But she is not subdued—she is always attentive and focused. She plays the drums with a power that seems equally intense and constrained, and when she does speak she is clear and knowing.

Many things about Sobonfu reflect this diversity of qualities, the balance of opposites and hidden meanings beyond what is evident. For example, she is deeply connected to nature and its elements, knows the language and the meanings of the natural world. And yet this connection seems to allow her access to energies and elements from different worlds, different dimensions. It is as though her complete presence with the energies of the earth allows her to reach realms far beyond the earth.

Also, Sobonfu has lived in the West for only several years, but her facility with English and her awareness of Western customs are very impressive, suggesting an ease with and acceptance of her life here. Yet her outward ease in this culture and this world belies a deep and intense longing to be somewhere else, whether back in her village in Africa, or in her real home with her ancestors in the place before she was born.

THE KEEPER OF RITUALS

In her native language Sobonfu's name means "The Keeper of Rituals." Sobonfu grew up in the matrilineal Dagara tribe of West Africa where, from the time she was born, she was guided to fulfill her purpose as one who makes the rituals of her people available for healing and transformation.

As we sit on her couch in her cottage, the sunlight shining through the large window that looks out to a green hillside in the back, I ask Sobonfu about her work.

"My purpose is to make sure that the rituals of my tradition do not become obsolete or dead," she says. "I bring rituals and share them—to help people in transition, to give them tools to draw on for healing or for their work." On a practical level, this means she presents the wisdom of her people through books, tapes, lectures, and workshops. She has an extremely busy schedule writing books, traveling all over the United States and Europe, speaking and giving retreats, and returning to her village in Africa at least once a year.

When I ask her why she came to America, she says emphatically, laughing, "Not because I wanted to!" and explains that the elders of her village sent her to the West in order to keep their wisdom and traditions alive.

"A lot of people in indigenous communities have basically become wounded from opening up to the rest of the world. So now they are closing down, and they don't want to share their ways or their wisdom.

"There are many things about the indigenous world that are being destroyed by the modern world. Young people are leaving the villages, and if they come back they are not wanting to embrace their culture; often they are not eager to learn the rituals. So the elders are having to decide, 'What do we do? Do we let the rituals die or do we do something else?' So the elders sent me here to share our wisdom. The elders understand that there is a connection between communities. What affects one community affects another."

Sobonfu offers the rituals of her people to those who want to learn them, even if that means living thousands of miles away from her village. But presenting rituals to people through workshops, lectures, and books is only the outer aspect of her work. On a deeper level, she must first gain access to these rituals, many of which do not currently exist in an outer form. Either they have been forgotten, or they have yet to come into consciousness.

As she describes this more hidden aspect of her purpose, I become increasingly aware of her capacity to enter different dimensions, to work with many levels of reality. "I bring rituals back from the unseen to the seen," she says, "from the non-activity to the activity. By making them active, you make them alive. I allow my spirit to be swallowed by Great Mystery, so that my spirit melts with it and is able to bring back this knowledge."

I ask Sobonfu to explain what she means by "being swallowed by Great Mystery," and she describes a relentless and rigorous training that has dismantled her again and again, and continues to dismantle her so she has increasing access to other worlds and realities. Her reality has been continually broken down through training and initiation, allowing her spirit and her consciousness to melt into the consciousness of a greater whole where rituals and wisdom exist in their pure form. Thus she can access the knowledge that exists beyond our world, and bring it back here as it is needed.

"Training in the village starts from the time you are born," she tells me. "There's an emphasis on who you are, and the kind of gifts you are bringing into the world. The training happens every day; we are taught how to work with different things, different vibrations that you see and feel in nature. Then, how do you relate to those for healing, for communicating? We learn about the language of nature, the language of the earth, the language of animals, how they communicate with you, and how to communicate with other dimensions. There are different initiations, which break down your barriers and the things you are resisting. It can be very painful. All the armors you have put up have to be stripped away."

Sobonfu's connection to nature and to the earth is real, and I see this during the "Circle of Women" retreat. She was upset one morning, telling us that a bat had flown into her room in the night and hit her on the head. In her tradition, bats are from the underworld. If a bat hits at your head it means that someone close to you will die. In fact, when I met up with Sobonfu after the retreat I told her I had been thinking about the bat, worried that something had happened. And she confirmed that a young family member had died unexpectedly. I was sorry that the harbinger had become real, and I saw more clearly how she lives completely connected in the natural world, how she relates directly to the earth and the spirit world. I can only assume the training that guides a person to this degree of openness must be extremely demanding and complete.

"I tell people that you have to have a willingness to break down at all levels," she says. "What you are most afraid of, the elders will make you go through it. What you resist most, they will make you do. You have to have a willingness to be dismantled, again and again. So that you always go beyond who you think you are."

Her own training continues; Sobonfu still faces her own limitations and has to be pushed beyond them. "I am still in the middle of my own initiation. For everything I bring back to this world takes a toll on me. At the same time, I see a hunger for the rituals; I see how much they are needed. The pain in seeing what is lacking can be overwhelming. It can be very difficult to think about what to do. Sometimes I feel it would be easier to just run away. Sometimes I have to say some vows of commitment over and over.

"Two years ago I was resisting being here. I was tired, I wanted to be in the village, in my community, and I didn't understand why the elders sent me to America—I had begged them not to. And then back in Africa during one visit, the children got my attention when they said to me, 'We see you.'

"And I understood that the whole community witnesses. I know if I don't do this work, I will fail other people. So, there is a sense of duty requiring one to open one's heart and to give. It comes from love, and from duty."

As Sobonfu reveals herself to me during our meetings, I understand why I had the initial sense of her being both here and not here. It is the presence and absence of a skilled spiritual teacher, or guide. When I ask her about this rare combination, she laughs and says, "In my village this is not a rare quality! Many people are trained as I was.

"This ability to be present and absent must be my shape-shifting quality," she continues, and when I ask her to explain, she says, "A shape shifter is somebody who can use the energy in many different ways. Being present here, but quickly shifting to another place to tune in to what needs to be said or done."

In my time with Sobonfu I become increasingly respectful of these extraordinary aspects that in her village seem so ordinary. I experience in her very little of an individual person, a person focused on her own needs or demands, but rather a person of community with a striking combination of duty and love, and any qualities needed to fulfill her role. I see mostly a purity of being and purpose, and the elements which keep her true to her name, "The Keeper of Rituals."

THE RESURGENCE OF FEMININE SPIRIT

Sobonfu works with men and women both, but she also works exclusively with women in specific workshops. "I like working with women," she tells me, "because I grew up in a society where women worked a lot together."

Her appreciation of women is not surprising, as one aspect of her work at this time—whether with men or women—is to help people develop their feminine qualities and help the feminine spirit in the world heal and grow. She explains to me that right now feminine energy and feminine ways will help us move forward individually and collectively.

"We're not going to solve our own problems or the problems of the world the old way," she says. "The masculine ways, the ways of the warrior, of violence, don't work. This is a historic time for women, and for the feminine. Women who welcome and live their own power can help shift the consciousness of the world, to bring out a more positive side of the feminine, to bring a new way of being into the world. Feminine spirit more than ever wants us to acknowledge its presence, wants us to be truthful and honest about where its energy is, and to use it to heal."

I ask Sobonfu to describe feminine spirit and feminine power, and she tells me, "Feminine spirit works in different ways. Its foundation is that it sustains everything, it weaves things together, it maintains harmony, it comes with intuition. Feminine spirit allows a way to be oneself without having to assert oneself. It affirms life, recognizes and sees the value in individuals. It can be a strong barrier to negative influences, especially in a community.

"Feminine power is different from masculine power because you can not see it so clearly. Hence the need to re-define what power is. Not as something that is seen, outgoing, but as something that is hidden. The one that is hidden can achieve a lot more than the one that is out there.

"People get confused. If they don't see it, they don't know it is power. But women can appreciate another way. Feminine power doesn't come out in showmanship, it doesn't overpower, it allows one to be oneself, it allows things to be as they are without aggressiveness or assertiveness. Unconsciously we know we have feminine spirit; it lives inside us, and it is important to consciously honor and appreciate it.

"Sometimes it's difficult because it can be so hidden," she reiterates. "But anybody who looks at the history of the world has to say there is something about women's strength that we can't define. It has kept us going.

"In many indigenous communities the women are very quiet. They don't say much but basically they use their power to protect the community, for example when an outsider comes. They question, 'Who is this person? Is this someone who is going to create chaos? What approach do we need to either curb this person back on track, or start to take action so that they don't destroy life?' And this power comes with intuition, with the knowledge of what to do."

I tell Sobonfu that I experience in her a great stillness, but also a great power. It is a strange paradox. "A lot of times we expect power to be displayed in a masculine way, an outward way," she says. "In my tradition, the best way to weaken your power is to display it. So, yes, I tend to be quiet and centered. This is the feminine way. My power comes from being connected to the wholeness of life, to the great web of life and light that connects everything together."

Sobonfu explains that feminine spirit used to be more prevalent, used to be a stronger force in the world, but that at some time in history feminine power retreated.

"At one point there was a feeling of there not being enough for everybody. Women have a very strong sense of survival, in bearing children and protecting them; protecting what is dear to us. When we were confined to limited choices we disconnected from others and our need to protect ourselves came through. This period created a dent in feminine identity, disconnected us from each other and from the source of life."

When I ask Sobonfu at what point in history this withdrawal occurred, she hesitated to answer, explaining that in her village there is no sense of time. She smiles at my confusion, and says, "If I were to put it in time, I would say it has been a gradual happening, and it's in the last few centuries that we have become aware of being disconnected, isolated, and competitive—fending for ourselves, protecting ourselves, not thinking about the collective. When we fended only for ourselves, the sense of sisterhood was gone; there was just mistrust. This made it easier for the masculine to overtake, and threw us into competitive mode, competitive with each other."

Sobonfu explains to me that a sense of disconnection and isolation is damaging to feminine energy because isolation is counter to the nature of feminine spirit, which is about relationship and wholeness. It is the turning against its own nature that is the real source of vulnerability in feminine spirit. "The only thing that can disempower feminine spirit is feminine power turning back on itself," she says.

I ask her to say more about this, and she continues, "In my tradition, we say in order for a woman to be hurt by an outside force, she has to be betrayed by another woman. Similarly, in order for the collective feminine to be hurt by an outside force, it needs to be betrayed by the feminine. In order for masculine energy to harm the feminine, either individually or collectively, there needs to be this betrayal. And that's what happened. Women turned against each other in order to guard what they had for themselves. Then there was a wounding that allowed external energies to come and do more harm. Then we were all left isolated and disconnected, from each other, from ourselves, from spirit."

But now feminine spirit is returning, Sobonfu tells me. "Feminine spirit pulled itself in, and now it is coming back. I see feminine spirit in people who I wouldn't expect to be acknowledging it. More and more women are coming out, becoming more open with their power. Men in various parts of the world are confused; they no longer know their place. They see they are no longer running the world.

"Many prophesies in many indigenous traditions say that feminine spirit is resurging. It is a rising energy. It rises now because there is a consciousness between women that is allowing it to surge again. We have an opportunity now to embrace it again. The most critical thing is to make it collective—if it stays individual, it will be every woman for herself, and it will stay turned against itself."

Sobonfu impresses upon me the importance of recognizing that it is against our nature to be isolated; we must work together, and for the collective. "Feminine energy is an energy of connection. The truth is, if I am happy, my happiness overflows to you. If I am not happy, my unhappiness overflows to you. We are connected."

I ask Sobonfu why it is that feminine power and spirit are coming out of hiding now. She explains that its resurgence will help humankind take the next step in our evolution, which includes making a conscious connection to a greater wholeness, a great web of life, light, and wisdom that connects us all, and connects our world here on earth to other planets and other dimensions. This web of light is itself feminine energy and thus it is the feminine spirit within us and in our world that will link us to it. Connected to this web, we will be able to live in a consciousness of oneness from which new solutions to our own evolutionary challenges and the evolutionary challenges of the world will become available.

THE WEB OF LIFE AND LIGHT

"There is a web of connection, life, and light," Sobonfu explains, "a web of feminine energy that goes from the earth, to the moon, and to all the other dimensions." She tells me that the web is a form of consciousness, a consciousness of oneness, like a network linking all elements of life together. "The web of life and light is how we stay connected to the earth and other worlds. Different energies flow into this web, and we can connect to these energies by connecting to the web. The web of life and light contains wisdom, knowledge, and a healing energy for the whole world. Healing energy that binds us together, and helps flush out what is not necessary from our lives."

I ask Sobonfu if this web of light has always existed and always been accessible to human consciousness, and she tells me, "The web of light has always been present. And through time women have always used it for tuning into each other's energy, tuning into it for healing, for doing their work, and strengthening feminine spirit and identity." Women have a special access to this web because the web itself is a form of feminine energy. Anything that works non-hierarchically, like a web, or a network, can be considered 'feminine.'

I ask Sobonfu if human beings are the only species that can be conscious of this energy, and she says, emphatically, "No! All beings are connected to the web of light. All beings are conscious of it. Animals are very conscious of it, and they don't struggle with it like we do. Their connection allows them to be more sensitive to their environment, more connected to and aware of their environment. So they can relate to and interact with the environment in ways we cannot. Keeping their connection to the web of light is very important to them, because it is the source of their information about the environment. So they are more dependent upon it. Of course it should be as important for everybody.

"The energy of the web flows from the earth through the trees to the moon and to other planets, to other worlds. The trees are like antennas, that direct the energy from the earth to the moon, which is the source of feminine wisdom and energy.

"Plants are always conscious of the web of light," she continues. "Trees do inter-dimensional traveling through the web, and communicate with trees on other planets without moving."

I am a bit speechless now, not sure what surprises me most, the idea that trees can communicate with other trees, or that the other trees are on other planets. I ask Sobonfu how she knows this, and we both laugh at my skepticism.

"When I was a girl, my grandmother used to take us to watch trees to see what they would do. She taught us how to look at things differently, to see things that you might not see if you were looking in an ordinary way. She showed us how trees in communication may seem very very still, but when you are underneath them there is actually a lot of motion going on."

Sobonfu has mentioned her grandmother to me before with such love and respect that I ask her to tell me more about her.

"My grandmother was a visionary in the village," she says, taking a sip of water. "She envisioned the future and helped people adapt to it. Grandmother's role was to take people where they were afraid to go, towards what the future holds, to where they could embrace the future. When she used to say, 'Last night I dreamt...,' everyone around would stop what they were doing to listen, because everyone knew that what she was dreaming was going to be reality."

The way Sobonfu speaks about her grandmother is enough to reassure me that there is truth in what she is saying about the trees, despite its being so far beyond my experience. We continue to speak of human beings connecting to the web of light.

I ask her what it feels like to be connected to the web, and she says, "I don't know if I can describe it in human language. But it feels like being so bound to something. No matter what, it gives you reassurance. Whenever you are in doubt that energy surges in you saying, 'Wake up!' And it won't let you go back to sleep. It gives me this feeling of being deeply connected.

"When you go through initiation you become aware of what you're dealing with because you are helped by this huge web of light, of connection, of wisdom. And when you come back and start to access it, there is no doubt what it is. That is why when I work here and I express something that someone else doesn't believe, and they tell me, 'You have no way of knowing,' well, there is a limit as to how much energy you want to invest trying to open the eyes of someone who has a sight and yet who refuses to see. Sometimes I won't argue because there is no point in arguing. When the person is ready, that is when things that confused them make sense."

Sobonfu explains that the first step to connecting to the web of light is to acknowledge its presence, and to offer oneself to its school. "We acknowledge that we are all connected; we acknowledge that we are part of this great web of life that gives us what we need. Then we offer ourselves to it with gratitude. Offering ourselves is the only way of keeping the energy going, for it makes us an outlet for this powerful energy. We have to be grateful, and to give something of ourselves. Like the Native Americans offer the corn, or like the women of our village offer their menstrual blood. Gratitude is the way to acknowledge that it exists, that we are connected to it. Gratitude allows the web to provide healing energy for the world."

She tells me that if one connects to this web one is immediately connected to the wisdom and knowledge that come from all dimensions. "Once you connect, then the knowing can come. It is like intuition, but more than intuition—it flows both ways. It is like looking for the path and suddenly the path takes you. The path takes you; you don't take the path. The web needs you, takes you into it, as much as you look for it, as much as you need it."

Once connected to this web of light, a person can no longer remain separate from the greater network that links all life together. The web has its own life, its own patterns and its own needs, which are the needs of the whole. Becoming conscious of this wholeness includes a new way of understanding oneself and one's relationship to life. It includes a surrender to something beyond oneself, a surrender in service.

SERVICE AND THE WEB OF LIGHT

"It can be scary to acknowledge a connection to this energy," Sobonfu says seriously. "When you are searching for it, it seems like you own it. But once you find it, it owns you! And then you have to serve it."

I ask Sobonfu how one can serve one's connection to this web of light. She tells me, "My grandmother used to say this to me: 'Open your heart and spirit to a life of service. And when you feel it, when you know that there's a presence in it, do something even if it's wrong.' Because once you act, you are going to start to feel connected to something and the life force will help guide your actions. The deeper you connect, the more knowing comes. This is how genius is born. And this knowing goes in both directions. You know it, and it knows you. It's like knowing the path is there and you are trying to intuit it, but all of a sudden there's a shift of energy that actually immediately takes you there. The web itself takes you to it.

"When you begin to connect to it, you are going to have to be willing to expand your way of looking at the world, and to expand your dreams. You have to be able to start to pay attention to what comes in your life, in your dreams.

"You will find the right way of doing it," she continues, "for all the pieces of the puzzle will start to reveal themselves. But you have to start somewhere, and you have to keep going until you get it right. Until then it's going to drive you and the world around you crazy, and you're going to grow so restless that you're going to burn down, basically. So it's important to do something with it. And at some point you'll get there.

"I was working with a woman once who was in the middle of a very important project, trying to figure something out—how the different pieces connect. One day she was hiking with some friends, thinking and wondering and trying to understand what she needed to understand about her life of service. Suddenly she stopped, and her friend said, 'What's going on?' She answered, 'I just know what it is!' She finally understood what she needed to know. But she had to start her project all over again. All the work she had done up till then wasn't what needed to be done. However, it helped her connect to what she had to do. So she had to start from the beginning. That's the attitude you need—you have to be willing to be absolutely wrong. You have to go forward with the best intentions despite not knowing what you are doing, and pray for the right thing to reveal itself. Sometimes you will have been right from the start, but sometimes you will have been all wrong!"

I tell Sobonfu that as I talk to her I sometimes feel extremely irritated because I'm not sure what it is that I need to learn from her. She suggests that my uncomfortable feelings are part of the process. "The spirituality of Africa is not a one-way street. It is a road with many forks, each of which comes with its riches. When you stand at a fork, you have to be willing to get your hands dirty as you choose a direction and surrender to the process.

"Sometimes it's not clear as we are talking," she continues. "And that's probably partly because of the way I work. I try not to spoon-feed people. So, there is that mystery. You say, 'OK, I'm getting close to something, but what is it? OK, I think I found it!' And then you say, 'But wait a minute, where did it go?'"

During all our time working on this chapter, this feeling does not abate. I feel as though I get close to something, and then it is gone. I remember the sign in front of her house, 'Undulations Ahead,' and associate this feeling with riding on gentle waves. Sometimes there is a feeling of fullness, or imminent completion, and then there is the feeling of something slipping away, and having to start with nothing.

"That's how the elders worked with me," Sobonfu continues. "They give you a little bit, but not so much that you stop thinking for yourselves. When the elders give us all the solutions, we don't do any work. But when they give us just enough, then we start to think, 'Ah ha, I wonder…' These are the moments when you surrender to the process and liberate your genius.

"Sometimes when I work with people, I try to do the same. It doesn't always make people happy. But there are certain things that can only be opened from within. Too much guidance drowns it, and too little stops it from waking up. You give just the right amount to fire it up.

"My grandmother was a powerful dreamer. And she would have us go through exercises that challenged us. And when we complained, she would say, 'Well, it is not easy, but if it were easy then you wouldn't know what to do if I weren't here.'"

Serving one's connection to the web of light includes more than persevering through mistake after mistake. It starts with letting go of our perceptions and expectations. It includes the development of feminine qualities within oneself because it is through feminine energy—in men and women—that the connection is strengthened. As our feminine wisdom grows, so does our capacity to relate to and serve the greater whole.

I ask Sobonfu what women can do to develop their feminine spirit, and she tells me it is by doing what comes naturally to us as women. "Honoring the feminine when we see it," she says. "Learning to be in harmony with our environment; stopping competitive behavior; supporting and welcoming life-giving energies; remaining in one's center and feelings and other things we call in the village 'women's ways of living.'"

THE HEARTBEAT OF THE COMMUNITY

"There are a lot of things you name here that we do not have names for in Africa," Sobonfu tells me. "If you went home and you said, 'women's spirituality,' everybody would frown, and look at you and say, 'What are you talking about?' but if you said, 'Women's ways of living' they'll all get excited!

"Women's ways of living are about the heart of community and also the earth," she continues. "Women are the heartbeat of the community. In many places in Africa, if you want something to happen, you really have to get the women involved. If the women are not involved, nothing is going to work. Watching women in my community, you see how they make things happen. They have that sense of knowing, that connection to something bigger."

Sobonfu explains that all the rain-makers in Africa are women because of their connection to the spirit world. This is extremely dangerous work. "You have to know what you are doing," she says. "Otherwise you are going to get struck by lightning. In many communities women get ready to perform the rain ritual. They are running around naked and once the rain starts it's going to be beating you and throwing you into many directions. You have to be courageous enough to let the rain come to a certain point before you move on to another part of the ritual.

"There are a lot of things that we do, a lot of rituals that we do with the earth, related to the earth."

Sobonfu tells me that in her village, women can make things happen. Nothing happens without the involvement of women. "Once, a Western company came to the community to start a project," she says. "They got all the men involved, and they ignored the women. Several years passed of pumping money into the project with no results. So they went back to the men and asked them why nothing was working. One of the elders said, 'What do you expect when you cut our tongue out from our mouth? What do you expect when you cut our heart out from our chest?'

"And the people from the Western company didn't understand, and the elders said, 'Look, you cannot isolate a part of the community and still get things done. You have disconnected us from our tongue and our heart, and you still expect us to do this. Women must be a part of what happens.'

"So the company involved the women, and the projects began to succeed. And they even had some projects that were run exclusively by women, and those were especially successful."

Here in the West, many women have lost their connection to the spirit world, their own feminine power, and also to the greater whole. Women live isolated or separate from themselves and also from their appropriate place in the community. To reconnect, Sobonfu tells me, women can focus on their own nature, their natural ways of living. When I ask her to explain more, she reveals the important and often hidden aspects of menstruation and the womb, emotions, connecting to the earth, relating to children, and being in silence.

Menstruation and the Womb

In our talks together, Sobonfu emphasizes the importance of women's menstruation again and again. Women's menstrual cycles are a direct and natural connection to the spirit world, to feminine energy, and to the web of light and wisdom.

"Women are vessels to many energies coming through us," she says. "During our menses the veil between the worlds is non-existent. Menstruation is a time when women connect most to the world, and to other dimensions. This is why menses is very powerful. It is a way to create and become conscious of a deeper connection. It is a time of power for women. In the village, people are respectful of the menstruating woman. When you menstruate, what you say, what you think, is very important because there is a lot of power in it."

Sobonfu tells me that it can be helpful to have a positive attitude of service when one is menstruating. "For women, we connect through menses. We are able to give more to our community during our menses. And when we give, we feel connected."

In Sobonfu's village, the women offer their blood to the moon. "According to the myths, the moon is the place of origination for women. It is the source of feminine spirit and wisdom. We need to acknowledge this connection, because our cycle follows the moon. That is also one of the reasons why when they are in their menses women of the village will take their menstrual blood and offer it to the moon in the night. Doing that brings them many gifts."

I ask her what gifts are given, and she answers, "When women offer their blood, they can make a wish, or bring a particular need in focus. Then the wish is more easily granted, and the need more easily fulfilled. So much can be given, if a woman offers herself or her blood with focus at this time."

I ask if a woman can make a gesture of offering without collecting her real blood. I'm thinking about women in the West who might not feel comfortable with the actual ritual of offering their blood. Sobonfu makes it clear that it is the attitude that is most important—the attitude and focus.

"When a woman menstruates, she is very open and very powerful," she tells me. "Many things—wisdom, knowledge, power, gifts of life—are available to her if she focuses with gratitude."

She also says that when a woman menstruates she is open to what she has learned at other times. "Menstruation is in tune with sacred energy. When she menstruates, a woman can strengthen the knowledge she has gained in her life."

Menstruation is not just a physical process. "It is really a deep energetic process," Sobonfu says. "The natural cycle flows through women. If we pay attention, we see that even after we stop bleeding, our bodies shift as if we are in a flow of energy. Menstruation still happens in elders. It's just that the energy is not being given outward; the energy becomes a blessing pool for others. Others can come to the elders and they can give to them from this blessing pool of energy.

"You see, elders have years of experience within. It builds up in our system. And then, when someone comes to seek the wisdom of experience, this wisdom can be given. In the village we call this wisdom the *water of life*. This water of life is held in a blessing bowl, and can be given to those who acknowledge it and need it. And during this time of menstruation the energy still flows into women and strengthens and rejuvenates the water of life so it can serve the community. But it only becomes valid when it is acknowledged, when someone seeks it out. Then it can be given. This whole process reflects how we are all connected.

"The womb is the center of creation," she says, "the center of our own energy." She explains that the neck and the womb are, for women, receptive centers, that they have a magnetism that draws energy inward.

"The womb is a place of strength, but it can also be where we are weak. The energy we encounter in the world is held there. If we hold positive energy there, it gives us power to create good things. But if we hold negative energy there it can poison the things that we do.

"The connection to the womb is very important. In the West we are very disconnected, and we must reconnect. In Africa, we wake up every morning and we hold the womb and ask, 'What is it I took in that needs cleansing?' 'What did I receive that is good or not?' We touch our womb, and massage it. Sometimes we eat garlic to cleanse it, or massage it with garlic.

"We receive so much through our womb," she continues. "We must keep it clean so our connection is clean. If the womb is filled with a mess, then we will have confusion and bring confusion into life. If the womb is clean, we will have clarity. We connect through the womb to all life and to the web of light, so we have a deeper, more conscious connection if we keep it clean."

Emotions

"One of the beauties is the way women use their emotions," Sobonfu tells me. "The positive use of emotion is very important. In fact, it is one of the ways women speak to spirit. True emotions are feelings from deep within that come out for healing.

"When women in the village are saying prayers, you will see them get very much into their emotions. The emotions become the way of conveying an important message to spirit. Emotions are one of the ways women connect to their inner knowing, their power, and to the web of light. Emotions keep things in balance, because they are a way of clearing out what isn't working in our life, and allowing spirit to come in. A way for us to bring in positive energy to keep life flowing.

"This is why all across the world women tend to speak emotionally. Yes, we can be very heady and talk about things in a heady way. But we have to come from the heart also. So if you see women doing prayers in the village, sometimes you see them crying as they say those prayers, because it is for them a way of conveying a particular kind of message.

"It is so important to say it from the heart. Because when you pray from the heart an answer will come to you, which is impossible if you do not connect with your heart.

And so as women in the village pray with the power of their emotions, the prayers start to open not only their own heart, but also the hearts of the people who are around.

"Emotions are necessary; otherwise they wouldn't be there," Sobonfu continues. "I find that being able to be in touch with my feelings is very important for me. If there is something I want to do, and I am not letting myself feel, then it can be very difficult to achieve it. But when I let the heart come in, then my feelings help me connect to what is real in the situation, and I can do what I need to do. In this way, emotions are like a bridge to intuition. If you can't feel, then you can't tap into your intuition. If you're shutting down your emotions you won't be able to connect to your intuitive wisdom. This has to do with the illogical nature of emotions. They don't get stuck in or limited by your rational mind. They are a direct connection to something else, something that one just knows, and then one can act upon it.

"Somebody was telling me recently, 'Sobonfu, when you're happy, you're happy, and when you're sad, you're sad.' And I think, yeah, that's because I know what I am feeling. Being happy or sad gives me information about myself and the world, and I need to stay connected in this way. If I'm sad, I know something is going on, maybe even in my village. Recently I had a feeling that something was happening back with my family. I get pulled back there. My feelings connect me to them."

Sobonfu tells me that one can connect with one's feelings by bringing one's attention to the energy that flows through the body. She explains that energy flows through one's body and out into other dimensions. This energy links us to the web of light and all the information in the web. We become conscious of that energy as it moves through our body and reveals itself through our feelings.

"You can start by putting your focus on your belly, and then bringing energy up from your belly to your heart," she explains, using her hand to indicate this movement up the body. "Concentrate at your belly, then rise with it through your heart, and then the energy goes up out of your head, to the moon and other dimensions. Then you bring it back down into the earth. You can do this all the time, especially when you are feeling disconnected.

"It takes attention and practice, but eventually you can allow this energy to be continually flowing. It's something I do all the time, especially if I feel disconnected. It can help you be focused and grounded. You can use it when you are overwhelmed or confused, especially. It's very helpful when you go to a new place and you don't know what's going on. For example, it can be helpful if you want to know if you are safe. If your stomach or your heart starts to contract you know you have to be careful. I call this 'navigating.'"

I am somewhat surprised at Sobonfu's emphasis on emotions, as she herself seems extremely stable and detached. I am aware of her being exactly who she is—there are times when I know she is sad, and she does not hide it. But she does not seem particularly emotional. When I mention this observation, she tells me that I am probably confusing emotions with 'drama.' Real—or positive— emotion is a simple way of connecting to what is happening in one's world. Drama, or a negative use of emotion, is being overly involved in what one feels, and this can cut one off from what is happening. Or you end up acting out one aspect or one piece of what you are experiencing.

"This negative use of emotion can get in the way of listening or being open," Sobonfu explains.

I ask her to speak more about the difference between positive and negative uses of emotion, and she says, "Well, it is like the difference between real grief and whining.

Grief is feeling something that needs to be healed; grief connects a person to what can help them heal. But whining is not seeking healing. Whining just wants to go around and around for more attention.

"Negative emotions, like whining, are emotions that are stuck. And they annoy all those around you. They are not healing emotions."

I ask her how to transform the negative emotion to something real that can be healed. "Most important is to be aware of what you are feeling," she answers. "Where are you touched? And where can you release it? If you are experiencing a negative emotion, you need to recognize it, and then it can be moved to the next phase of real grief, for example. Then the healing can come, because emotion draws the healing in. This is why in the village some prayers are only done by women. Women's ability to feel real emotions means we can draw in the spirit, draw in the healing."

Connecting to the Earth

"The earth is a living entity," Sobonfu tells me. "An energy that grounds us, keeps us connected to our own spirit, deep in our soul. The energy of the earth can give us a sense of being home—it helps us know where we are. If we disconnect from the earth we feel out of touch, ungrounded, in la-la land, as they say. Being connected to the earth gives us a sense of *being*, and through our *being* we connect to our intuition, and to the web of light.

"The earth is where we, as spirit, have come to contribute something, to share our different experiences as spirits, here. It is like a great flea market—many different spirits coming here to contribute to a greater energy. We all offer our own gifts to the whole."

Sobonfu tells me that one simple way of relating to the earth is directly through the body, and specifically through bare feet. I share my skepticism with her, and tell her that walking barefoot sounds a bit "new-agey" to me. Sobonfu says very seriously, "It doesn't have anything to do with new-age, because it's ancient-age. We might have this as a new-age thing, because we have basically taught ourselves to go away from this ancient wisdom, and so now we have to learn it again.

"I did not grow up here," she continues, "so you cannot say that I suddenly came up with this idea to walk barefoot. I know that when I am not walking barefoot I start to feel disconnected. I know for me that when I have my feet on the ground, then I feel rooted, grounded.

"Actually, in my village we tried different things, including giving shoes to women. And they went crazy. Some women would not put shoes on. And if they do, then they are sure they have some time with earth under their feet.

"It is very important to be directly touching the earth. But I know some people live in cities, and there isn't direct access to the earth. So it is important to have some potted plants in the house. Relating to the earth is very powerful. It allows you to shed what is not good for your spirit, what basically holds you back, and changes it into something good. It's very important; it doesn't have anything to do with new-age at all.

"There are many other dimensions beyond this one," she explains. "But the connection we need to keep, in order to connect to the other dimensions, is to the earth."

I understand from Sobonfu that the earth is like a gateway to the conscious energy of the web of light that flows through all dimensions. The living organism that is the earth is a part of the greater web. By being here, by directly relating to the earth, we access worlds and potentials beyond it.

Children

At the "Circle of Women" retreat I attended, three young girls were present. I was surprised when I first saw them, unsure of how their presence would affect the group. But I soon saw that their inclusion was extremely natural. They were allowed to be children—nobody insisted that they remain still, or quiet or controlled. They came and went from meetings as they wanted. Sometimes they participated, sometimes they just watched, and other times they even played together while the adults continued with what they were doing. And they were surprisingly at ease with the intense circumstances and emotionality of the retreat. I had never seen children fit in so naturally to an adult event.

During the retreat Sobonfu tells me, "Children make everything all right. Even if someone is doing something wrong, if a child is present it is all right." Later, during one of our talks, I ask her to explain what she means by this, and she says, "There is an energy that children come with. It is life; it is energy that opens us to life. In the village, there are certain rituals that can only be done with children. This energy allows a direct connection to the web of light."

Sobonfu explains that sometimes women who give birth can feel this energy and then become dependent upon their children for their connection to the web of light. When a woman associates her own connection with what the child offers, it can be very difficult to allow her children to grow up and leave home. "She might be left with nothing if her children leave. Sometimes the access through the child lasts till the child is seven or eight, or sometimes it can even last until adolescence.

"In the village, sometimes the mother and child will exchange a gift or ritual object, so the mother can keep the gift on her altar. Then she can let her children go; that allows her to develop a way to be connected." Sobonfu tells me that it is important to understand that all children—not just one's own—are a link. "I think this is one of the reasons why in the village we all get together with other people's children. So there are other people's children to help you stay connected."

Of course a woman is always connected to the web of life and light, Sobonfu reassures me. But whether she acknowledges it as such is another question. "Where the challenge comes in is for the mother to expand her connection beyond her child, so she can let go and connect on her own."

When I ask her about women who don't have children, Sobonfu tells me that often women without children can develop stronger connections to the web because they expand their connections beyond the limitations of dependence upon a child. When I ask Sobonfu if she herself has children, she answers that all the children in her community are her children. In her village there is no sense that one is only a mother to those she gives birth to. At the retreat I see her reflect this tradition, as she relates with great care, affection, and authority to the children present, as if they were her own.

Silence

At one point when Sobonfu and I sit in her cottage talking, I find myself unable to think, or to even ask her questions. I remember feeling this way while speaking with other people for this book. Sobonfu notices that I'm not responding to what she is saying, so I tell her I feel drawn very far away. She assures me that sometimes it can be like that. Sometimes there is nothing that you can say. It can be as though the silence has a life of its own and takes over.

"There can be something very powerful about silence that you cannot get when you are talking," she tells me. Even in the village you see two people just sitting there; no one is saying anything. And no one is uncomfortable.

"We have been conditioned to have to say something. But it's natural to just sit without saying anything. It's one of the things I've noticed people have the most discomfort around. Silence can be very healing for me.

"It is universal that women love to talk," she says laughing. "But, also women value silence. Silence allows the intuitive side to come forward. Silence is a way to tune in to what is out there, a way to observe, sense, and open up. Silence is a feminine quality because it allows integration; it allows men and women alike to be centered in their own power. Silence is not about doing, but *being*. It brings things together in wholeness. In silence, one integrates, and this integration happens naturally, but it is best to be conscious of it, so we can focus on what we are embracing.

"This is like meditation in Buddhism, for example. In Africa it can be those pauses in conversation between people. Just those moments when people are mingling and then they just stop talking. And there is no need for words."

HEALING WOMEN AND THE FEMININE

Sobonfu and I have spoken a lot about the need for feminine spirit to be acknowledged and nurtured, for it to gain a more central place in our collective consciousness. This process includes a healing of feminine spirit, and a healing of women. Many women individually have suffered abuse, and this abuse has damaged women's connections to the web of life and light. When women became disconnected, that in turn damaged our collective connection to the web, leaving people isolated from each other, and from the whole. In the West, especially, this disconnection is prevalent, and the need for healing extreme. If the healing doesn't take place, the connection to the web of light and wisdom will not serve its highest purpose. The energy or information from the web will get caught in patterns of abuse within women, and will reinforce patterns of abuse and ignorance in the collective.

"The abuse basically shatters your connection to spirit, and shatters the connection of the collective," Sobonfu explains. "Whatever information you get, it's in small different pieces and you can't put it together.

"Women who have been abused can tune in to the web," Sobonfu explains, "and will receive the correct messages. But the shock stage still overrides what you receive and so they tend to think that it's whatever they are still processing from the trauma. The trauma creates the blockage, so the energy from the web gets stuck there. The energy comes in, but you can't recognize it as something separate from the abuse. So healing and transformation never happen."

The abuse of women is something that must be healed in order for wider transformation to take place. Some of the work Sobonfu does in the "Circle of Women" retreats is to create an environment that encourages women to find their own skills and power, and learn to trust themselves, and then to have that feminine spirit reflected back to them by the other women in the group. In this way, the collective feminine spirit is strengthened. "In the 'Circle of Women' I help women discover their own strength," she says. "We come up with activities that slowly lead them to a place where they can start to recognize, 'Hey, I can do that.' They can acknowledge what they know and take it out into the world. Unconsciously women know they have power, but consciously they are scared to acknowledge it. So we need a witness, and the witnesses in the retreats are other women.

"We want the acknowledgment from men. And yes, they give it to us, but we still want more. Which simply implies that we have to get it from somewhere else—from other women. Because the women have drunk from the same source that we have. Only they know what it is like, so they can say, 'Yes, this is really good!'

"If someone who has never tasted something says, 'This is good'—well, how do they know? On what basis do they say this? On someone else's experience? How do they know? The people who know are the other women. There is a tone, a chorus between women, a shared experience. Women can hold the mirror up so other women can see."

Sobonfu explains that women themselves are woven together in a web of feminine spirit and energy, and healing can take place within this web that can help all women. "When one woman becomes healed, it reverberates onto others. The web between women is something that we tap into," she tells me. "When you see me you see my pain, when I see you I see your pain. Even when we don't talk about it, we know there is something there. That's why we feel the pain when things are happening around the world. Like in the village. They don't watch TV or anything like that, but they'll sense and feel what is going on in the world."

I ask Sobonfu if women's connection means that the healing of some women can affect the healing of other women, and she explains that this is correct, and that there is a real opportunity now for a widespread healing to happen. "Since we are all connected, one woman's healing affects another woman. If enough women can be healed, it is like an electric connection that will spread throughout the web. It is as though the right plug is put into place. All of a sudden there will be a jolt, and 'Wow!' Things really start to shift.

"What is feminine has a tendency to flow, naturally," she continues. "As women heal, feminine spirit heals, this healing affects us all. These connections can change the world very quickly."

SURRENDERING TO INITIATION

"We are all going through a time of initiation," Sobonfu tells me, as we sit on the couch in her living room, the breeze coming through the open window in the back.

"We are shifting our consciousness regarding how we look and act towards each other and towards the world. This shift has something to do with moving out of isolation and back into community. Breaking down the ways we are disconnected from each other and ourselves, and embracing ways to open up, and reconnect."

The events at the World Trade Center took place during our time working together, and I asked Sobonfu about it. "The World Trade Center attack brought changes in consciousness," she says. "Anger changed to care and connection. We started to talk to one another again. People opened up to one another for a while.

"The attack is also a symbol for what could be in the future if we do not change. We need to accept that the ways of violence are over; otherwise there will be more fighting. We are not born with violence, with hatred. We are born with a connection to the web of light. We are born knowing our role is to support life, to sustain life. This is feminine power and spirit."

Sobonfu tells me that many women are hesitating to claim their role and responsibility in this time of change. "There is a lot of reluctance in women to do what needs to be done. I was at a recent conference and we asked, 'What keeps us from coming together, what keeps us separate?' And the most common answer was the fear that if we speak the truth, no one will hear. This is our biggest resistance."

Sobonfu explains that we have to overcome this fear, come together, and claim our own power which will connect us to the web of light. "It is important to surrender to initiation, to be willing to let initiation take you," she says. "Initiation is the chance for your boundaries to be broken down, your perception of yourself and the world to be dismantled. And then initiation helps reconstruct your world. But it only works if you surrender to it.

"I had an initiation when I was five," she says with a smile. "The elders brought me to a gateway between the worlds, and they asked me to jump. And I jumped, and I landed in water. And when I was sixteen, there was another initiation. The elders brought me to a gateway that I thought was the same, and asked me to jump again. The elders told me, 'When you jump, look. And be careful!'

"But since I thought it was the same place as before, I was sure there would be water where I landed, so I had an attitude when I jumped. But it wasn't the same dimension, it wasn't water!"

I asked her what was there, and she said, "Rocks!" laughing at her error. I asked her if she had looked at all. She said, "No, I hadn't looked. If I had looked I would have seen where to jump. But I wasn't paying attention, I thought I knew what was coming.

"In initiation you have to be willing to be open and let the initiation take you. And be willing to listen to the voice of intuition. I wasn't paying attention. My ego was saying, 'I've done this before!' And, 'My god, I'm going to do this and they're going to see I can do this because I know what I am doing.' But this wasn't the right attitude, and I hurt my legs in the rocks."

She tells me that the initiation we are all now taking part in depends on the participation of women, the claiming of women's power and their appropriate place in the collective. With the empowerment of feminine spirit, women themselves can heal and transform very quickly, and through this transformation can help all humanity connect to the web of light—giving us a new consciousness and a new relationship to life.

"This is a time of initiation for everyone, but especially for women and feminine ways," she says. "Part of the initiation includes healing from abuse, and going back to a place before the abuse. It will be very helpful if we can acknowledge this process. Women are very intuitive; they see what is coming. But we have to work with what we see, and take responsibility for the part we are playing. It is as though we are still in the shock stage—we are in the middle of change and it takes us by surprise and confuses us. But if we can see it for what it is, we can move through it more easily. This acknowledgment is like a seal, as though we stamp this experience with our acknowledgment, grounding it.

"When we don't acknowledge that we are coming through a time of initiation we get caught in a bottomless pit. We stay in a vortex in which we create the same initiatory circumstances again and again. And we will stay there, not because we want to, or need to, but because we don't know the exit. Conscious acknowledgment helps us exit."

When I listen to Sobonfu's words I remember an image I had when I started writing this book—an image of women's longing to be connected to the source. It was as though there was a vessel of great longing, a disembodied vessel, caught between worlds. It seemed to be the collective longing of women's souls, the longing of women who have been cut off from their own natural way home due to centuries of disconnection and abuse. Lost, like a ghost-ship, it circles around and around in abandoned waters. The longing continually cries out, but something keeps it from drawing the energy or circumstances needed to complete its cycle.

As Sobonfu speaks of incomplete initiation, I remember this image and think, perhaps women are caught in an initiation that could either end soon or repeat itself again and again. If women themselves take the next step to live who they really are, then they can contribute to the changes taking place around us. In Sobonfu I see a woman who puts aside her own fears, her own needs, in unrelenting service. And I know if she can help more women do the same, then this vortex that holds the world in a state of isolation and incompleteness will not be able to hold us anymore, and great changes might finally be realized.

THE UNKNOWN SHE

a meeting with

Lynn Barron

THE UNKNOWN SHE

The ascent is work, effort. You take one step at a
time, pass through one stage after another, move closer
and closer to the light. But suddenly the light becomes so
bright it is black. And the descent begins. The descent is a
pull. You have surrendered and it's not up to you. You
are pulled by love. You are gone. You are lost in the
luminous black, the sweet silence, the dynamic,
living emptiness of the Unknown She.

Lynn Barron

THE HOUSE IN THE DESERT

At the meeting point between the endless dry out-pouring of the Mojave Desert and the gentle green uprising of the San Gabriel Mountains, amidst Joshua trees standing silent and still against the horizon, protected by three vigilant and untamable dogs, sits the small yellow house where Lynn Barron lives.

During the four years that she has lived here, the house has attracted more life than one would expect in this seemingly empty landscape. Hornets come from an unknown source and swirl around the bathroom, even though Lynn persistently puts them outside after they collapse on the windowsill, disoriented, she suggests, by the intoxicating energy in the house. Mice scurry around the kitchen until they, too, become suddenly stilled by whatever it is that brings the wasps to rest. Then Lynn wraps the swaying little creatures in a napkin and places them outside where the air is a bit less inebriating. In the evening, strange noises float through the darkness as parts of the building seem to moan and sway under a great pressure. And an intermittent stream of people come and go from nearby Los Angeles and as far away as the East Coast to sit in meditation with Lynn, sleeping outside the little house on handmade wooden structures, skeletal and exotic, set up amidst the sand and sage of the property.

In the night, unruly dogs from miles away can howl for hours, and cries from unknown animals—coyotes or other hunting creatures—incite the dogs. Strange rumbling sounds travel the roof of the house, giving someone trying to sleep the impression of lying under a bowling alley. First thing in the morning enough songbirds for a grove of trees swirl around the single elm outside the front door, introducing the sun into the darkness of the house with a demanding and urgent wakefulness.

Lynn tells me that while all the activity at the house can sometimes be conspicuous, there are also times when it is hidden within great stillness. I visit her twice, and the first time I meet with her I feel this stillness. The whole time I am with her, I find my mind being drawn somewhere dark and sweet, lulled and blanketed by a heavy and soothing feeling. I am deeply relaxed, and can barely think. Even as I drove the five hundred miles to her house, I had to pull into a gas station to rest and meditate because I was so overcome by a soft opiate-like state of peace.

But the next time I stay with her for almost a week, I am awake most nights, constantly alert to noises and movement. The days are intensely focused and full of activity. The second day I am there, a strange and massive dog shows up in Lynn's yard, allowed in, it seems, by her three dogs who usually drive off intruders. Lynn and I spend much time managing this new addition to the pack, even taking one dog to a veterinarian after a long and vicious fight. Sleepless nights, meditation sessions throughout the day that involve continuous attention and focus, the emotional weight of caring for wounded dogs, and the demands of this book all add up to an energetic and exhausting trip for me— a stark contrast to my first stay at the house.

During both visits, Lynn's demeanor and attentiveness remain constant. Despite the activity around her, Lynn is still and detached, emanating a feeling of peace as well as spontaneity and freedom. She is an empty human being, made so by a lifelong devotion to the Truth and a two-year mystical experience that annihilated her ego, leaving her with little or no individual identity or sense of personal need. Since then, she has undergone five years of continual dismantling and integration. Endless space exists within and around her. Yet, as I saw during my second visit, it is not the empty stillness of a cloistered monastic life, where one has no responsibilities, nothing to pull one back from absorption somewhere else. Rather, it is an emptiness that demands heightened attention, and drives one towards constant participation in the fullness and chaos of life.

DRIVING ON EMPTY

Lynn is a beautiful and generous woman in her fifties, with medium-length brown hair and bright blue eyes that seem to open up to endless light. She is herself extremely light and easy to be with, joyful and spontaneous. And yet she is also unrelentingly focused and hard-edged, signs of the discipline and commitment needed for the journey she has made and for the work she now does.

She would describe herself as an unlikely candidate for mystical life, never having suspected that she would be sitting in meditation most of the day and night, living in an odd little house in the desert with tilted floors and awkward aluminum windows that sometimes don't shut, her only companions three wild dogs, two of which are part coyote. She laughs at her life now, a far cry, she says, from the Four Seasons, to which she had become accustomed.

Before her mystical experience, she lived a full and busy life in New York and Paris as an artist and makeup artist. She traveled around the world for her work, sometimes in royal circles, and was married to a businessman. While she was continually drawn towards the Truth through intense longing and disciplined studies, she had no idea that she would undergo complete transformation, that her life would become so unconditionally not her own.

Hints of her previous life are hard to miss. Fine Italian linens, impossibly white, cover the antique brass bed in the one bedroom and the goose-down duvets that are carried around the house for meditation. Beautiful oriental carpets, brought back from India, lie on the small slate living-room floor. A simple, striking calligraphy in red ink of a rearing horse sits on a shelf in the bedroom. In the tilted little bathroom, the shelves are filled with fancy soaps and bath salts, expensive lotions and shampoos, signs of an urban elegance from a time and place before Lynn's life in the desert.

Lynn now lives in a timeless dimension, a state of oneness beyond our three-dimensional reality. She seems rarely disturbed by events around her, moving quickly from one moment to the next, trusting that what is needed to resolve a situation will be given, lost in remembrance of God while continually attentive to the demands and lessons of daily life. She earns money from makeup-artist jobs offered just when her funds become low. When she is not working she takes care of her house, meditates, and sometimes travels to meditate with others.

At times during my visit I feel unable to keep up with her freedom and detachment; I am sometimes anxious, unsure of how to address the needs of our days while being at least somewhat absorbed in and distracted by the energetic emptiness around us. One day we are driving in her car when I notice Lynn's gas gauge reads 'empty.' Lynn doesn't seem to mind driving on an empty tank. But we are at least thirty miles from the nearest gas station, and I worry that we won't make it there in time.

We finally do get gas as we drive her wounded dog to the vet. I am anxious in the back seat, caring for the wounded dog, hoping we will make it to the gas station. The arrival at the gas station only momentarily relieves my anxiety when, as we turn off the road, four cars collide behind us. Lynn is aware of the unsettled events around us, but she never seems worried or threatened; rather her interest is in learning their meaning, understanding what they can teach her.

Everything does get done and everyone is taken care of, even though I'm not sure how. And much of the time the feeling of being lost in way too much emptiness gives rise to fun instead of fear, the freedom and energy Lynn carries often spinning us both out into endless and disorienting fits of laughter. Whether we are watching a poor little mouse swaying by the dog's food dish, obviously stilled just before it can enjoy a great snack, or trying, unsuccessfully, to meditate while the new dog snores like a chainsaw and drools all over Lynn's beautiful linens, we are often buckled over, laughing desperately, tears streaming from our eyes.

Many of my reactions to being with Lynn—deep peace, elation, disorientation, and anxiety—are in part reactions to the tremendous energy and power of emptiness and oneness that she embodies. It is not always pleasant being swept into an energy field that takes little account of one's separate individuality, that allows for chaos and does not impose order or even the restrictions of time, that has its own life and agenda. The moments of peace, joy, or even ecstasy are the moments when I forget my own needs and really let myself be with Lynn.

It has taken years for Lynn to learn how to live in the emptiness that has been created within her. Her mystical experience located her almost completely in an inner dimension, seemingly without a bridge to this world. With the help of Hazrat, an Indian *Sheikh* in the Naqshbandi Sufi tradition whom she met after her experience, Lynn has learned to become, as the Sufis say, more 'sober.' She has learned to be attentive to the details of life, despite constantly working on other planes of consciousness.

Living in this state requires certain adjustments. One night Lynn and I laugh as I struggle to cut the vegetables for dinner with what seem impossibly dull knives. She can't risk having sharp knives in the house because she could easily hurt herself if she is suddenly lost in remembrance while cooking. Eating squashed tomato slices on one's sandwich is just a small sacrifice one has to make at Lynn's house.

The sense of protection around Lynn is almost palpable, as though special considerations have been made for whatever state she is in. While she slowly becomes more capable of daily demands, she still requires systems in place to assist her in the world. It didn't seem like a coincidence that the dog who suddenly arrived on her property is a pure-bred neapolitan mastiff, one of the fiercest and most loyal guard dogs in the world.

Lynn needs the help that is given, as her mind so often functions beyond a linear or rational state of awareness, her attention so predominantly on her inner work. How else does she feed and care for her dogs, or even herself? How else does she remember to fill the car with gas? How else does she live, safely, in an isolated environment that could be too demanding and dangerous for any single woman?

And how else does she work in a traditional line of Sufism, located in an Islamic framework, dominated, historically, by male teachers, and remain free from the prejudice and even physical threats that might normally assault a woman in that context?

Annihilated—as the Sufis say—in the fires of divine love, Lynn has been shown a unique vision of what is possible in the evolution of human consciousness. Within her understanding, there exists a state of consciousness currently available to all humanity in a way it has never been before. This is a consciousness of oneness beyond duality, a pure and formless state of being whose essence is love. It is, as Lynn calls it, the "Unknown She."

THE UNKNOWN SHE

Lynn and I sit outside under the elm tree in two large Adirondack chairs drinking tea; Lynn's three dogs and the new mastiff lie in different areas of the property, carefully watching us and each other. It is now late fall, and the weather is cool in the evening, heating up during the day. The temperature is lovely and warm where we sit in the shade of the elm; the sunlight sprinkles down on us like rain as the light wind plays with the leaves above our heads. We drink tea made from herbs of the Amazon that guarantees, on the package, the 'clarity of the rainforest,' and laugh because the rainforest evokes, in both of us, a rich darkness and multiplicity that are far from what we associate with clarity. Laughing, we are happy and optimistic as we begin discussing the state of consciousness Lynn refers to as the Unknown She.

"When I talk about the Unknown She," Lynn explains, "I am talking about a state of being beyond concept, idea, or form—a timeless state. All sense of duality has been dissolved. There are no biases or distinctions born of conditioning, culture, or tradition. The illusory boundaries have disappeared. You have let go of all that is confined in time and space. You have given up all ideas of individuality.

"The Unknown She is a state of love, in which there are no intermediaries between you and the divine," she continues, between sips of tea. "You have sensed the subtle connection to the essence, the divine energy. You have rid yourself of any sense of separation, for nothing in the world of relative truth is real for you.

"This is a state of silence and emptiness. It is an active, dynamic state of radiating luminous black light. In this state of being, silence and emptiness exist in oneness. It is a pure state of being that contains itself within itself. Here, God rests in action, as when God spoke, '*Be*.'"

Lynn tells me that it is difficult to conceptualize this state of consciousness because it is beyond concept, and not reflected in our current forms of perceiving and knowing. I also feel it is difficult for her to talk about it because she herself exists in a place without words and explanations. I sense her struggle to express herself to me within the limitations of definitions and my own understanding.

"It's so hard to recognize," she says, "because we want to bring it back into the old forms of this world, and what I'm saying is it isn't there. It's a turning within, a *new* way to be in this world of time and space. The visible outer picture is being formed in the moment, and yet this state itself is timeless. It is a consciousness of love and being, and conception before conception takes form. It is the formless form, it is a non-dimensional state of being here in ordinary reality."

One particular aspect of Lynn's understanding is that it was given directly during her mystical experience, without any established outer spiritual context. She had not studied

Sufism or any other mystical system before she was thrown into her two-year process of annihilation during which experiences in meditation took her deeper and deeper into her own being and beyond. Hence, she has had to search for conceptual frameworks for her experiences in order to convey those experiences in terms others might understand.

"When you start to investigate this concept of a consciousness of love in which all is contained within itself," she explains, "the closest thing that comes to it is Mary—if you're within the Judeo/Christian/Islamic mystical tradition. Mary had a pure consciousness; she was in a virgin state. She conceived from a pure state. In this state impregnation, conception, gestation are all self-contained within the principle *love*."

Lynn now begins to talk about what it is like in this state, often using the word "you" when she describes her own experience. When I ask her why she talks this way, she apologizes, and explains that it's difficult to speak with reference to an "I" that she can no longer locate.

"In this state, you don't have the mechanism anymore of 'do'—What do I do? Can I do? How do I do?—because only '*be*' is there. When you are shown what you really are, '*be*' becomes your reality. And this state of being is a surrendered state. It embraces you; you don't embrace it."

We sit for a while in the quiet shade, drinking tea and watching the shadows flitter across the ground. I ask Lynn why she describes this consciousness as feminine when she also says it is formless, beyond duality.

"Just because I call it 'She' does not mean that it is female," she says. "It isn't a gender, it is neither masculine nor feminine, but for some reason you want to say 'She.' It is a *feeling* state, and feeling is a female quality. You just feel it. You can't think, or put thoughts around it. It stays in the formless realm. For example, you feel as if you are enveloped by presence. There is such intimacy, as if you have been embraced." Lynn reminds me of the state of peace I experienced when I first visited her. "It is as you felt it then," she says, "a feeling of peace, harmonious oneness, and joy.

"In my understanding, when you are in this state you are in the female element. Love, the Essence. She embraces you and you embrace this feeling—the She—with your heart, so it can live inside of you as *you*. This feeling emanates from the source. It is a state of pure transformative love."

This state of pure being, as Lynn describes it, is the beginning of a journey that takes you to the most hidden chambers within your heart—into the beyond of the beyond. Love itself embraces you and takes you further into the mysteries of love. One enters the Unknown She, *becomes* Her luminous black light, and can then be guided by this light into deeper states of consciousness. The journey happens beyond ordinary consciousness, and, as Lynn tells me, is only remembered later, when one comes back into the ordinary mind. The memories are sometimes images, but sometimes just exist as direct knowledge, as though one simply understands the meaning of one's experience.

Lynn says that the journey in the Unknown She can take one through tunnels under the sea, or under the earth—tunnels that lead to hive-like caverns where golden streams of honey flow. This is not the physical earth or sea of our ordinary awareness, but rather the earth and sea of another level of reality. This golden honey, this amber light, is another form of love, a sweetness that exists in the deepest chambers of the heart.

"Remember," she says quietly, "the Prophet said that there is a hidden treasure that wants to be known. Enter Her light and Her light will take you to the treasure. Enter this luminous blackness, and She who is love itself will take you deeper and deeper into love, into the sweet honey, into golden amber streams of light.

"You go under the water, dive deep into the endless sea," she continues, her voice becoming soft and lulling, as though she is drifting away. "She lives deep in the earth, under the heavenly sea. Not the earthly earth, but the heavenly earth, the earth of your heart, the source of all being that is deep within each of us. There is a sense of returning to the source, the origin, to the primordial. It is ancient, ancient, ancient. Formless, empty, endless, She.

"When you hear Her singing heart calling, 'Come to me, Come to me,' dive, willingly, into the dynamic luminous black sea. There is a death, a dying into life, into eternal truth. There is a small opening of golden amber light. You hear, 'Come to me, Come to me.' Dive!

"You are deep in the earth under the heavenly sea, hearing Her call to you. The Unknown She helps you find your way. Guided by light, you travel in the earth of Her heart, through a labyrinth of tunnels where you find a chamber. It is an elliptical space, like a beehive. There are rows of niches, as if in a hive. You are suspended in this golden amber light. This is a state of absorption and merging. Like when the drop hits the ocean. It is light upon light."

Lynn sighs, looking at me and at the same time looking somewhere very far away. "The sweet honey, the amber light. It's like being inside a flower. Such intimacy, peace, softness. You have reached the treasure, the Beautiful One."

She puts down her tea and says quietly, "Pure consciousness is waiting, pulling us. We don't go to God so much in the way you might think. God comes to us. There is a Sufi saying, 'You take one step towards God and God takes ten steps towards you.' And this is how it was for me.

"God comes to us. This is where the serious pull is. The ascension can be work, effort, one step at a time. But the descent is the pull. It's not up to you. You're going.

You have surrendered. You're gone, in the beyond. And then you give conscious recognition that God was there all along. You *remember!* You are awake in what you have always been. Love itself. A state of harmonious oneness."

Lynn tells me that many spiritual paths do not help a seeker enter this dimension of love. "Many traditions can help you realize your higher Self," she says. "Your awareness of what you are changes from a limited, ego-oriented identity to a more natural expansive state of unity. You realize a higher or divine Self, the divine manifested in what some call the 'perfect man.' Yet there is a next step; any sense of 'higher' and 'lower' goes. Even any concept of God goes. Everything dissolves into a state beyond all concept.

"The Naqshbandi Sufis have been accessing the beyond forever," she says. "Sometimes Sufi poems can lead to a feeling of diving. It's not beyond in an upward way; it's a descent into depths of meaning. In the descent you give conscious recognition to the deeper meaning of the eternal truths. It's as if meaning is contained in consciousness as part of itself. In the ascension you become aware of God, aware that God is all there is. In the descent God is integrated into consciousness of who you are, who you have always been. It is a descent back into the luminous black sea. You are guided to the core of your being, where you are empty. It is your breath that takes you. You are told to follow it. You hear, 'Come to me. Come to me.'"

Lynn looks at me, and says, "How can I explain what can only be experienced?"

After a moment she continues, almost whispering now, "Abide in the silence and She will come. Remember Her, so She will come.

"She is lost in the shadows behind many veils. Remember She, She wants to be known.

"Peace She is. She wants to be known."

THE BIRTH OF THE UNKNOWN SHE

We sit quietly in the sparkling shade. Time passes, and I feel the difficulty of asking for more explicit descriptions of this state of being. The words and terms are hard to understand, and hard to explain. I would prefer to just sit in meditation with Lynn, the atmosphere around us drawing me into a place of smooth stillness. I have never felt anything like it, and I can't help but want more of this deep and soothing silence. It is as though I am drinking from a well I have never known existed.

After a while, we begin to talk again, and she tells me that the Unknown She is a state born from the intermingling of the male and female elements. Individual seekers come to know this state as a balancing and intermingling of opposites taking place within. Similarly, a balancing and intermingling must occur on the level of universal consciousness before humanity as a whole can enter this state. Lynn tells me that the intermingling has taken place, and the Unknown She is available to us all in a way it has never been.

"In the beginning of our spiritual evolution," she explains, "we had the tradition of the 'Mother' or 'matriarch' followed by a long period in which the 'Father' or 'patriarchal' aspect of consciousness was developed. Now it seems as though the era of patriarchal consciousness is coming to a close. But it is not the matriarch that will come back around. One could say we are turning towards a new awareness in consciousness.

"The evolution of consciousness is circular," she says, gently waving her hand in a figure-eight motion. "It develops in one direction, and then comes back upon itself. Perhaps this is what the infinite eternal is. An outward movement and then a return—again and again and again.

This movement creates an intermingling, an inter-blending. And at this time in history this intermingling brings us to a feeling state. It is a feeling of harmonious oneness that comes from the male and female being in union.

"When the male and female come together, something new can come to life, a new child born in the heart, a child that is 'true being.' This is the immaculate conception. You have to remember the evolution of consciousness doesn't end. We circle back around on a deeper level. It's a circle within a circle within a circle. We've understood the male and female and there's been a union. And from that comes a new consciousness. As the Koran says, 'a brightly shining star kindled from a blessed olive tree that is neither of the East nor of the West.'

"You know the basic underlying principle in our nature is harmony," she continues. "So, after the male joins the female, after the East meets the West, the duality, the opposition falls away. It all dissolves. You don't know what's male or female anymore, they become so entwined. In consciousness, there is concord and agreement and equanimity. The struggle disappears. The union happens, you are in harmony, the *isness*, this state of being. What would happen if all conception came from this state?

"Maybe this is what I am saying when I speak of this virgin consciousness which is available to us all. There has been a transition in our awareness—it has already taken place. If you look around carefully you can see it. It became evident especially after September eleventh. Suddenly people who do not know each other at all are feeling connected to each other in new ways."

Lynn goes into the house for a minute and brings out a letter from her cousin who lives in New York City and was at the World Trade Center on the morning of the attack. "My cousin was there on the eleventh," she says.

"She could see this shift. I think many people noticed something similar." In the letter to Lynn, her cousin wrote:

> After running from the explosions at the Trade Center I had a long walk of about six miles with thousands of others. The tragedy we had witnessed that morning was not comprehensible. Yet amidst the horror was a tangible peace and order that is difficult to describe, far beyond our relief at having survived. This peace was all-encompassing, like an embrace that protected us in our sorrow as we walked. There was a collective unity being generated from everywhere. I will always remember the silence as we walked across the bridge.

"Grace is ever present," Lynn says. "Grace is present in our normal daily lives in simple and more subtle ways. Perhaps it was made more apparent by the magnitude of that event.

"When someone experiences the consciousness of this unity, duality begins to have a new reference. We can no longer completely see duality as in opposites, but within likeness. We see ourselves as individuals, but also feel deeply connected. It is a tremendous shift at every level of our structure. This energy, this light is emanating from the source of being and has descended into consciousness. There is potential for people to receive this transmission, receive it directly in their heart. There are many people who did not have a mystical bone in their body and all of a sudden they too find themselves in this state.

"This state of pure consciousness has always existed, because it is who we are. We've never given it conscious recognition as part of who we are because we hadn't evolved there yet in our understanding of ourselves as THAT. But we *are* this pure consciousness. This is our natural harmonious state of being. It's the underlying principle in the nature of our being. And now we can give conscious recognition to this natural state so it can become manifest."

INTUITING YOUR WAY HOME

Lynn and I are walking in the desert behind her house. Her three dogs, Hunter, Bandit, and Girl, run through the sage hunting rabbits or snakes, rolling in an old animal carcass, and occasionally limping back to Lynn, the signal for her to remove a cactus needle from a paw. The new dog waits in the house, separate from the others so there won't be a fight. The sun is setting and the sky is streaked with purple and red. There are few houses in view, and the only other suggestion of human life comes from the dirt road we stroll on.

We have been meditating most of the day, and now begin talking about how we can realize this state of consciousness, how we can live from this place of harmony and oneness and pure being. I have the sense that Lynn's own path has been guided by and within this consciousness of love from the beginning. So I ask her to tell me about how it was for her, and how she thinks a person can come to be in this state of love.

"It's not as though people can suddenly just live completely from this state," she says. "It is still a journey, a process. We just have to be open, listen to what is there, within us, present. Everything is within us, waiting for conscious recognition, waiting to unfold.

"Sit silently, be patient, wait. Know She will come. There is a potential in consciousness for this awareness to be spontaneous. All can give recognition to this as a possibility.

"I think one of the most important things about my life and my experience is that there was no established form to it. I just intuited my way home. I never followed prescribed rules, I never had a spiritual/mystical teacher, and I never did any spiritual practices except what came to me to do." She says, laughing now, "And even those weren't your normal practices!"

Lynn tells me that she always had the idea that she could go home, and she was not home yet. She always felt as though she had been dropped here by accident. Even as a young child she had the awareness of another place, another way of being. She let her longing for this home, the sorrow of being away from it, and the intention to go there lead her through her life. These feelings helped her prepare for the two-year mystical experience of being taken into the beyond.

"I would say the longing, sorrow, and sincere intention I had are more important than all of the practices of a tradition. It seemed as if everything that I needed to make the journey was given to me. Whether I went to the movies or read a novel or it came from the scriptures, every step of the way I was shown what was needed. The idea that you had to have a practice and do a certain amount of something and then move on to the next practice wouldn't have fit in at all.

"The sorrow wasn't sadness or depression. Just a sadness that came from knowing that there was more than what I was able to experience. I knew I wasn't home and I wanted to go home, but it never had a demanding feeling, or included a hatred for the earth. I've loved my experience here. There's been a great deal of joy in my unfoldment. No matter how frightening or devastating, it has been filled with joy. Even the sorrow was not a depression; it was really sweet.

"And then there was longing. They go hand in hand. I think this longing is always driving you home. Like when you start to settle into a 'normal life'—it wakes you up, shakes you up, makes you move. It's just always there. Just saying—'Is this looking like Reality to you? Is this what it's all about? A nice house, nice clothes, all those things? Are these things Spirit?' And sometimes with this sorrow, this longing, you just start crying and you don't stop.

"All my life, my thinking and my feeling were always around this longing. I was always saying, 'How do you get there? There have to be maps, or roads, or a means to travel there!' And that's what I did—I followed maps wherever I found them. I traveled there in all different kinds of ways. And one day you wake up in the morning and you begin to realize the potential to actually make it home is right there. It's like two blocks down the street—right around the corner. You see this finally, how close home really is, and then this reality, this life as you've been living it, slowly starts to slip away from you."

"I had the sincere intention to do what I needed to do," she continued, matter-of-factly, revealing the unwavering commitment and discipline I have felt since first meeting her. "It had to do with not wanting anything for yourself. I mean, I never ever thought I would get anything from my experiences, except the information that would allow me to make all the changes that were necessary so that I could get home. For me, home didn't have a picture—not like in scripture when they say there's a paradise waiting for you. That isn't what I was seeking.

"I was seeking the truth that would set me free. I can even remember going to the movies—it's amazing how much the movies really participated in my journey. This whole pop culture really helped me get home. Even the music I listened to was like a *mantra*—it was soul music. It wasn't any lovely piece of classical music or chants. I would just sing James Brown's 'I Feel Good' again and again. That was my *mantra*. It had deep meaning for me. You can sing your way home!"

Lynn and I laugh now at the absurdity of singing James Brown's "I Feel Good" as a spiritual practice. She keeps speaking, shaking her head. "Or, I was watching a movie— E.T.—the scene where it says, 'E.T. call home.' I'm in the movie thinking, 'OK, I'm going to start calling. That's what I'm going to do. Call home.' And this is when I started to pray. When I started saying 'Grandfather, Great Spirit, Grandmother, Great Mystery, hear my voice.'

"Prayer can be anything you want!" she says, laughing again and looking out into the open space of the desert. "I never had a specific prayer that I got out of a book or that somebody gave to me. It seemed as though it was already present within me as a part of myself. My prayer was around calling. I was actually sitting in a respectful way, with the intention that I was going to sit and wait, and not ask for anything, but I was just going to let the Great Spirit and the Great Mystery know that I was there. And it was as simple as that. I was totally convinced that you could call, and they would come. I guess I had kind of a sense that there was a '*they*' that would participate in this. Like the elders. Though I never would have called them that."

Lynn tells me that the '*they*' in her childhood was never God in the traditional sense. "I would say nature was very present as a reality. That was probably the first thing. I saw nature as the mother of all mothers, and this made sense to me. I spent most of my childhood on my back looking up to the sky, the clouds, the stars, and having all of them come alive. God was nature. I lived in New Orleans and we had hurricanes. She had the ability to make the waters rise so high that they came into your house. And make the winds blow so hard that all the trees in your yard bent down so you'd have to pull them up and tie them to poles till the next hurricane.

"So I lived in a place where nature was very present. I lived on a bayou, and on a lake, and it was very primordial. The word 'God' never made much sense to me, but one day when I was shown God as 'consciousness, the primal element,' it had a great deal of meaning for me."

I ask Lynn to tell me more about what guided her later in life. I ask her if she had specific beliefs or any internal structure other than her longing to go home.

"I had the belief that we are all God, but we just hadn't given conscious recognition to that state, but that one day I would arrive there. And I believed in the all-ness of good: that everything that happened to me was for the good, that everything could take me home. So I believed everything that was in front of me was given as an opportunity to come closer to what is good.

"And I had my studies—I studied a system of metaphysics called Eschatology which, translated, means 'the science of last things.' This was a path of truth, in which one had proposals about reality and proved them as a way to realize the truth. One had to live this truth in one's daily life. Every day I had my studies.

"I also had the idea from my studies that you have a human disposition, but your true nature is inherently perfect and good, not influenced by our human conditioning, parents, or culture. There is this sense of the perfect being. Or the higher Self that is perfect. So I did have a sense that I had to empty out anything that was unlike God. When I was jealous or judgmental, for example, I knew those had to go. Because I just never thought God would be envious or jealous or backbiting. I emulated the qualities and virtues I thought God was: patient, courageous, forgiving. I thought in my true nature I had the same attributes as God, that they were inherent within me as a potential.

"Most importantly, I knew that a moment would come when the spirit of Truth would come and guide me. So I prepared myself, I worked on myself in this way, and waited patiently for that moment when the 'invisible guide' would come and I would begin my journey in love."

PULLED BY LOVE

It is dark now, and cold outside. Lynn and I sit in her small living room, the woodstove burning for the first time this year. We sit on cushions on the floor—the house is too small for real furniture—under soft cashmere shawls Lynn bought in New York years ago. Incense burns on the small table near the front door that also holds candles and a picture of Hazrat, Lynn's Sufi guide. The giant new dog lies next to me, snoring, and Lynn and I begin to talk about the two-year process of annihilation and revelation that left her empty and barely able to live in the world. Lynn tells me that everything she did in her life brought her towards that one moment when love pulled her deep within herself and then beyond. Her life and all the studying and effort were a preparation and purification for what would be the beginning of her real training in the 'unseen' world, the world beyond concept, the beyond of the beyond, where even she no longer existed.

"The first experience was a huge jolt," Lynn says, wrapped in her shawl. "I had never had visions before. I was staying in Los Angeles at my Eschatology teacher's house and suddenly I had the experience of being a bird in a birdcage, and my soul was being set free. I was shown all of the things that still bound me, where I didn't have a limitless sense of self. I was sitting under a tree in the backyard, and I couldn't move for weeks. I could hardly eat or sleep, and the pain was unimaginable.

"I started off with a very simple cage. Like when you come into being. Then it became more ornate, and very beautiful. And another room was added, and beautiful drapes of jewels. And it was a big ornate thing at one point. I was taken through these stages, and many lessons happened at each stage. And as I passed from stage to stage the cage would change.

"At one point the door was opened and I could come and go as I pleased. In the beginning, I didn't travel too far, returning to the cage for my sustenance. One time I returned after a long day's journey to find the door shut. I could no longer go in. I was a little bird at this point, holding on to the outside of the cage, thinking it offered life. Then one day the cage disappeared. I was told to fly. I was free.

"This experience left me dazed and confused. It lasted for weeks, and when it came to an end I was completely disoriented. The very foundation of my being shaken. I would ask, 'How could what I have been shown be true? How could I be so free?'

"For months after, I was left with the sense of being a caged lion. Roaming back and forth in a very small cage. Restless. In a sense the lion was an energy, or a state of consciousness within me, one I was not familiar with. This lion would roar, and wanted to be set free. And even though my soul was uncaged, I was still contained in a space that was way too small. I hadn't reached the infinite eternal. Something had been set free, but something so much deeper was becoming available. The lion had to be released because I was going to need the energy of that lion; I was going to need that state of consciousness in order to make the next step of the journey. You could say, also, that this lion represented a courage within me. I needed the courage to trust what I knew to be true; I needed that courage in order to continue on."

After these initial experiences, Lynn spent months doing inner work, praying for qualities she needed for the journey, asking people she had hurt over the years for forgiveness, and doing other purification rituals that she felt she should do. It was a time of preparation and agreements, in which Lynn committed herself completely to realizing the Truth. Then came a time when she understood she needed to go into meditation.

"In my studies I would say I was still conceptually moving through things," she tells me. "Even after this experience, that was so dismantling and so freeing and took me to the next stage, I was still limited by concepts. You see, many spiritual experiences are within a conceptual framework because they include visions or pictures, experiences within time and space. And I always wanted to keep moving, not let myself get comfortable or stuck in one state. So I decided to sit in meditation because I thought that could deepen my understanding and experience. And I thought something had to happen with my breath and that was the best way to do it.

"So I just sat in a chair and closed my eyes, and in an instant I found myself being taken to where the primordial is, the source from which I came. The energy was so strong— I was just holding on to the chair for dear life as the energy was just ripping through me. I was thinking, 'My God, what have I done?'

"I was wrestling with the energy," Lynn says, laughing now at her confusion at the time about how she ended up in such a strange and intense situation. "The energy was trying to take me out of the chair and I was trying to stay in the chair. I was at the house of my Eschatology teacher and there was only just a little space in front of the chair—

the rest of the room was filled—it was like a storage room. And there was just enough room for my body to be on the floor in a prone position, my face flat down on the floor. And eventually the energy just took me out of the chair and I was on the ground face down. And I had one thought, which was, 'If there's a fire in this house I'm just going to burn, because I can't move!' I couldn't move; it was like being paralyzed.

"The energy pulled me down and my face was ground into the floor. I couldn't breathe at all. I felt like I was dying. The duality of my breath—the presence of an in-breath and an out-breath—was gone. The ebb and flow of life was gone. I was told to give my life to the one who owns my breath. And it didn't mean my own breath, but the one breath that we all are. And that was what happened. I gave my life to the one who owns my breath.

"For months and months the energy had its way with me." Lynn says, shaking her head. "I would just have to sit down and the energy would take me. Just take me. It was a constant pull. And those were the months that I couldn't leave my house. I stayed in my room. You don't have to eat really. I put a 'Do Not Disturb' sign on the door. You're just gone. All the time gone, and being taught. All of the time I was being taught. And I don't know even now all that I was taught. The pieces come back little by little.

"The experience lasted for about two years, with times to integrate. But there was a point when I wanted to put myself away. I didn't think I would ever be able to live in the world again, safely. I was living in New York, and I was always afraid that I would get hit by a bus because I wasn't really seeing so well yet.

"I remember one time when I tried to go get soup. I went to a restaurant about four blocks from my house—a neighborhood place. I arrived there after lunch; I got there just fine. And I was standing at the counter and I had ordered. I knew I had ordered. I was standing there waiting for my food. And suddenly I was gone. Right in the middle of it all. And I came to, with the wait staff yelling, 'Hello...Hello...Hello!' Just standing there. But nobody home. Nobody at all. So I waited a while before I went out again. I wasn't really ready yet."

FINDING LOVE THROUGH TRUTH

"When you read about the process of annihilation," Lynn tells me, her face barely lit by the flames of the fire and the glow of a nearby candle, "it can be described in a way that seems attractive. But it's not. Your heart is exploded and imploded again and again. Your heart is totally pulverized, broken and beaten to a pulp. You come out confused, bewildered, disoriented, with no reference point. And then you can read a poem by Hafiz or Rumi or Kabir and you see clearly something about what has been happening to you. So you're ready for the next onslaught to dismantle you. All the while you melt and merge into the emptiness, silence. Into the beyond, into the Unknown She, the dynamic living luminous black She. And this is where I was taught—in the unseen. I would be led somewhere, shown something, all in meditation. I was in a state of conscious awareness in the beyond. Beyond thought, beyond concept. And of course even I wasn't there. It all happened in the beyond. But you see I had no context for this experience. I hadn't been studying any tradition. I had no background for it.

"Before my training in the unseen, I would say that all my training was male. It was a path of truth, not love. It was scientific. I never even thought of love, really. In a way

I could even say I was figuring it out, figuring out what reality was and trying to realize it. The process was like mathematics for me, really high mathematics, very abstract mathematics. Trying this—'If I put this and that together then I get that.' Or, 'This and that don't work.' I was definitely figuring my way home to what is real.

"And at some point you reach this obstacle, this brick wall. And you know you're not going to get through it by figuring something out. And that's when this idea of sitting in meditation makes sense. Things would just dissolve. Things would just fall apart. Whatever conceptual walls I had built around myself would collapse. But I didn't know the whole house would collapse!

"There is an expression," Lynn continues, feeding the woodstove, speaking softly, "'To surrender your will to God.' This is what happened to me, and I wouldn't wish it on anyone. The surrender is an experience; it's not a statement. It's an experience. An intense struggle. During the experience I had to find everything I had swept under the rug. You think you're surrendered, and then there is more resistance, more of you. And I was broken into that surrender. I was taken kicking and fighting. There were times that you feel you don't have any fight left in you anymore, but then you are taken deeper, become aware of more barriers, and then they are broken down. At one point I was so weary from this intense struggle, and then the surrender came. Love took me.

"This was a very beautiful moment," she says, her eyes becoming soft and shining in the dim light. "My whole chest was lit with a beautiful light. I could see into my heart. I was standing in the front of a beautiful tree, a two-edged sword in my hand. It was bejeweled and glimmering in the light. My sword was taken from me and was placed into my heart. I was told I didn't have to be a warrior any more. All the things I had to fight in that kind of way had been conquered.

"And so in the midst of it—when I sat down and surrendered—I consciously said, 'I take everything I know to be true and I'm going to put it in my heart, in love, and I'm just going to see what happens.' And that was the end of one stage and the beginning of the next.

"In order to be completely surrendered, everything has to go. Every thought and concept was dismantled until the only one that remains is 'I AM.' Everything else is gone. The 'I am' is with you during the journey, and then even that goes in the unknown. Every concept you ever had about God, self, life, is gone. You are made empty."

I ask Lynn how all her discipline and work in the earlier stages of her life relate to this moment when it seemed that nothing was up to her anymore, this moment when God finally seemed to embrace her completely. "Through effort, attention, and discipline," she explains, "some sort of space gets created for the experience to take you. A vortex gets created and then you are pulled. When you sit in a state of surrender, there's a flow, there's a pull. Sometimes it becomes very, very strong—like a rapid running river—and sometimes it's just a still brook. It's all love, and the love just takes you."

BEING OF USE

Still sitting by the fire, late in the night, Lynn and I talk about what happened after these years, about how it was for her to try to come back to this world after being so completely on a different level of reality. While she remains in a state of freedom, she continues to become more present here so she can be of use. In order to be able to function in normal life, Lynn needed a great deal of help, and was given it by Hazrat. The Naqshbandi Sufi path emphasizes 'sobriety'—the capacity to be present and attentive on this level of reality despite working at the same time somewhere else.

"The experience brought me to a place of pure being," Lynn says. "But then you are sort of dumped back here. I definitely had that feeling of being abandoned. There were some arrangements made, just as they are made at other important stages on the journey. I had to say 'Yes' to being here. And I was cognizant of these arrangements. But when you're in certain states of consciousness you don't realize things—I didn't realize I would be back in such a literal picture again.

"After the experience I felt abandoned with no help or directions," Lynn tells me, and I can feel some remnants of her desperation and confusion. "I wasn't even part of any tradition. I had no outer teacher who could help me understand what had happened to me. But as I stick in that surrendered or that '*Be*' state, things show up to help me, or guide me. I was sent here, or there's relief there. It all eventually started to organize and systematize. I could see the intelligence at work.

"It has taken many years of help," she continues, speaking more slowly now. "It was difficult for a long time—just to live—after being so much somewhere else. It was as if I was a child and I had to remember what I had known as an adult. 'OK, I know how to drive. I used to drive.' And living in California you have to drive. So I had to remember to drive. Or small things like taking showers and changing your clothes. You have to learn it all again. And so often it is like being a child, you are so vulnerable, in so much need of help, you are in such a child-like state.

"Within the Sufi tradition, there is an emphasis on selfless service. I think it has something to do with the idea that once you are free, once you've been set free, there's a possibility for use. I had to say 'Yes' to coming back. And it is still a process. Subsisting in God is a learning process. I try to stay in a surrendered state of being, and the experience gave me that opportunity. And now, through integration I am stabilizing that state.

"I remember one aspect of the agreement was that I would bring everyone home," she says, then laughs, "I'm assuming it doesn't mean a population of people!" Then she becomes serious again. "This agreement was made during what I would say was a Buddhist training in which I was brought to a deep, deep state of compassion and I committed myself to helping everyone come home. It's not about making sure every individual person realizes the truth. This agreement reflects the understanding that we are all one and the same, we are all contained within a state of oneness. It looks like there's a multitude. But in actuality we are all one and the same. So this is part of my work. All I am doing is remaining in this state of consciousness, sitting in what has been revealed to me, offering one example that people can use to come home, if it is God's will."

WOMEN'S PATHS

"What's important is that you can intuit your way home," Lynn says as we walk along the dirt road behind her house in another beautiful and bright desert morning. "All I did was *remember*. It's so much more direct than you think. I was shown what things are—without concepts. What the truth is. And it is so silly what we have made things into. What our minds have created. And it's really so simple. All you have to is '*be*.' But we like to '*do*.'

"Many of the practices of many traditions can actually be obstacles. They create dynamics of expectation, progress, failure, all of which don't leave you free, don't encourage you to listen for what might be needed in that one moment. You can do and do, and want and want, but all that has very little relevance to what and when something really happens.

"'Unfortunately so many people have bought this idea that there's a program—that you do step one and it leads to step two and to step three. But from my perspective it didn't work that way, and it doesn't work that way now. I didn't have any preparation as far as I'm concerned for what actually happened to me. I had years of training in Eschatology and every day I am grateful for that training." Then she says, laughing again at the strangeness of her own life, "But it was never to lead to this!"

"There is also this sense that as women we can use our everyday experience to activate a process. Whereas for men, maybe they need practices. Like *mantras*. But maybe as women we don't need those kinds of practices. A simple humming song that has a particular repetition that starts a particular kind of breathing, and you arrive at the same state you would by saying a *mantra*. But in this way it is not imposed, it comes from within.

"During my experience, it was songs from my child-hood. For other people, I don't know. I mean, whoever thought James Brown's 'I Feel Good' would have taken anybody anywhere in consciousness? But it did. I also sang, 'Love Is all There Is' and, 'Open Up Your Heart and Let the Sun Shine In.' I sang them over and over again, and before I knew it I was in another state.

"But they were very particular verses from songs that were real for me. I was trying to open up my heart so the sun could shine in. Or, when it was all said and done I felt good and I knew that I would!" Lynn's freedom and joy are so contagious, I find myself laughing with her for quite a while before she continues. "It sounds ridiculous, but it worked! I never had any mantras; I didn't know any mantras. So I had my own that came, that lulled me into a state so I could slip away, where you're so totally surrendered that you can just go. So maybe it isn't about this kind of training that we traditionally think is necessary.

"I knew I had to meditate, so I meditated. It was the same with prayer. I had no idea what prayer was, so I basically made one up.

"In my case, and maybe this is true for other women, all this—the inner environment, inner conditioning, ripeness—was created in life. I had a busy and full life. I had a very stressful job, and was under constant pressures. But I didn't let those pressures or demands distract me from what I knew was possible. I used everything in my experience to teach me. It seems to me that there must be a possibility that women can make this journey just by staying in a state of awareness conducive to seeing what it is you need for the next step. Of course, maybe this is true for men, too, I don't know. I just know it was true for me, and I'm a woman. And again, this is possible if there is a trust that what is needed will come, that the unfoldment is a process within yourself, a natural process that comes from within and takes you where you need to go. This is a mystery you're going into.

"I still have experiences sometimes that are very powerful and very strongly suggest something about the work I'm involved in now. At the beginning of the year I had an experience in meditation which helped me see why perhaps women are a bit more naturally attuned to this state of being we are talking about.

"In the experience I was standing in an archway or a niche and I was all by myself; I was in the unseen where you have no awareness. And all of a sudden you're punched into awareness. That's really the only way I can describe it—suddenly you are aware in the unawareness. And you just wait knowing something is coming. You don't know when but you just patiently wait. It's a very surrendered state.

"I was in this archway, this niche, alone," she goes on. "All of a sudden illumined beings were showing up. And there were a handful of us standing at this niche. Then the luminous black just opened up. When I see the luminous black I just walk right into it. There was an oil lamp. The flame was in here and the glass was out here," Lynn says, indicating a lamp surrounded by a glass. "I was inside between the flame and the glass. The only thing that was left of me was my right hand. And I immediately put my hand into the flame and I was gone.

"When I told this to Hazrat, he asked me, 'What about the other people?' And I told him they wouldn't come. I had the feeling that the illuminated beings just wouldn't enter that luminous black light. They were given the opportunity to glimpse the nature of that luminous night, they were at the threshold of the beyond, and they wouldn't come. I don't know why. I can speculate—maybe they thought it was darkness, or they were afraid of the hidden meanings that are contained within the night. I don't know.

"You see, to me the illuminations felt male in quality and character. And they wouldn't enter this space. Perhaps something holds men back from embracing the female element. But in order for people—men and women alike— to enter this new dimension, this new consciousness that is now present, we must undergo a change in orientation. The Unknown She is love itself. And love is the female element. I thought that perhaps this is why women seem to me to be a bit more naturally drawn to this state, more willing to embrace it."

OBSTACLES FOR WOMEN

Lynn has recently bought a new parcel of land with a small cabin a bit higher in the San Gabriel Mountains, behind the house she now rents. She and I are walking on her land in the high desert. Some of her property looks flat and scrubby; a grove of Joshua trees suggests the Mojave that stretches out below us. Looking from another angle, her property is home to rich greenness—pine and juniper trees, and the mountains rising behind us. She is more remote here, and her small cabin more rustic than the little yellow house below.

We walk along a ridge overlooking the desert. The new mastiff dog runs beside us, having moved up here and claimed it as his home. He looks feline, like a mountain lion, as he runs along the dirt road that winds through Lynn's property. Unlike at her old house, here we seem more part of the sky, not beneath it. We follow the currents of clouds and light for what could be hundreds of miles out into space. It is early evening, and the sunset begins to transform everything around us into gentle streams of purple, blue, and white. We are talking now about obstacles for women, what holds women in an older model of spiritual transformation and limits their realization of this new consciousness.

"One of the greatest obstacles for women, I would say, is to understand that all is within," Lynn tells me. "Because women are so relational. We want to be in relationship to something outside ourselves for the qualities and elements we need. We want to look to a teacher or a husband, or lover, to be the authority. But I just turned within myself for what I needed.

"I knew I had to learn how to become a person who was capable of making this journey. I knew I would have to be totally self-contained. I understood that all of the qualities, emotions, characteristics, everything was going to have to come from within me. I couldn't have any sense of 'other' involved. No attachment whatsoever on any level to anyone or anything.

"With my Eschatology studies you had to live what you understand, you couldn't just study it. You had to live it; it had to be part of your daily life. So, when I started to recognize that the male and female concept were not two, but one, and that they were contained within consciousness as aspects of the primal element, I understood that I had to develop all of the characteristics that you would call male as well as female in order to be a whole being.

"So, assumptions that you can rely on things like protection, strength, or security from your husband or partner had to go. I had to develop these qualities within myself, and so I did. And finally one day I was living in Paris working as an artist and I woke up one morning, and it was as clear as could be that I'd become the man that I'd always wanted to marry. So there was this marriage that had taken place between the male and female within myself. I had become totally self-sufficient. Totally sufficient in Self."

I asked Lynn to tell me more of the qualities she had to develop in herself in order to realize the self-containment she was talking about.

"During my experience when I was pulled by love into those deep states of meditation, I heard, 'Take on the journey only that which I want in the circle of being. I and my relations.' I had no idea who or what or where my relations were because all had been either given or taken away. But I understood I had to choose what I needed in order to go home.

"And what I said was: 'Power, purity, love, wisdom, patience, courage, and understanding.' I also knew that I needed an emptiness and a compassion for the journey I would be going on. I knew that there would be the full force of God, and I needed to prepare myself. And that would require humility, surrender, courage, patience, wisdom, and strength.

"There can be so many obstacles for women," Lynn continues, as we walk along the ridge near her cabin. "Just the conditioned roles in our relationships. Just the idea that we nurture and care. If you are the type of person who will nurture and care for every individual who comes into your experience then you are in big trouble. Because you will never find the time or inner dimension necessary to develop that quiet contemplative place within yourself that will allow the grace to come.

"If you aren't on the path in a very sincere way you can't make it. These are obstacles that will keep presenting themselves so you don't do what is necessary. One of the hardest things to accept is that you have to learn to be completely alone, whether you are alone in an empty house or alone in a room full of people. It's the idea of living completely within yourself. And if you aren't willing to accept this aloneness you will be given one diversion after another that will draw you away from the path.

"What about being at home?" Lynn asks, unknowingly addressing my next question. "Women can be home taking care of children, and also be in a constant state of remembrance, a constant state of being alone with God. But still it is good to have time apart. For me, time set aside was key. I did take hours, sometimes days, off to shift from a worldly idea of self into the depths of my studies. I had to be willing to say 'no' to jobs, to take a week off and protect that space. Set and keep priorities. This is the sincere intention I was talking about before. It would have been really easy never to take time out, never to set that time aside, because just like every one else I was so busy; I could easily have never found the time.

"For me, the longing was just always there. It was what moved me. But if you're really busy you won't have the awareness of it. The awareness has to be there, it nurtures the longing. Longing is the motivating principle in a way. It's what moves you forward and keeps you from getting stuck. It's the same with the sorrow. It's like a driving force. So you need to be sincere, and you need to develop qualities within yourself to help you on your journey, whether it be patience, endurance, courage, sagacity, discernment, or peacefulness; it all comes from within."

THE NICHE OF THE HEART

"This is a state of consciousness we're talking about," Lynn tells me, as we sit at her new cabin looking out across the Mojave. "It's a state of being, a consciousness of love. And love is the transformative element, it does not teach. It transforms, forms, and reforms. Traditionally, the *Sheikh*, the teacher, had authority, and you had to be obedient. But this new consciousness works so differently. Nobody has authority over anyone else. It is a state of oneness and equanimity, everything in its right place, aligned vertically with what is highest in itself.

"The only thing I do with people is sit in meditation with them. And maybe they are given a taste of something. I have no role as a teacher, as an authority; there's just a grace that is always present.

"Recently I was in India, and I experienced how I now live and work in situations of conflict or polarity, how this energy comes into such situations and changes them. I was visiting Hazrat," she says. "And when I visit Hazrat, we often go with a group of his students to the tombs of the saints where there is always a mosque. And it can be disturbing for many women, because women are not allowed to pray in the mosques, where the men pray. The men go into the mosque, and the women are to go pray in another room. At the time of the Prophet this wasn't the case. But over the centuries cultural and social ways have influenced the tradition."

Whenever Lynn tells me stories of her times in India, the atmosphere shifts, as though suddenly she sits with the scent of thousands of years of incense clinging to her clothes, as though thousands of years of prayers flow along with every word she speaks. Sometimes she can talk on and on about her trips to India, where the traditional elements—with all their restrictions and inadequacies—give a special substance, an ancient and soothing certainty to her experience. And as she tells me of a recent trip I can feel a change in atmosphere. The desert light itself seems to be changing, suddenly becoming more excited and alive, as though it found new joy waiting for the wild colors of the coming sunset.

"In India," she tells me, looking into the sky, "when you go by a mosque and you hear the Koran being recited, immediately there is a shift in consciousness. The grace, the beauty, the *baraka* (energy of the path) are just so strong. So as a woman, when you're not allowed in the mosque to pray, you can feel like you're missing something.

"One time, Hazrat knew the women wanted to pray at the tomb. So, he indicated a line in the dirt of the courtyard by the tomb and then a student put a row of flowers along the line. There was this beautiful line of flowers, indicating the men could pray up front and the women could pray in the back. And we said our prayers, and the *baraka* was strong and we felt it intensely.

"So some of the women wondered why we couldn't pray at the mosque where Hazrat has his home and his school, why we had to pray in the basement. You see, it can be very difficult to be praying in a basement with five women when right up above your head the men are sitting in the *baraka*. The prayers can be so exquisite. You can become full of light, in a total state of remembrance. But when there are five women in a basement it's just not the same.

"So the women asked me to speak with Hazrat, to see if perhaps we could pray in the mosque at his home, since he let us pray at the mosque at this particular tomb.

"The night before I was to talk to Hazrat, in my meditation, I had a vision with a *sura*. The *suras* usually come as a disc, and they come in Arabic, and I can't read it because I don't know Arabic. But I am left with a meaning that I can understand. And I can usually translate it into something that makes sense for the situation.

"The next morning, I told a woman from Pakistan what had happened in the night. I described the meaning of the *sura*. I told her that the *sura* described a niche, and a lamp inside of the niche, and a light that comes from the East and from the West but it's not of the East or the West—like a new light.

"The important thing was that I was told during the experience that the women were to pray in this niche. We were not to go pray with the men at the mosque. We were to pray in this niche.

"And so based on my understanding of what I was told, the Pakistani woman found the sura, and it's a beautiful sura. She said it's one of the more mystical suras. It reads:

Allah is the light of the heavens and the earth.
The likeness of His light is as a niche wherein is a lamp.
The lamp is a glass. The glass as it were a brightly
shining star kindled from a blessed olive tree that is
neither of the East nor of the West.

Whose oil well nigh would shine though fire does
not touch it.
Light upon light.
Allah guides to His light who He wills.

"This *sura* is very open to interpretation on many
levels," Lynn goes on. "And we ended up having many
interesting discussions about it. And I didn't go to Hazrat
and ask to pray in the mosque.

"You see," she tells me, "once the East and the West
meet, and there is this intermingling or this union, there
is still something beyond. And for me this is what was
indicated in the *sura*. The light is neither from the East nor
the West. It is from a place beyond. Beyond the mosque,
beyond the rules, beyond the distinction between male
and female, beyond separation. There is something beyond
the beyond.

"What is this niche where we are to pray?" Lynn asks
me, as the darkness starts to fill the sky before us. "It is the
niche of the heart, the light of Allah," she answers softly.
"Here, there is peace, there is expansion. If you pray in
the niche of the heart, you are in a place of oneness,
beyond separation, beyond the forms and structures of
the world. This is where we can be, all of us.

"When you pray in that light, you feel enveloped," she
continues. "Something comes and embraces you. Peace
comes over you. There is a huge expansion in your heart.
You fall away. Light is all that is left. It is light upon light."

I ask Lynn to tell me more about how her state affects
those around her. How does she live from this place of
expansion in the world?

"It is like my time in India. There was conflict; there
was polarization. When I am in a situation like that, I am
in a contracted state. When someone presents me with

something that is not real, that comes from a limited place, it cannot come into me. Physically I can't breathe so easily. My heart closes down; the light in my heart becomes dim. These are all signs that what is happening is not real for me.

"I then open myself back up by pouring love and light into my heart. I just *remember*. And then there is expansion, and sometimes those around me feel it as well. And they can give themselves to it. They can go beyond the separation, into oneness, into the beyond of the beyond. And there, there is no need to resolve conflict, because there is no conflict. It is so simple; you have to laugh. There is no conflict, there is no polarization, there is no exclusion or separation. So there is nothing that needs to be done about it!

"I come from an empty space now. I look around situations of conflict and I see that conflict is not me, that I am not within separation. This state is another way of being. In India, we did not have to stay in a place of separation, in which we were excluded from something. How can we be excluded from God? As the *sura* says, 'Allah guides to Allah who He wills.' If God wants you to come Home, He will find a way.

"What is this resurrection that's happened in the world? The child we have given birth to? It is just wisdom. An ancient, ancient wisdom that will come into our modern time. It is as though this wisdom has been sleeping in women, in the female principle of all of us, for we each contain the wholeness of God. And She has awoken. And She whispers 'Come to me, come to me.'"

That night I hardly sleep, and Lynn and I meditate together while the sun rises. The energy is still and deep, silent and soothing, like waves on an endless ocean— coming from nowhere and returning to nowhere. We eat breakfast and then I drive out of her dusty yard, her dogs watching quietly from the shed. Soon I pick up the flat and monotonous stretch of highway and begin the seven-hour trip to my home in northern California. The aloneness, the intense freedom, and the great stillness of my experience with Lynn have left me deeply exhausted. The highway, with its few demands, is a welcome change. Stopping only for gas, I let myself put the car in cruise control and take the smooth ride out of the desert.

Grand Mother, Great Mystery
Absolute One
   I send a voice to you
   Hear my voice
I am here   I am you

I want to tell you a story
   One you may already know
It is of a remembering
   Of someone you knew
   Long long ago

In the silence of the *NIGHT* comes
The Unknown *SHE*
   Whispering sweetly
   Come dance with me
It is the primal dance
   From time before time
   Beginningless
   Endless
   Dance of *ONE*
Call her
   The Hidden *ONE*

Have you danced this dance of
The Unknown *SHE*
   The Aurora Borealis
   The Mid-Night Sun
Dance of *ONE*
Call her
   MAJESTY
Mysterious *ONE*

In *DAYBREAK* comes the
   Radiant *ONE*
Her Golden Arrow
   Pierces your HEART
   LIGHT upon LIGHT
   Diamond Bright
Call her
   The Most Hidden *ONE*

She is the *SWEET HONEY*
   Pure LIGHT
   The Golden Halo
   Queen of Hearts Heart
Call her
   BEAUTY
Call her
   LOVE
The Camel *SHE*

CALL The Unknown SHE

Grand Mother Great Mystery
Absolute One
   I send a voice to you
   Hear my voice
I am here I am you
Come to me Come to me

Have you heard Her singing *HEART*
   Remember and Return
   Remember and Return
Come to me Come to me

Sing the sacredness of
   The *Unknown SHE*

LOVE *HER*
   Praise *HER*
   Be Still Awake
   Face Down
SING
   Come to me
   Come to me

Have you been given the
   Emerald of *Her* HEART
Has *SHE* laid down *Her*
   GREEN mantle
That you may find your
   WAY
Guided to LIGHT
The Perfect Way

LISTEN
   Is *SHE* singing
   Come to me
   Come to me

SHE lives deep in EARTH
   Under the *Heavenly Sea*
The luminous BLACK
   SHE makes *ONE* see
The *Heavenly EARTH*
   Thou Art *SHE*
The Holy ESSENCE
   Compassionate
   Caring
Call her
   LOVE
Call her
   SHE

Lynn Barron

Everything Holy

a meeting with

Myosho Virginia Matthews

EVERYTHING HOLY

*"In the vastness of love we can really
meet each other."*

Myosho Virginia Matthews

BEGINNINGS

 Ginny Matthews lives less than an hour from my own house, but I had never driven in that direction before. The gentle rain which has fallen all morning slowly stops as I travel the thirty miles of coastal highway to her town, and the hills and valleys spread out from the road in shades of glowing green. Cows, stark against the grass in their steaming patchwork coats of black and white, spread across the fields up to the horizon. Rivulets of rain-water flow down almost every valley, and bushes with golden yellow blossoms line the road in occasional bursts of floral sunlight. The sky is luminous gray with wild slashes of light cutting through the clouds, back-lighting the fog from above.

I arrive a bit early for our meeting, and Ginny is picking flowers from the small garden in front of her house. She has medium-length brown hair, with a bit of gray, that hangs loose and slightly curly just below her shoulders. She wears a long brown-and-green skirt and a matching vest, and greets me with a smile and an immediate introduction to her black lab mix who waits eagerly at the door.

Ginny lives with her husband and two sons—the oldest is off at college—in a cozy neighborhood just a few blocks from the center of a quaint northern California town. She is a modern dancer by profession, having danced and taught dance for over thirty years in the San Francisco Bay area. On one living-room wall are five black-and-white photographs from her younger years as a dancer—showing a bright and focused, incredibly strong and light woman with large eyes, lifting high in the air as though completely at rest in that state of suspension.

She is also a lay-ordained nun, having taken vows, the same vows as a fully-ordained nun, in her Rinzai Zen tradition in 2000, receiving her Buddhist name of Myosho (*myo,* meaning the feminine form of the great unknowable mystery, and *sho,* meaning pine tree). Her dance studio doubles as a *zendo* where anyone can come and meditate one Sunday a month and where Ginny hosts occasional workshops or lectures on a variety of spiritual topics.

Ginny has practiced Zen Buddhism since meeting her teacher, Kyozan Joshu Sasaki Roshi, in 1973. And in the thirty years since, through raising three children and pursuing a successful dance career, she has never doubted her connection to her teacher and has remained committed to her path.

Her first introduction to Zen was at a two-day retreat she attended with her husband who had been meditating already for a few years. "I was not particularly drawn to Zen," she says as we drink tea at her dining table at the edge of her kitchen. "But I wanted to see what Jim was so passionate about. At that time Roshi was leading training periods lasting three months up at a new center on Mt. Baldy, outside of Los Angeles. I thought it would be interesting to go for a few days."

As she tells the story of her first encounter with a Zen practice session, I sense I am in for a fun ride with Ginny, in which my traditional image of Zen as a path of almost desolate simplicity, emphasizing detachment from the body gained from intense physical trials and a warrior-like approach to spiritual accomplishment, will give way to something quite different.

"I really didn't know what to expect," she tells me, sipping her tea. "The first day we meditated. I hadn't ever meditated before, but it didn't seem too difficult. I liked the quiet, the stillness. I was a dancer, and I think that training helped me to sit. *Zazen* (Zen meditation) is a yogic posture. It's physical, and dancers are trained to pay attention to the physicality of the body.

"So the first day was quiet, and it was nice. But on the second day there was this wedding going on. It was a very odd couple—an old woman who was kind of crippled was marrying a much younger man. I guess they were Zen practitioners from the community. So there was this strange wedding, and Roshi was organizing it. And this is how he worked—he never explained anything about the ceremonies, he just pointed and said, 'Move this!' or, 'Do that!' or, 'Over here!' And his monks would have to respond spontaneously, so it was totally chaotic. Everyone rushing around, changing everything, trying to get it right. Roshi yelling out commands, everyone scurrying around trying to figure out what he meant. And the rest of us in our black robes in a row in the back, chanting away, which at the time seemed incongruous with the wedding. I remember we all sat down, and Roshi thought we were in the wrong place. So we had to get up and move. All the while with the drums beating, and us chanting!

"Really, it was just wild. And I was sort of awe-struck, thinking, 'Wow!'

"Probably the strongest initial impression was of being totally enraptured by this community. This was a really active community of young people living and working and eating and meditating together. There was something I just responded to immediately.

"And then I met Roshi, and I was in love. I just totally fell in love with him. I had seen him at the ceremony, and then I met with him alone in *sanzen* (interview with the teacher), and that was it. I was just in love, and I haven't looked back since. Well, I guess I have looked back," she says laughing. Then she says, laughing even harder, "I've looked back a lot actually. But the heart-to-heart connection was just so strong. I knew I loved him. Just loved him. I made a commitment then and there, and plunged into the practice.

"It was such an amazing time for me, it was a time of many beginnings. Roshi had only been in America for ten years or so, and it was really the beginning of American Buddhism. Jim and I had moved from the East, and we loved the West Coast. Jim knew he wanted to study with Roshi; I knew I wanted to be a dancer. We didn't particularly want to live in Los Angeles where Roshi was, and San Francisco in the seventies was really great. It was so beautiful; it was still such a soft city. It was so easy to live on so little. You could get a terrific tempura dinner in Japantown for a dollar and ninety-eight cents. We had a great apartment with a view of the Golden Gate Bridge in the Upper Haight for such low rent. It was just a good time to be there. The whole dance scene was just starting too.

"At that time Roshi was so fun. He was always cracking us up with his humor. He had a certain wildness. We all had this wildness. There was a particular *sesshin* (retreat) in 1973 I remember well. I would say ninety percent of the people on retreat had had some experience with psychedelics. And some of those people were still doing them! Rumor had it that one participator liked to drop acid and sit behind Roshi's cabin and listen to everybody's private talks with Roshi.

"Roshi was so energized. He had come recently to the country, and mostly he felt Americans were refreshingly free. We weren't coming to Zen with a lot of baggage—

Buddhist baggage. It was so free at that time. The *zendo* was not a quiet place. It tried to be, but the energy was wild.

"This was the beginning. It was so exciting. I love beginnings. I loved being at the beginning of Zen in America; I loved being in San Francisco at the start of the modern dance scene. I'm very good at beginnings. When I choreograph dances I love the initial phases, and I hate finishing. In the beginning there are all those possibilities! I'm not a conservator, someone who wants to conserve, to hold it, to keep it. We need those people to conserve, but that's not my nature.

"I guess I'm a creator. I love the creative process. Jim is a good conservator. When we finally decided to have children," she tells me, smiling, "Jim said to me—and he really has a great sense of humor—he said to me, 'Well Ginny, I just want you to know, I don't want this to be one of those projects you start that I have to finish up!'"

FULLNESS AND SIMPLICITY

One morning I sit *zazen* with Ginny and her meditation group in Ginny's studio which doubles as a *zendo* one Sunday a month. During *zazen* one's eyes are somewhat open, one's back is straight, one's legs either folded or in lotus or half-lotus position, and one's hands rest just below one's navel in a specific *mudra*, or gesture. During *zazen*, one tries to remain motionless and attentive for at least a half-hour, the length of meditation of this particular lineage.

Ginny's studio is a lovely open rectangular space with wide, dark, soft floorboards, white walls, and a large skylight above. One wall has a small mirror for the dancers to see their form while practicing. After meditation, I tell Ginny how much I liked the feeling in the room, the simple and warm spaciousness. She says to me, "I've realized there are two kinds of people in the world—those who like simple, and those who like baroque. I like simple too."

In that moment I began re-conceptualizing simplicity. Ginny's life seems far from simple to me. It is filled with constant activity, many personal relationships and responsibilities, and also many professional obligations. Ginny is one of the busiest people I know. She is focused on her family, her dancing, and her spiritual practice from morning to night. So when she tells me she sees herself as someone who likes simplicity, it becomes a *koan* of its own. Where is the simplicity in so much activity?

It is a new form of an old *koan*, as it has shown up in many of my experiences with the people in this book. But with others, I felt that the activity often held the most visible position, while the simplicity was more hidden. But despite Ginny's busyness, I feel her simplicity very directly.

Throughout our time together, I come to see that her simplicity lies in a particular quality of attention she has. It is pure and focused, like her shockingly clear green eyes. It is a quality of consciousness that is constantly attentive and also detached. It seems to be able to relate to what is needed, and ignore, gently, what is not necessary.

I'm used to the image of the Zen monk, sitting quietly in his simple hut, with little to distract him from his meditation or contemplation. But as Ginny clearly illustrates, the simplicity of detached consciousness does not only come with a pared-down or ascetic outer life. Her clarity and detachment manifest through an often confusingly complex web of family, professional, and spiritual endeavors. Her own spiritual practice, three boys, a husband, a dog, and a dance career that includes her own dancing, teaching, and sitting on at least one arts council, require her constant attention. And she is currently involved in the establishment of a new retreat center in her lineage, a retreat center for women.

Ginny's detachment embraces the fullness of life. All areas of her life reflect this ability to live within a variety of relationships and obligations from a place of simplicity. And it seems that thirty years of Zen practice have helped her develop this quality.

EARLY ZEN

"In these early years," Ginny tells me, sitting in her dance studio and *zendo*, the sun streaming in through the skylight above us, "Roshi really didn't want us to study Zen or read any books, he wanted us to just *do* it. And at that time, for all of us, this really meant to learn to sit *zazen*. He taught us about *zazen*, about the breath, and about dissolving the self. We had to learn to stop our minds, to stop thinking and dissolve. Most of us were former college students! We really had to learn the basics about letting go of the rational mind, being able to be still and quiet, to rest in spaciousness.

"In Japan, Rinzai Zen developed as samurai training. The practice can really push you. You are taught to embrace every experience, even if it is the experience of wearing no socks in your shoes as you're doing walking meditation in the snow. You embrace the cold; you meet your resistance.

"The early *koans* helped you experience this state of true meeting, in which you really meet whatever experience you are having at the moment. They were basic *koans*, like, 'How do you realize your true nature when you see a pine tree?'"

When I ask Ginny what this means to her, she answers, "Well, for me it has to do with really meeting the pine tree, being in real relationship with the pine tree, a state in which you and the pine tree are one. In those years we were really learning the basics—how to dissolve our limited or separate self in a relationship of true love with another. And true love doesn't mean love in the sense we are used to, but rather is a state of being in real relationship.

"Roshi never talks about enlightenment. All he talks about is deepening your experience. Going deeper and deeper. Practicing being born, practicing dying. It is very pure. You meet the pine tree, your small self dies into that relationship, that state of oneness. This is one step. Of course you can't stay in this state of dissolving, you have to come back into your limited self.

"And then the question is, How are you going to be born again? How are you going to manifest? What happens when you have to come back to your limited, separate self again? Are you going to manifest into all your attachments and all your tendencies to polarize? Or are you just going to separate from the oneness? That's the manifestation practice. There's dying, and then there's being born.

"Roshi always leaves us very alone to figure out what this means in our own lives," Ginny says. "He doesn't speak English very well, so we never were able to rely on language with him. When we meet in *sanzen* we don't have a translator. And those meetings are very brief. So we are very much on our own, in a way, struggling to relate to our practice and to Roshi and each other without the crutches of language, rational mind, etc.

"I never minded this language barrier. I always felt I had an advantage because of my training in dance. I was very familiar with a way of being and expressing yourself that had nothing to do with the mind. Jim ended up leaving the practice a few years after I began, in part because he was a writer; words were his passion. The fact that Roshi didn't speak English was very difficult and frustrating for him.

"But what a great tool!" she says, suddenly smiling, excited. "When you come face to face with your master and you can spout all the philosophy you want and he's not going to understand any of it. What a great opportunity!

"I don't think I exchanged a word—or very few words—with Roshi for almost twenty years. And that suits my nature. I didn't need words. I knew, through dance, that there was another level of communication."

Ginny then tells me more about what it means to her to dissolve into, or be in true relationship with, things around her.

"Zen is really very practical," she says. "I think it really trains you to be present in every moment. To really be there, not to let your mind take you away from your experience. When you wake up, you really wake up! You jump out of bed and really meet the day; you feel the cold of the floor on your feet. When you brush your teeth maybe you can really be with your teeth brushing, instead of thinking, 'I wish I was back in bed, or drinking a cup of tea.' Just to meet every moment fully and completely.

"This *koan*, 'How do you realize your true nature when you see a pine tree?' points to the possibility of relationships. When you meet your experiences without the interference of the mind, you are actually in your real nature. And from there you understand the true relationship with the pine tree. This is a relationship within oneness. Your real nature is not different from the nature of the pine tree. This is the knowing, the being, of true love."

I ask Ginny to explain what this feels like, and she tells me, "Well, you are really talking about returning to the source. Returning to the source from which you and the pine tree both manifest. And there are so many aspects of being in the source. You can be totally gone. No body, no mind, no anything. Or, you can be in true love, or true relationship, which is simply meeting something else. Two beings, meeting.

"It feels like I am just there. I am really alive. I am participating in the content of the universe. My *me*, my limited self opens up and connects with all. Roshi calls it true love, and it's hard for Westerners to understand because we have such a limited vocabulary for the word 'love.' The Greeks have four words for love. We could really use a few more definitions. For me it is a state of luminosity and peace, that contains all feelings—it is all-embracing. It vibrates at a much higher frequency than the ordinary mind. I can't describe it very well, and really I experience it so rarely!" she says laughing.

"Of course there are shallow experiences of this state, and deeper experiences. Regardless of how deep or shallow, I am talking about a state of being that embraces my experience, or whatever I'm in relationship with. My mind stops. I'm not in some emotional state that keeps me separate from what's happening. I'm *here*.

"If I'm chopping carrots I am chopping carrots. And it's wonderful! That orange glow of the carrot is beautiful! As though I've never seen it before. It doesn't matter that I had a crazy mother. Or it doesn't matter that I didn't feel loved that day. Nothing interferes with chopping the carrots. It's really so simple. Zen trains you over and over again to stop the mind, be with the activity, and dissolve the limited self.

"And for me it has a great deal to do with the body. Sometimes Roshi will say, 'Buddha is the center of gravity.' Dancers have to deal with their center of gravity all the time. It's actually a physical location—two inches below the navel. It's the force that holds us on the planet. Gravitational force is a relationship. A pulling together, a coming together. And it includes the physical in a very direct and intuitive way for me because I have so much training on that level.

"In all the universe there is dissolving and manifesting. These early years I felt I was mostly learning this first part. How to dissolve into an experience, how to be in real relation with something, a relationship in which there was no separation, no separate self."

THE MYTH OF TRANSCENDENCE

Ginny and I sit at her dining table one day talking when one of her sons returns from a friend's house with two companions and one of the boys' mother. Ginny gets up to make some further arrangements for the afternoon and helps her son find his sweatshirt. The children leave again for the next leg of their adventure, and Ginny returns to the table with more black tea. It is a blend of teas I hadn't tried before, and Ginny tells me she enjoys trying all kinds of teas.

As we drink the tea, we talk about the tendency in the West to use Buddhist practice as a way to avoid life and the simple experiences of life. "I think this process of dissolving into a pine tree, or into the space in meditation, can become sort of co-opted by the Western mind and habits. It starts to be used as a way to avoid things in life, instead of as a way to engage with life. It gets hooked up with ideas and ideals about transcendence. I suppose it's because it can be so nice to be in this state of oneness, of merging. It feels so peaceful. Who wouldn't want to stay there? I know I wanted to! I loved coming up to Mt. Baldy to meditate for a week. I loved being in a relationship of true love with Roshi.

"And I don't think I'm alone!" she says, laughing. "How many people use their meditation practice as a way to avoid problems or issues? I think we tend to wrongly define spiritual states with the word 'transcendence,' as though when one experiences these states one is above or beyond something. So we are encouraged to strive for something 'above' and 'beyond.' Of course it's true—one does go beyond the limitations of the ego, but isn't it more accurate to say that these states are states of real presence? They reflect something of us really being *here*? For me, these states even depend on a rootedness to the earth. They include my center of gravity, my physicality.

"Everything dissolves into formlessness and emerges back out of formlessness. Everything dies and is born. But *transcendence* is neither the dying nor the being born. Transcendence is just an escape."

I ask Ginny what it is that makes 'dying' into something not an escape. She answers that it has to do with balance. "When you merge into a relationship of oneness with something else—a person, a pine tree, whatever it is—you don't disappear. You remain present. You remain alive. You are embracing an experience, not cutting yourself off from an experience. Transcendence is a way to leave something behind. But dying in relationship with something is an embrace. It is inclusive, born from an awareness of wholeness and oneness.

"It's pure, and you do it the middle way, you do it in balance, here in the world. The Buddha said you don't go into denial, you don't transcend in an ascetic way, nor do you totally indulge. You try to find that middle ground. I think the intent of this practice is balance. And this is what I, personally, really needed to learn.

"Thirteen or so years after I began practicing, I realized I was using my practice like so many others as a way to avoid being here. I was avoiding things that needed attention. I was leaving my young son to go on retreat because I liked the quiet, I liked my relationship with Roshi; I liked dissolving into the pine tree.

"I understood that it's easy to dissolve into a pine tree; it's easy to dissolve into a full moon. But could I dissolve into three a.m. feedings? Could I dissolve into a screaming baby and a husband who sometimes couldn't be there to help? That became the real question, and a whole new challenge. And that was when I realized Zen wasn't really helping me in my life, in my life as a mother.

"Roshi kept saying, 'You guys, it's easy being a pine tree!' This is the easy part. I realized the next step was to really be in relationship to my kids when they had been screaming for hours, when I was tired. What good is Zen practice if it's not going to work then? Personally, I couldn't make that bridge.

"I think in the beginning, as a group, we just really didn't understand what the practice was about because psychologically, culturally, Americans are trained to dissociate, to be distracted, to not really be part of life. If we're sad, we go shopping. If we're bored, we watch TV. This is how we are conditioned. So it was a natural mistake, to prefer meditation or states of peace to really dealing with the demands of life. But still, it's our responsibility to be honest with ourselves and see that this escapism, this use of the practice to perpetuate transcendence, is not what the practice is really about.

"I don't think Roshi had any idea of our American conditioning at first. Especially our conditioning around self-loathing. There are many aspects of Zen that feed our tendencies to dissociate from ourselves, like references to violence in Zen literature. It took him a long time to understand that we weren't having a very pure response to being hit by the stick. He couldn't help us with those issues. Zen really doesn't address these collective psychological dynamics, and I've seen people be caught in them for a long time, and it keeps them from really doing the practice. People had to get their own healing work. And Roshi didn't really encourage that because he was suspicious of Western psychology... and rightly so!"

I ask Ginny what it was that really showed her she needed to find help outside her tradition. "There was a moment one day," she tells me, "when I started screaming at my son. And it disturbed me so much. I thought, where was this coming from? And I saw it was something from my mother, my relationship with my mother. I knew I needed help. This episode with my son, and also chronic back problems that just wouldn't go away. I knew I needed to do some personal healing work. And as I said, I knew that my Zen practice was not going to answer this need."

ZEN AND MOTHERHOOD

"You know, I never had any intention of being a mother," Ginny tells me, laughing. "Jim and I were going to be bohemians! He was a writer; I was a modern dancer. We had no money. But I reached a point where I realized we weren't growing any more. We'd been together since high school, and I saw I was standing still in our relationship. And there was a dimension that my Zen practice just wasn't reaching. I was yearning for the experience of being a mother, to have a baby. And it was scary as hell for me because I didn't have a good example of a mother. My mother had been mentally ill since I was a year-and-a-half old. So it was scary to think I could do an adequate job. But we did it; we took the plunge.

"We'd been together seventeen years already. I had a full-fledged dance career. We were living in an old 1890's fire house then with a huge space for a dance studio. It was a heck of a place to have a baby! The roof leaked, I had to carry laundry down three flights of stairs, and the stairs had no railings because the landlord didn't want to put them in.

"In the early years, I felt that being a mother was something totally 'other' than my Zen practice. That practice wasn't helping me be a good mother, a better mother. In those days we were especially focused on the form of sitting meditation. I suppose you could say, like most of us, I identified 'Zen' with formal sitting practice. You were supposed to be doing *zazen* every day. And I really wanted to. I'd try to get up before my children in order to sit. But if I got up at six, so did they! If I got up at five, so did they! If I got up at four, so did they! They just knew I was getting up to go to this place where mommy wasn't present for them. They would come up and pull me off of my cushion. They really did not like me being in meditation.

"So it left me resentful, but also curious. I was wondering, 'OK, how do I do this?' and so," she says, pointing around at the small altar to the left of the telephone, "I went a bit beyond the prescribed form. I put altars everywhere. There's one there, there's one outside. Or I would sit in my car for ten minutes before I came in the house. I meditated whenever I could. But even so, I wasn't sure how meditation was helping in life. This was so long before all this talk about everyday life, about ordinary *Dharma*. This was an inevitable aspect of Zen coming to America, of the transition from a monastic practice into a householder practice. I guess I lived out some of the difficulties within this transition.

"I did go to *sesshin*. The first time was when Ian was two-and-a-half, and it was a mistake. I think you should not leave your children for a week until they are at least three or four. With Kyle I really blew it. I left him when he was one-and-a-half. He didn't even know me when I got back. He didn't even know me. It took him a few hours. It was really very scary.

"When Damion, my youngest, was three-and-a-half, Roshi was coming up to our center in northern California so it wouldn't be so far away if I went to retreat. And he was doing shorter retreats. I thought maybe I could do three days. Damion must have finished nursing by then; otherwise I wouldn't have left him for that time. So, I asked him if I could go, and he said, after a moment's reflection, 'Yes, mom, because we're never separated in our hearts.' So I went for three days, then the next year I went for five, and the next for the whole week. It's still not easy, but clearly those cords are starting to unravel."

I ask Ginny to speak more about some of the difficulties she experienced trying to bring together her Zen practice and being a mother. She explains, "Roshi really encourages relationships—marriages, love partners, committed relationships. In fact, he's quite a matchmaker! But what I don't think he really understood was that some of these relationships would end up with children. And he didn't really understand they really come first. He knew children would come, and you'd have to take responsibility for them, but he didn't understand how completely they would affect life and practice.

"I remember when an ordained couple had children. Roshi forbade her to go into the *zendo* for a year-and-a-half, which is good, I think. But she got upset; she wanted to be in the *zendo*. And eventually she left her children to go sit. She found people to help care for them. At one point when the children were between eight and ten they stormed into Roshi's room and said, 'Our mother is never here! She's at this *sesshin* or that *sesshin*. And she's not with us!'

"He was very surprised!" Ginny tells me, smiling and shaking her head. "He had very little understanding of children's needs.

"So it did feel like motherhood wasn't entirely integrated as part of practice. And especially in the earlier years when we were really focused on formal practice and meditation. Everything took place on the cushion then.

"The point is, I just knew I had to be a mother and really learn to do that well before I could return to Zen. It's not that I ever stopped meditating, or stopped seeing Roshi, or loving him. I was completely committed to that relationship. I feel that heart-to-heart connection, and I'm not going to let go. But I had work to do around motherhood, around my relationship with my own mother, around being a woman.

"My Zen practice had really been feeding the shadow side of my masculine qualities. Detachment I could handle, pushing through a *sesshin* I could handle. But the shadow of all that is that one keeps going when it's time to rest! One keeps pushing through when it's really time to receive. It's no fault of the practice; I think mostly it's my own and our general cultural conditioning.

"I had to learn a whole new way of doing things. As I said, in my practice, I was used to pushing, pushing. And as a mother you push, too. You have to! You need a lot of endurance. But it's such a different kind of pushing. You can't just keep pushing through, you have to let go. You have to respond to what the baby needs. So you need these receptive skills, listening skills, and you need to develop patience and a loving attention.

"It took me a long time to really learn to be a good mother, to respond to someone else's needs while still taking care of myself. It took three children before I learned to do it right. By the third I had figured it out. I realized, No, I don't put my child in daycare if I can help it. I stay with my children. I don't leave that relationship behind for other things. And I really wanted to learn how to be with them, in a real relationship. Just like with the teacher on the mountain."

INTO THE MUD

"I really love the image of the lotus," Ginny says as we eat bagels at a café near her house. "It's so perfect—to have those roots in the mud. More and more I feel the importance of being grounded, earthy; and for me that means to be able to take care of simple things, to be grounded in the simple things of life. In the early years I never felt earthy; most of my experience was of feeling out of my body, weightless. On the mountain, I was transcending. I could not find peace when I came back from retreat. I could not connect with difficult things in life.

"Zen practice for me is in part about being in relationship with one's experience. Dying into those relationships, being born into those relationships, and deepening those experiences. Being present with the pine tree, the carrots, the screaming baby—whatever it is. But I wasn't really being present as long as I was carrying around all the baggage I had. Whether it was baggage from my childhood, baggage from my family, whatever. I had to look into those wounds. Until I did that I would not be a good mother, or a good Zen practitioner.

"You know, the wounds are not the problem. It's the masks we create to hide the wounds, or to protect ourselves from more pain. The structures we build to keep ourselves from being vulnerable in life. My Zen practice just didn't help dismantle those masks. And so I just had to do it somewhere else. I heard this wonderful saying that I think is Sufi, 'We have to accept the limits of everyday life, the heat and the dust of the moment.' Well, here in northern California where we get forty inches of rain a year, all that dust turns into mud. It's the mud of life. For me, I needed to get into the mud. I needed to dismantle the masks, and cry for three years, if that's what it was going to take. Then the mud becomes simple, grounding material. Allowing me to be here, physically, connected to life. Present in whatever I need to do.

"I was at a retreat recently. And one day I got very upset. We are served tea in the morning before we chant; it's part of the tradition, part of the form. And there is a monk in charge of the tea, the *shoji*—it is part of his job in the *zendo* during retreat. But this person just wasn't paying attention. He was giving us a kind of tea that dries out the throat—not what you need before chanting. And I asked him about it later, and he said that he just took whatever tea was there at the top of the bin. There was no care; there was no attention.

"Taking care of the tea is earthy. When you're really picking the right tea, that center of gravity is there.

"If I walked into my house ten years ago exhausted after teaching all day, having to face cooking dinner, most likely I'd be like—'I've been teaching five classes! Why is my husband just sitting on the couch?! I'm exhausted! Grr!' I'd be chopping the vegetables, missing the moment, burnt out, and not able to renew from the source. I'd be bringing all my demons in, and they would take up the space. Now the demons come, but I know it. I see it more clearly. Sometimes I even invite them in for dinner too! I say, 'Oh, OK, there you are, come on in!' And then they're quiet. They're included.

"There's this great children's story of a boy who finds a tiny dragon in his room on the floor. He tells his mother, who says there's no such thing. So the dragon grows and follows him around. One day the dragon is at the breakfast table eating pancakes, and the boy tells his father about it. But the father says there's no such thing as a dragon.

Each time the dragon is denied, he gets bigger and bigger. Finally, the dragon grows so big the house ends up sitting on top of him. So the father comes home from work, and he's still in denial. He walks up the neck of the dragon to the front door and the boy says, 'Look what's happened to the dragon!' And his father starts to say, 'There's no such thing.' Finally the boy screams, 'There is too a dragon!' And gets his father and mother to admit it. And suddenly the dragon shrinks and becomes a pet.

"I love that. If we ignore them, all our demons just get bigger and bigger and fill the space so there's no room for anything else.

"The idea is that one's demons might always be around. But if you acknowledge them, and relate to them appropriately, they're going to behave better! They'll be small compared to all the space. The space can accommodate them. When you're in a real relationship there is so much space. It is truly vast. There is room for everything. Roshi used to say to me about my dance performances, 'You've got to perform for the ants in the back of the auditorium. You've got to expand the space.'

"Before I took care of these personal issues I wasn't living in a lot of space. They took up my time and my attention in a distracting and controlling way. But after this healing process they are not so demanding. And my attention can be where it needs to be. A new balance was established. A deep and nourishing balance.

"There was a point after I had been dealing with some of my personal issues, when Roshi said something to me that helped me live in this place of balance more and more.

"It was a gorgeous hot October day in 1989. I had spent the night at Green Gulch Zen Center, and hiked to Muir Beach in the morning. Then I went off to teach in Oakland. Coming home across the Bay Bridge, I was in endless traffic from the World Series. And I thought about an earthquake and how it would be if it was to happen when the country's attention was turned to San Francisco. Well, I made it home, and Jim had come home early that night, so we could watch the game on a TV set we borrowed from our friends. The whole family was home together, which was rare. And as we sat down to dinner, the earthquake started.

"Jim and our son Ian dove under the table. And I stood under the kitchen doorway with Kyle. What I remember almost more than anything is that the noise was horrific. It was really amazing, as though the earth was breaking up into pieces. It felt like the whole house was coming down. Standing there in the doorway with my baby, I thought, 'This is it!'

"And I left my body. I was so gone. I thought I was dying. I thought, 'I'm going Home! Yea!' It was such an ecstatic experience.

"I don't know how I came back, really. I don't know where I found the resources to pull myself back. But I yelled Jim's name, and that was enough to pull me back. When I returned to my body, I went under the table with Kyle.

"I was absolutely depressed for a week after that. It wasn't just that I had to come back, though it did feel terrible returning from the ecstasy of going Home. But also, I realized I had basically abandoned my baby! I left my body, but this one-and-a-half-year-old was still there, in my arms! It was devastating to think that I had left him like that, and in such a dangerous situation. I was racked with guilt.

"It bothered me for over a year. And then I finally talked with Roshi about what happened. Probably it was the longest I'd ever talked to him. I told him the whole story. He just listened, sat quietly for a moment, then looked at me and said:

"'Death OK. Resurrection OK too.'

"And for me that is really the essence of the teachings. Death OK, resurrection OK too."

EVERYTHING HOLY

"You see," Ginny says, as we talk again at her dining room table, drinking herb tea this morning, "so much of the early teachings stressed the dying part. You die out of your limited self. But during the earthquake, I saw that the dying part had become maybe a bit too easy. I had focused too much on the dying part, and I was leaving something behind. And there are consequences to that. In a way, when Roshi said what he did, he gave me permission to come back. To begin the process of manifesting myself, cleanly. Not with guilt, not within woundedness. I had done enough personal work, and now I could begin to see that dying and being born can both take place in the vast space of love. Dying into true relationship includes being born into true relationship. I think I really understood this for the first time. Probably because it was finally accessible to me. I didn't have to split the dying part from the manifesting part. And I no longer had to prefer one over the other.

"Roshi said, 'Death OK. Resurrection OK too.' And I understood I could be here, alive in the world. And it didn't have to be a problem.

"There's a saying I really love," she continues, "from the great Patriarch Bodhidharma when he was asked by the emperor of China to describe the essence of Buddhist teachings. He replied, 'Vast emptiness and nothing holy.' I try to remember that a lot. It indicates all the space that exists. And in this space, nothing is holy. I love this saying because it indicates a way to live, a way to manifest in the world. It suggests a purity, a way to stay detached and also involved.

"It's easy to get caught up in things. Everything from dancing to motherhood, and especially spiritual practice. It can be so easy to make spirituality into something special. But everything is equally special. That's what I'm trying in *zazen*. Vast emptiness and nothing holy."

I ask Ginny how this saying relates to the sense I have from her that life is very full, and very holy.

"Well," she asks, sipping tea, "What is vast emptiness? It is *sunyata*—the womb. The source. It is the source of all things. It is not empty in the sense we are used to, but full of potential, full of energy.

"And the 'nothing holy' part is simply that nothing is more special than anything else. Everything is equally holy or equally not holy. It simply refers to the basic equality between all things, all beings, all experiences. It refers to a formless essence of things. In form of course we have to discriminate, we prioritize. But in essence, all things are equal. All things are equally holy. So one learns to hold these different views. One prioritizes, one takes care of what needs to be taken care of, but one rests in the understanding that all things are essentially equal."

I tell Ginny that I see in her this capacity to be very attentive to many things. That she seems to go from one task to the next with equal enthusiasm. She says, "Well, I suppose I would expect this kind of practice, this kind of attitude to allow for that. If one does not discriminate so much between experiences—if they are equally holy or not holy, then there is such great freedom! One can do what needs to be done without attachment, without prioritizing too much. Then one can really care, really be involved.

"This is the real freedom of detachment. Not the denial, the 'getting rid of' or the transcendence that we as an American culture have so often identified as detachment.

Detachment is freedom to really be with an experience, to really engage. Not disengage.

"I think back on the tea episode during the last *sesshin*. Why did I get so upset? Because the *shoji* wasn't being attentive to the tea. He wasn't caring about what he was doing. I suppose he was thinking that we would be meditating soon. We all go through that, don't we? We all tend to start with a prejudice for the 'spiritual' practice, ignoring the simple details of finding the right tea for people to drink. Of course, it's my responsibility to meet that situation truly. With the patience and freedom and space of true love." She says, laughing, "That was of course *my* shortcoming!

"More and more, I tend to think that this might be one of those areas where you could actually use the word feminine. I think feminine attention tends to be a bit more egalitarian and embracing than a masculine focus. You don't skip ahead so much. You do what you need to do and then you move on to the next thing you need to do. And you do it all with a certain care. Mothers know this. You have to pay attention to all the details, and love is present. It's relational. And it is a caring attention. There isn't so much hierarchy in that, so much interest in focusing on one thing to the exclusion of others.

"That day with the tea, you can ask the *shoji* rushing down the line of students, pouring tea, 'What are you in relationship with? Where are you? What are you nurturing? What are you attentive to in this moment?'

"Do the work in front of you, choose the right tea. Be with the person receiving the tea when you are in front of him. Don't think ahead to the moment when you are on your cushion! Work with the *koan*, 'How do you realize the Buddha when you choose the tea?' And for me realizing the Buddha means to be in a relationship of true love. The vast space of true love."

REAL AUTHORITY

Ginny and I talk about how her practice has changed over the last thirty years. She tells me, "You know, the form hasn't changed, but my relationship to my Zen practice has changed profoundly. I guess I would say it's matured! For one thing," she says, beginning to laugh, "I'm not waiting around to get enlightened!

"Or, I'm not always telling myself, 'Hey, I just passed that *koan*!' It's no longer *nirvana*—no longer, 'Ahh, up to the mountain!'

"It has something to do with really giving up enlightenment as a goal. Yes, I have to admit I thought I would get something from this practice. And I don't think I was the only one! At the beginning, this was really my attitude. I would think, 'I passed the *koan*, I got somewhere!' And of course two years later Roshi will give me the same *koan!* And I'd think, 'Wait a minute, I passed that one already.'

"You know that's the näivety of not knowing anything about Buddhism. Isn't that very American too? We've been trained in this materialistic culture that we're going to get something. And you can hear it again and again—that you're not going to get anything, arrive anywhere. But you really don't believe it, do you? Not for a long time, anyway.

"I suppose one day I just finally saw it. There's no direct road. The path really just brings you to the place where you start over, again and again. Every moment is new. It's not so much one linear moment after another. It isn't linear; it isn't direct. This lineage, practice, is developed to express this nonlinear element. You really spiral around and around. One day you just accept it. You're just going around in circles!"

I imagine that as a dancer she is very at home spiraling here and there. I tell her this, and she laughs, agreeing. "Yes, sometimes it seems there's not a big difference between Zen and dance!"

I then ask Ginny where she is now, what issues is she addressing now?

"Well," she says, more quietly. "I would say I'm facing a lot of issues about authority. In a way, letting go of this goal of enlightenment sort of reflects the idea of letting go of an outside authority. If there's no enlightenment, if there's nothing to achieve, to gain, where does that leave you? It just leaves you with yourself in life. It's your life, and you need to live it. No one is going to tell you what to do. It has to do with accepting a certain level of inner authority and maturity.

"It's an interesting time in our community. Roshi is ninety-five. He is going to die soon, and right now he doesn't have a successor. So that authority might go. We are all going to be faced with this issue of authority. How do you live and practice if there's no teacher to guide you? There is such fear in that degree of letting go, in that degree of aloneness. Maybe it's not even fear…but I hesitate, for sure. To step off that cliff into that complete unknown. I try to remind myself that it's also where the real freedom is, and the real power.

"Personally, I have no real authority in the community. I'm just a lay-ordained nun. I'm not an *osho*, an authorized teacher and leader in the ceremonies. And I'm grateful for this, because it means I have to begin to really let go of this hierarchy that we have in Zen, and find an authority in myself. I think it's interesting timing, in a way, that Roshi is leaving and we are all left to make certain choices. And being free to choose is part of what Zen practice is about. How are we going to be in relation to one another? Are we going to relate through hierarchy? Are we going to keep ourselves separate through structures of thought, structures of authority? Or are we going to be together differently?

"Maybe this is where women are facing a particular challenge," she continues. "Women, especially, seem to have difficulty finding and trusting that inner authority. I know very few women who trust their truth. I could count them on one hand. But I know hundreds of men who trust their truth because they're validated from the beginning by their culture, at their schools, in their professions. So women are going to have to find their authority, their courage, their confidence in their perceptions and understanding.

"About ten years ago I was at a book-signing with Brother David Steindl-Rast, a Benedictine monk, one of the first people to learn Zen meditation in the sixties. He told us that earlier that day a reporter had asked him to identify the one thing that would change the world. And he replied 'If women regain their power.'

"What does it mean? For me, I think it means accessing my truth, and really living it in the world. Being able to manifest it with confidence. And in my case I think it means to live in a non-hierarchical, non-judgmental way. It definitely means to be in relation. To connect with people heart to heart. And I think this is so natural for women. It comes naturally to us, because women are relational.

"Roshi says Buddhism has tended to emphasize the feminine aspect—the return to the source. But then there's being born; you're manifesting your limited space. Roshi's teachings describe the universe in terms of 'Thus coming, thus going.' How are you going to manifest that self? Are you going to polarize or are you just going to separate? Are you going to totally identify with your emotions, your rational mind, with your attachments? Do you want to do it with hostility, or neediness, or whatever baggage you've been carrying around? Or in some other way? In true love? In true relationship?

"I had a dream recently that really spelled it out for me. I am in a lamp-manufacturing warehouse to receive a lamp to bring home. A man gives me a lamp with a beautiful crystal base. And I'm somewhat dismayed because I have bags to carry, and I'm afraid I won't have my hands free enough to carry it safely.

"But I find a way to balance all the bags, which include my dance bag, my kids' backpacks, and Jim's golf bag. And so they aren't too heavy, and my hands were free. So, I pick up the lamp and see that the bottom of the base is broken.

"I say to myself, why should I accept a broken lamp? I try to get a man's attention, to give me a new lamp, but they are too busy, and I'm not going to get a new lamp.

"Do you know this saying of the Buddha?" Ginny asks me. "His final words to his disciple Ananda? He says to Ananda, as he is dying, 'Be a lamp unto yourself, Ananda.' This was my first association with the dream. There is a light that belongs to me, a state of consciousness. And it is connected to the lineage, all the way back to the Buddha.

"But in the dream I am disappointed because it is broken. The light works, but the base is broken. A friend helped me understand that the broken base had to do with my own perceptions of myself as flawed, or broken. Why was I looking for someone to give me a new lamp? I was the base, whole and complete, the place the energy flows in. I carry a consciousness my lineage has helped me develop. I have to accept myself as my own authority.

"And part of that means accepting that I am a mother, a dancer, a woman, a wife. These bags I am carrying—that I have gotten balanced enough so I am free to carry this lamp—these are my relationships, and they will always be there. I remember in the dream feeling this dismay at carrying the lamp with all the bags! And it reminded me of the dismay I felt—still feel—at being a mother, being a householder. Sometimes I look at my life and think, 'How did this happen?' But I think the dream shows a way to balance these responsibilities in a state of freedom, in a state of consciousness that is detached and at the same time in relationship.

"And more and more I think it is not unusual for women to be terrified to take this step. To accept one's own authority includes an aloneness and a detachment that can be so frightening for women, because women are naturally relational, naturally connected. And we tend to think that to be detached means to fail in our relationships, or worse, leave them behind. But there is a way to be detached and alone while still within relationship. One's own wholeness, one's own inner authority, is the basis of real relationship, of real love."

THE WORK OF TRUE LOVE

One evening Ginny and I eat dinner at my house, after meditating with a Sufi group near where I live. Over salmon and mashed potatoes, we begin to talk about Ginny's future, how she sees the next challenges in her life.

"I know that in the last phase of my life I want to do the work of true love," she says. "And by true love, I mean what Roshi has been teaching me. Being in real relationship with life, with all experiences. A relationship of oneness, in which you know that your own nature is connected to the nature of what you're relating to. And you can't experience true love when you are limited by your small self. You have to get bigger. Because love includes everything.

"As I said, Roshi used to tell me that when I dance, I have to really fill the space. I have to be dancing to the ants in the back of the auditorium as much as to my husband in the front row. Love includes the ants as much as the husband. Love doesn't discriminate; it doesn't pick and choose.

"This is really where I am right now. To live in this state as much as I can. To have the intent of realizing the content of the whole universe as my own being. That's the big space. The content of the universe means the starving people in Afghanistan as much as the corporate heads of Monsanto.

"We die; we resurrect. And the question is, how am I going to resurrect? In the limited space of my self? Or in the vastness of true love? And in the end, is dying different from resurrecting? In all that vast space, is there even a difference between dying and resurrecting?

Ginny and I sit quietly, candles lighting our faces, rain tapping on the roof. She smiles and says softly, "I think you can keep manifesting more and more from this bigger place, this place of love, this place of real relationship. That's what the practice is for, to help you die and live more and more in this space. Love is so simple. It is not hierarchical; it is not judgmental. Love is so big, isn't it?"

Later, as I finish working on this final chapter of the book, I think about these last words from Ginny. "Love is so big." I understand that this is something most people in the book have expressed in one way or another. Love is so vast. It includes so much. And in love, I think, everything is holy.

Contributors

ANGELA FISCHER

Angela Fischer lives in northern Germany where she takes care of a small meditation center with regular meditation meetings. She leads seminars and retreats and is the author of three books on feminine spirituality and mysticism.

For further information, please visit:

www.einheit-des-lebens.net

English: Oneness of Life: www.einheit-des-lebens.net/englisch

PANSY HAWK WING

Pansy Hawk Wing lives in South Dakota and leads ceremonies in her Lakota Sioux tradition across the country and internationally. At the time of this reprint (2012) no contact information is available.

ANDREW HARVEY

Andrew Harvey is author of thirty books, and travels extensively, teaching on a wide range of subjects. For more information about Andrew, and for his lecture schedule, please visit:

www.andrewharvey.net

JETSUNMA TENZIN PALMO

Jetsunma Tenzin Palmo was raised in London and became a Buddhist while still in her teens. At the age of twenty, she traveled to India, becoming one of the first Westerners to be ordained as a Buddhist nun.

The international bestseller *Cave in the Snow* chronicles her twelve years of seclusion in a remote cave. Deeply concerned with the plight of Buddhist nuns, she established the Dongyu Gatsal Ling Nunnery in northern India in 2000, and remains as Director there. Following the heart-wish of her teacher, the 8th Khamtrul Rinpoche, she aims to reinstate at the Nunnery the 'Togdenma' (yogini) tradition.

In 2008 His Holiness the 12th Gyalwang Drukpa, head of the Drukpa Kagyu Lineage, gave her the rare title of Jetsunma (Venerable Master).

For more information about Jetsunma Tenzin Palmo and her projects, to receive the Dongyu Gatsal Ling newsletter, or to make donations to the Nunnery, please visit the website:

www.tenzinpalmo.com

JACKIE CROVETTO

Jackie Crovetto lives with her husband in Glastonbury, England. A weekly meditation group is held in their home. Jackie holds regular gatherings for women on the sacred feminine and the soul of the world. She also offers talks on dreamwork and individual help with dreams.

To contact Jackie, please email her at: post@crovetto.plus.com, or for more information about her Sufi path, please visit The Golden Sufi Center website at: www.goldensufi.org

SOBONFU SOMÉ

Sobonfu Somé is a respected lecturer, activist, and author. She is the founder of Wisdom Spring, Inc., an organization dedicated to the preservation and sharing of indigenous wisdom which fundraises for wells, schools, and health projects in Africa. She is one of the foremost voices of African spirituality to come to the West, bringing insights and healing gifts from her West-African culture. Sobonfu often tours the United States and Europe teaching workshops. Her books include: *The Spirit of Intimacy: Ancient Teachings in the Ways of Relationships*; *Welcoming Spirit Home: Ancient Teachings to Celebrate Children and Community;* and *Falling out of Grace: Meditations on Loss, Healing and Wisdom.* She is also the author of the audio cd set *Women's Wisdom from the Heart of Africa.* Sobonfu Somé can be reached at: Sobonfu@aol.com. For more information about her projects and teaching schedule, please visit her websites: www.sobonfu.com · www.walkingforwater.org www.wisdomspring.org

LYNN BARRON

Lynn Barron lives in Southern California and travels to meditate and lecture. To contact her, please email circlelight@me.com or write to: P.O. Box 375, Pearblossom, CA 93553.

MYOSHO VIRGINIA MATTHEWS

Myosho Virginia Matthews lives with her family in Sebastopol, California. A women's Rinzai Zen meditation is held in her studio, "Downtown Dance/Art Space" and full-day women's retreats are offered at various retreat centers. For more information please email her at: myosho@sonic.net.

NOTES

CHAPTER 2: IN RELATION

1. Since the time of our interview, Pansy has moved.

CHAPTER 4: THE STORMING OF LOVE

1. Henry Corbin, *The Man of Light in Iranian Sufism*, Omega Publications, New Lebanon, NY, 1994, pp. 72–73.

CHAPTER 5: THE TWENTY-TWO TARAS

1. First verse of "Praise of and Requests to the Twenty-One Taras," addressing Green Tara, the female Buddha of Compassion, the mother of all Buddhas.
2. Rituals or ceremonies, often performed for members of the lay community.
3. Dharma refers to the literal teachings of the Buddha as passed on in written and oral form. Also, Dharma can be a reference to the general path of Buddhism, the living energy of the Truth that leads one to liberation.
4. I visited Dongyu Gatsal Ling in September of 2000. Since then, more nuns have arrived.
5. Samadhi is a spiritual state of awakened consciousness which can include experiences of peace, emptiness, oneness, pure being, or pure consciousness.
6. Taking the Bodhisattva vow is a step on the Mahayana Buddhist path at which one vows to return to this world again and again until all sentient beings have reached enlightenment. This vow arises from and generates deep compassion for all beings.
7. Guru devotion is an element of practice in which one arouses devotion to one's teacher. Devotion to the guru helps generate the conscious awareness of a state of merging in which the disciple is one with the teacher.
8. Loving-kindness practices arise from and engender compassion for all beings. Through loving-kindness practices one deepens one's experience of the interconnection between all beings.
9. Engendering bodhicitta is one means of entering the heart, arousing compassion for all beings. Often one engenders bodhicitta at the start of practice in order to allow for compassion and wisdom to inform and guide practice. On the absolute level, bodhicitta is the wisdom of emptiness that is alive with clarity and luminosity, the source of all compassion.

Photo Acknowledgements

Photo of Andrew Harvey courtesy of Andrew Harvey. Photo of Ani Tenzin Palmo and the nuns of Dongyu Gatsal Ling courtesy of Monica Joyce. Photos of Sobonfu Somé courtesy of Tania Barricklo. Photos of Myosho Virginia Matthews courtesy of Michelle Montalbano. All additional contributor photographs by Hilary Hart.

ABOUT *the* AUTHOR

HILARY HART currently lives in Taos, New Mexico. *The Unknown She* is her first book.

For further information, or to contact the author, please visit www.hilaryhart.org

~⌒

ABOUT *the* PUBLISHER

THE GOLDEN SUFI CENTER publishes books and other resources on Sufism and mysticism. A California religious nonprofit 501 (c) (3) corporation, it is dedicated to making the teachings of the Naqshbandi Sufi path available to all seekers. For further information about activities and publications, please contact:

THE GOLDEN SUFI CENTER
P.O. Box 456
Point Reyes Station, CA 94956-0456
tel: 415-663-0100 · *fax:* 415-663-0103
www.goldensufi.org

~⌒

ADDITIONAL PUBLICATIONS
from THE GOLDEN SUFI CENTER

by IRINA TWEEDIE

DAUGHTER OF FIRE:
A Diary of a Spiritual Training with a Sufi Master

⁓

by LLEWELLYN VAUGHAN-LEE

PRAYER OF THE HEART IN
CHRISTIAN & SUFI MYSTICISM

FRAGMENTS OF A LOVE STORY:
Reflections on the Life of a Mystic

THE RETURN OF THE FEMININE
& THE WORLD SOUL

ALCHEMY OF LIGHT:
Working with the Primal Energies of Life

AWAKENING THE WORLD:
A Global Dimension to Spiritual Practice

SPIRITUAL POWER:
How It Works

MOSHKEL GOSHA:
A Story of Transformation

LIGHT OF ONENESS

WORKING WITH ONENESS

THE SIGNS OF GOD

LOVE IS A FIRE:
The Sufi's Mystical Journey Home

THE CIRCLE OF LOVE

CATCHING THE THREAD:
Sufism, Dreamwork, & Jungian Psychology

THE FACE BEFORE I WAS BORN:
A Spiritual Autobiography

THE PARADOXES OF LOVE

SUFISM, THE TRANSFORMATION OF THE HEART

IN THE COMPANY OF FRIENDS:
Dreamwork within a Sufi Group

THE BOND WITH THE BELOVED:
The Mystical Relationship of the Lover and the Beloved

edited by LLEWELLYN VAUGHAN-LEE
with biographical information by SARA SVIRI

TRAVELLING THE PATH OF LOVE:
Sayings of Sufi Masters

by **PETER KINGSLEY**

A STORY WAITING TO PIERCE YOU:
Mongolia, Tibet, & the Destiny of the Western World

REALITY

IN THE DARK PLACES OF WISDOM

⁓

by **SARA SVIRI**

THE TASTE OF HIDDEN THINGS:
Images of the Sufi Path

⁓